D0635496

THE CARIBBEAN

CENTRAL & SOUTH AMERICAN COOKBOOK

THE CARIBBEAN
CENTRAL & SOUTH AMERICAN COOKBOOK

TROPICAL CUISINES STEEPED IN HISTORY: ALL THE INGREDIENTS AND TECHNIQUES AND 150 SENSATIONAL STEP-BY-STEP RECIPES

JENNI FLEETWOOD AND MARINA FILIPPELLI

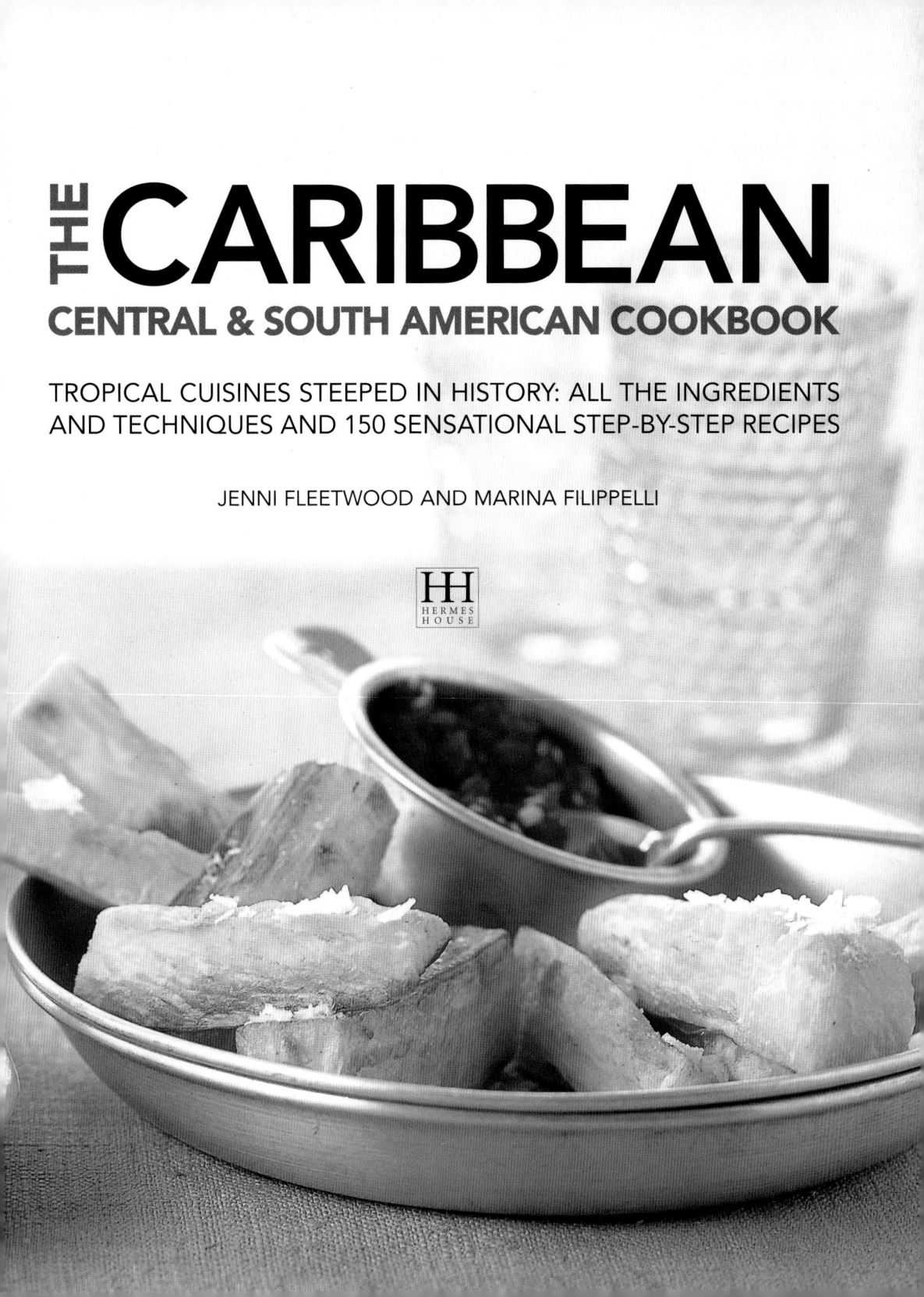

This edition is published by Hermes House, an imprint of Anness Publishing Ltd
Hermes House, 88–89 Blackfriars Road, London SE1 8HA
tel. 020 7401 2077; fax 020 7633 9499
www.hermeshouse.com; www.annesspublishing.com

If you like the images in this book and would like to investigate using them for publishing, promotions or advertising, please visit our website www.practicalpictures.com for more information.

Publisher: Joanna Lorenz
Editorial Director: Judith Simons
Editor: Clare Gooden
Photographers: Nicki Dowey, Will Heap and Patrick McLeavey
Home Economists: Fergal Connolly, Joanne Craig, Tonia George and Lucy McKelvie
Stylist: Helen Trent
Designer: Nigel Partridge
Jacket Design: Chloe Steers
Additional recipes: Rosamund Grant, Elisabeth Lambert Ortiz, Maggie Mayhew, Kate Whiteman

All rights reserved. No part of this publication may be reproduced, stored in a retrieval system, or transmitted in any way or by any means, electronic, mechanical, photocopying, recording or otherwise, without the prior written permission of the copyright holder.

© Anness Publishing Ltd 2004, 2010

ETHICAL TRADING POLICY

Because of our ongoing ecological investment programme, you, as our customer, can have the pleasure and reassurance of knowing that a tree is being cultivated on your behalf to naturally replace the materials used to make the book you are holding. For further information about this scheme, go to ww.annesspublishing.com/trees

PUBLISHER'S NOTE

Although the advice and information in this book are believed to be accurate and true at the time of going to press, neither the authors nor the publisher can accept any legal responsibility or liability for any errors or omissions that may be made nor for any inaccuracies nor for any loss, harm or injury that comes about from following instructions or advice in this book.

NOTES

Bracketed terms are intended for American readers.
For all recipes, quantities are given in both metric and imperial measures and, where appropriate, in standard cups and spoons. Follow one set of measures, but not a mixture, because they are not interchangeable.
Standard spoon and cup measures are level. 1 tsp = 5ml, 1 tbsp = 15ml, 1 cup = 250ml/8fl oz.
Australian standard tablespoons are 20ml. Australian readers should use 3 tsp in place of 1 tbsp for measuring small quantities.
American pints are 16fl oz/2 cups. American readers should use 20fl oz/2.5 cups in place of 1 pint when measuring liquids.
Electric oven temperatures in this book are for conventional ovens. When using a fan oven, the temperature will probably need to be reduced by about 10–20°C/20–40°F.
Since ovens vary, you should check with your manufacturer's instruction book for guidance.
Medium (US large) eggs are used unless otherwise stated.

ACKNOWLEDGEMENTS

Jenni Fleetwood would like to pay tribute to Elisabeth Lambert Ortiz, Elisabeth Luard and Judy Bastyra, experts on the food and drink of Latin America and the Caribbean, whose books have been an inspiration for many years. In addition, she would like to thank Jane Raphaely for sending her to South America in the first place, and the 107ers for decades of support.

Marina Filippelli would like to thank her friends and family who were always present with suggestions, advice and a healthy appetite. This book would still be in the making were it not for Lizzie's help and Nick's infinite patience and encouragement. Special mention also goes to her parents who instilled in her a love for the food and culture of Brazil.

Additional picture material provided by South American Pictures: pages 7–25.

CONTENTS

INTRODUCTION 6

A BRIEF HISTORY 6
THE CARIBBEAN 8
BRAZIL 12
ARGENTINA, URUGUAY AND PARAGUAY 16
PERU, BOLIVIA AND ECUADOR 18
CHILE 20
COLOMBIA AND VENEZUELA 22
CENTRAL AMERICA 23
MEXICO 24

THE LATIN AMERICAN KITCHEN 26

EQUIPMENT 28
CORN 30
RICE 32
POTATOES 33
BEANS 34
CHILLIES AND SWEET PEPPERS 36
OTHER VEGETABLES 40
FRUIT VEGETABLES 43
FRUIT 44
NUTS 49
HERBS, SPICES AND FLAVOURINGS 50
DAIRY PRODUCTS AND EGGS 52
FISH AND SHELLFISH 54
MEAT 58
POULTRY 60
DRINKS 62

STREET FOOD AND SNACKS 66
SOUPS 82
FISH AND SHELLFISH 96
MEAT 122
POULTRY 146
VEGETARIAN DISHES AND SALADS 162
SIDE DISHES AND SALSAS 184
BREADS AND CAKES 206
DESSERTS 222
DRINKS 236

NUTRITIONAL INFORMATION 248
INDEX 252

A Brief History

The Caribbean and Latin America is a vast area comprising a large number of individual countries, each with diverse ways of preparing and serving food. The only thing they have in common is that they have all been subject to a Spanish or Portuguese influence, even if only, as is the case with some Caribbean islands, by way of exposure to their neighbours.

The events that led to the domination of the continent by two European powers began when Christopher Columbus petitioned for support for a voyage of discovery across the Atlantic in search of a sea route to India. At first he was turned down, but King Ferdinand and Queen Isabella of Spain eventually agreed to his request, largely out of a desire to find a new source for the spices the people of southern Spain had learned to love when under the control of the recently expelled Moors.

Columbus set sail on 3 August 1492, and in October of that year he reached Watling Island in the Caribbean. Convinced he had reached the Indies, he continued to Cuba and Hispaniola (now Haiti and the Dominican Republic). In 1500 the Portuguese explorer Pedro Cabral landed on the coast of Brazil, and two years later Columbus reached the South American mainland. The early explorers were not interested in conquest, but individuals such as Hernán Cortés and Francisco Pizarro were dedicated to it. During the 16th century they invaded Mexico and Peru respectively, while other parts of Latin America fell to other conquistadors. In the process, great civilizations were overthrown and the stage was set for the total take-over of the continent by Spain and Portugal.

It was Napoleon III, the 19th century French emperor, who coined the term "Latin America" and applied it to those countries on the American continent where Spanish and Portuguese were spoken, including the Spanish-speaking Caribbean islands and Mexico. The term is now used to include all the islands.

The term "Latin America" suggests that nothing of value existed before the conquest, and it does not acknowledge the indigenous peoples nor the great civilizations – Maya, Aztec and Inca – they spawned. However, the term has value, if only as shorthand, in giving some indication as to the major cultural and culinary influences in this part of the world in the post-Columbian era.

NEW SETTLERS

When the first conquistadors landed in Latin America, they found many foreign ingredients. The most important of these was corn, which the indigenous peoples called *maïs*. Like wheat, corn could be used to make bread, but it was more versatile. The husks could be used as wrappers; the stalks for training beans; and the silks as ties. The cobs could be eaten fresh or stored for the winter.

Where corn and beans grew, so did squash. This remarkable food also kept well and yielded delicious seeds. Tomatoes were another important find, as were chillies. When Columbus first tasted a dish made using these fiery red and green pods, he assumed its heat came from black pepper and named the pods peppers.

The ships that brought the invaders sailed back to Spain laden with produce, then returned with settlers who brought their own bounty – cattle, pigs, sheep, wheat, sugar cane and nuts.

Below: The Caribbean islands and Central America have a vast coastline and fish and shellfish play an enormous part in their cuisines.

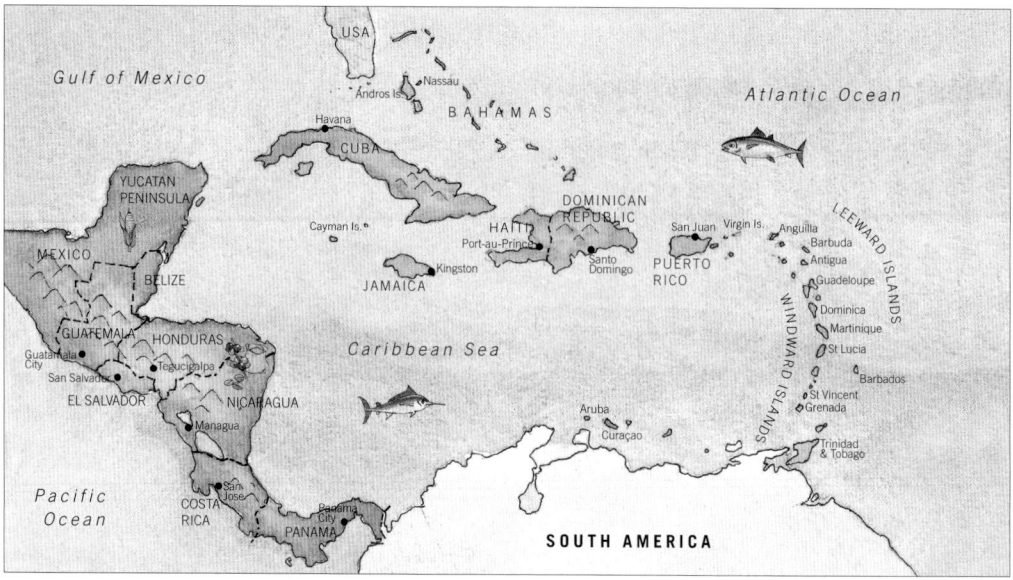

Priests came to Latin America too. Their aim was to convert the native population, but they also had valuable horticultural skills to pass on. The South American wine-making industries were started by priests who needed a ready supply of communion wine.

Lands were settled and crops were planted, but such activities required labour. At first the native population gave their assistance, but soon rebelled. The situation grew worse with the *encomienda* system, which gave Spanish individuals land rights. The indigenous peoples were forced to work for no payment other than Spanish lessons and religious instruction. They were shockingly exploited and the work was hard, especially for those already weakened by disease. They died in their thousands.

SLAVES AND SETTLERS

The colonists responded by importing African slaves to work the burgeoning sugar plantations. The Africans made a huge contribution to the regional cuisines, especially in Brazil. The climate was similar to their homeland, so the many vegetables and fruits they brought with them flourished.

Below: Native South American ingredients are sold daily at a busy traditional vegetable market in Peru.

The Spanish and Portuguese settlers intermarried freely with indigenous and African women and, as a result, the *mestizo* ("mixed") population grew.

The food became *mestizo* too. Many of the cooks were either indigenous or African women, and they prepared a mixture of their own recipes plus the dishes their employers wanted. Spanish ingredients – such as onions, garlic and rice – were incorporated, and Spanish dishes were adapted to include chillies, tomatoes and even cocoa. This two-way trade led to a vibrant Latino cuisine,

Other nations made a valuable contribution too. Indentured labourers from India, South-east Asia and the Far East have all contributed their own styles of cooking, and some Caribbean islands are, in culinary terms, forever England, France, Denmark or Holland, depending on their settlers.

Above: Although the cuisines of Latin America differ from country to country, there are some common ingredients.

Latin America is a turbulent part of the globe where the only certain thing is change; this is as true of the cuisine as anything else. Immigrants continue to introduce new dishes, and tourists take away memories of delicious meals they hope to recreate at home. This time the trade is between Latin America and the world. While pizza becomes commonplace in Brazil, ceviche is enjoyed in Canada, and Californian chefs hanker for *huitlacoche* (corn truffles).

Latin America still has secrets to divulge. In the jungles and hidden Andean valleys there are undoubtedly new ingredients waiting to be discovered. These will add another layer to a cuisine that is as exciting as it is extraordinary.

THE CARIBBEAN

A culinary cruise around the Caribbean is richly rewarding. Having feasted your eyes on beautiful turquoise sparkling seas, palm-fringed beaches, green velvet mountains and exquisite gardens, you can dine on dishes that are as diverse as the islands themselves. These islands offer some of the best seafood in the world, plus fragrant stews, spicy side dishes, unusual salads and sweet treats such as coconut ice cream and luxurious Caribbean fruit and rum cake.

EARLY HISTORY

The earliest inhabitants of the Caribbean islands were the Ciboney, hunter-gatherers who had themselves migrated from northern South America. They were supplanted by the Taino, Arawak-speaking fishermen and farmers, who in turn were harried by the warlike Caribs in a pattern that would be repeated again and again down the centuries as nation after nation fought for control of the islands.

The Taino were peace-loving people who lived in small communities and grew cassava, corn, squash, (bell) peppers, beans, sweet potatoes and yams – crops that remain the mainstay of the Latin American diet. Those who lived on the coast caught fish, which they often ate raw, and their diet was supplemented with ducks, turtles, snakes and small rodents.

The arrival of Christopher Columbus in 1492 spelled the beginning of the end for the Taino. Many of them succumbed to diseases, such as measles and smallpox, never before seen on the islands. Others died in the service of Spanish settlers who worked them cruelly on the land and digging for gold. The Caribs fared a little better. Most of them were now confined to the more eastern islands, and their fierce reputation and remote location acted as a deterrent to would-be settlers. However, by the end of the 16th century, only a handful of the former inhabitants of the islands remained.

In their place came Spanish, English, French and Dutch settlers, the latter occupying the islands that Christopher Columbus had overlooked: Aruba, Curaçao and Bonaire. These islands, which would eventually become part of the Dutch Antilles, were "discovered" in 1499 by Alonso de Ojeda, one of Amerigo Vespucci's henchmen, and settled first by the Spanish and then by Dutch traders in the first half of the 17th century. The British and French, meanwhile, were becoming solidly entrenched in the Caribbean. Having already taken St Christopher (St Kitts) in 1623, the British quickly set up colonies on the islands of Nevis, Barbados, Antigua and Montserrat, while the French settled in Guadeloupe, Martinique and St Lucia.

Below: The Caribbean islands are a beautiful, lush and fertile place.

Above: A local woman inspects the produce at a Caribbean street market.

SPANISH POSSESSIONS

The Spanish continued to dominate the most strategically important islands of Cuba, Jamaica, Puerto Rico and Hispaniola (modern day Haiti and the Dominican Republic).

During the next 200 years, the islands of the Caribbean became pawns in the hands of the European powers. They sometimes changed hands so frequently that would-be settlers set sail from home in the belief that they would be ruled by their compatriots, only to discover on reaching their destination that it was now under the control of someone else. The island of St Martin, for instance, was tossed between Holland, Great Britain and France more than a dozen times, the shortest period of occupation being just 10 days. The island is still half Dutch and half French, which explains why it is today known by two separate names: Sint Maarten and Saint Martin.

Today, most of the islands have achieved autonomy from their European conquerors and have banded together to form Caricom, the Caribbean Community and Common Market.

FOOD AND DRINK

The turmoil of the early years meant that recipes tended to do the rounds. The Spanish dish, *pescado en escabeche* became known as eschovished fish, caveached fish or *escovitch*. *Callaloo*, a soup made from the leaves of a plant similar to spinach, is another successful migrant, being known variously as *le calalou, callilu, callau* and *calaloo*.

The French brought *bouillabaisse* to the islands, even though the fish used in the Caribbean version is very different from that found off the coast of Brittany. On Dominica and Montserrat they found frogs so large that their local name – mountain chicken – does not seem inappropriate. These French settlers wasted no time in teaching local cooks how to prepare frog's legs.

The Danes contributed recipes such as herring gundy, a dish of salt herring with potatoes, peppers and onion, and *croustadas*, which resemble savoury waffles. From the Dutch came *erwensoep* – a hearty pea soup – and the utterly delicious stew cooked within a whole cheese, *keshy yena*.

Made from fermented sugar cane, some of the world's best rums are still produced in the Caribbean, and rum cocktails are always a popular choice.

Below: Hard-working Caribbean fishermen bring the daily catch ashore, ready to be sold at market.

Creole cooking

This term is used to describe many traditional Caribbean recipes. It generally refers to dishes that have their roots in both Europe and Africa, and is also used in Louisiana and some other southern states of the USA. There, Creole cooking has French, Spanish and African influences, whereas in the Caribbean, the Spanish and African influences are dominant. The expression *cocina criolla* is loosely applied throughout Latin America as a catch-all term for the native cuisine.

Above: Sugar cane is a major export for the region; the annual harvest in Cuba is exhausting but rewarding work.

NEW CROPS

It is widely believed that Columbus planted the first sugar cane on the Caribbean islands. By the start of the 17th century, the crop's huge potential was being fully appreciated, and large sugar cane plantations had been established, together with plantations of other crops new to the islands, such as bananas, plantains, coffee, coconuts and oranges.

Growing all of these new crops required a large amount of labour, and since the indigenous population had been largely wiped out, this led to the importation of slaves on a massive scale. They arrived in their thousands, enduring dreadful journeys by sea and harsh lives after reaching their destination. The slaves often had to subsist on dried fish or meat alone, since they were forbidden from raising cattle and denied the opportunity to catch fresh fish. The many traditional Caribbean dishes based on salt cod, such as Jamaican salt fish and ackee, originated during this period. The slaves, who came mainly from West Africa, introduced ingredients such as yams and okra, which were quickly incorporated into the Caribbean cuisine. They improved their bland diet even further by the imaginative use of spices, laying the foundation for the hot pepper sauces that would become synonymous with the islands in years to come.

When slavery was eventually abolished in the 1830s, indentured labourers from the Middle East, India and the Far East were brought to the islands; these labourers introduced yet more ingredients to the melange that is Caribbean cooking. Spicy curries and dishes such as lamb pelau entered the repertoire, along with *roti* and *dhal puri*, large flat breads filled with curried meat, fish or potatoes.

Today it is mainly tourism that drives the economy of the Caribbean islands. Although this has had some negative effects on the local cuisine, mainly due to the introduction of the "international menu" that some travellers demand, it has also stimulated interest in regional specialities. The more dynamic Caribbean chefs are revelling in the wonderful ingredients that are at their disposal, especially the superb seafood on offer all year round. New and exciting dishes continue to emerge alongside old favourites.

STREET FOOD AND SNACKS

Snacking is a popular pastime on the Caribbean islands, which goes some way towards explaining the abundance of food available from roadside stalls and bars, or beach vendors. In fact, street food accounts for 20–30 per cent of urban household expenditure on the islands, Whatever the time of day, wherever you are, tasty morsels can be found to satisfy your hunger pangs.

Among the items traditionally offered by street vendors are deliciously light fritters, made from conch, salt cod or perhaps split peas, with spring onions (scallions) or chillies for extra flavour. Barbecued jerk chicken is another favourite, and for easy eating and instant gratification you cannot beat a bowl of crispy plantain and sweet potato chips or lightly cooked coconut king prawns, served with a glass of ice cold beer or one of the rum cocktails for which the islands are famous.

The quintessential Caribbean fast food, enjoyed by locals and tourists alike, is *roti*, a large flat bread with a tasty curried filling such as conch, goat or a selection of vegetables. Plantain dumplings are also a popular choice.

Below: In Havana, Cuba, a street vendor prepares sausages, delicious stuffed pastries and fried potatoes.

Above: The "Day of Kings" festival, which celebrates African gods, is a time for partying on the streets of Cuba.

FEASTS AND FESTIVALS

Carnival is the highlight of the year on the Caribbean islands. The build-up begins with the calypso season, which starts in January, then as Ash Wednesday approaches, signalling a period of sobriety and self-control, the streets ring to the sound of steel bands. In Aruba and Trinidad and Tobago, Carnival is a particularly extravagant affair. Local festivals are also held throughout the year. Puerto Rico commemorates the island's African-American heritage every June, and Jamaica has a popular reggae festival in July. Saints' days are always a good excuse for a celebration too, and they inevitably offer the opportunity to sample local food.

Special occasions are often marked by the roasting of a suckling pig. Slow roasting and regular basting ensures that the meat is beautifully tender, but the best part for many diners is the stuffing. This varies from island to island and from cook to cook, often being made to a recipe that is a closely guarded secret. It may be hot and spicy, fresh and fruity or made from offal, with the heart, liver and kidneys of the pig mixed with sausage, onions and herbs. Rum or brandy is often added to give an extra kick.

No festival would be complete without food, and traditional Caribbean festival fare, available from street vendors, includes fish cakes, Jamaican saltfish fritters ("stamp and go") and rice and peas. More adventurous regional delicacies include *griot* (hot Haitian fried pork), jerked chicken and curried goat. Street-side food vendors can often be seen serving up more exotic foods, including fresh catfish and red snapper, Thai noodles or Mexican empanadas. In addition, hot dogs, sweets (candy), fresh fruit smoothies, soft drinks, ice-cold beer and rum cocktails are always popular.

The rum tradition

Not much goes on in the Caribbean that doesn't involve rum. It was developed in the 16th century by colonists who distilled molasses to trade for slaves in Africa. From here it was sent north to European markets, where a Spanish wine merchant, Facundo Bacardi, developed a process of charcoal filtering, to make rum taste better. Bacardi is now the leading brand of white rum and the best-selling spirit worldwide. Aged rum is darker, taking on the colour of the barrel in which it ages. It has a mellower taste that makes it perfect for sipping. Not all dark rums are aged, however – some have colour and flavour additives. There are dozens of rum cocktails available throughout the Caribbean. Three favourites are the daiquiri, the mojito and the pina colada.

BRAZIL

Whether it is because it is the largest country in South America or has such rich cultural and racial diversity, Brazil is a place that celebrates excess. The Brazilian people love to eat, love to drink and love to dance. A trip to this, the only Portuguese-speaking country in South America, is a glorious assault on all of the senses, and never more so than during Carnival, when the streets throb with the sounds of samba music and the vibrant colours of the costumes fizz like the fireworks that explode overhead. The food is just as exciting, Sample delicious seafood in Rio de Janeiro, unusual pork dishes in Minas Gerais, tender beef in Rio Grande or the spicy specialities of Bahia, where Africa meets South America in an explosion of unusual and fiery spices.

Below: The Amazon river and rainforest cover much of Brazil and are home to many unusual species and crops.

EARLY HISTORY

Some 50,000 years ago primitive peoples crossed from Asia to America by way of the Bering Strait land bridge and began the long trek south. Nobody knows for certain quite when they reached South America, but hunter-gatherers were certainly enjoying the fruits of the Amazon basin by 8000BC. Fish, manatees, turtles, game animals and birds were plentiful, and they supplemented their diet with cassava (*manioc*), nuts and fruits that grew in the area. Some migrated to the coast, and survived mainly on shellfish, as is evident from the huge shell mounds that they left behind.

Above: Coffee berries are picked by hand when ripe, then exported around the globe in huge quantities.

Brazil did not have the great civilizations that evolved in Central America and the west of the continent. Instead, as the indigenous people abandoned their nomadic lifestyle for farming, settled communities or chiefdoms were established. As well as cassava, corn, sweet potatoes and squash were grown, often on the shell mounds left by their predecessors. The existence of these early settlers was not as peaceful as it sounds, however. At least one of the tribes, the Tupinambá, were cannibals who not only ate their enemies, but fattened them up first.

PEDRO CABRAL

In 1500, the Portuguese explorer, Pedro Cabral, claimed Brazil for Portugal, but he only stayed long enough to erect a cross, say a few prayers and take on board his ship some unusual wood that yielded a red dye – *pao Brasil*. His compatriots at home were not very excited about this new territory, but Portuguese merchants considered that the wood might be worth exploiting, and a few expeditions were mounted to cut down the trees. Trading stations were gradually set up along the coast to the north and south of Salvador de Bahia, and the country came to be known by the same name as the wood, Brazil.

In the beginning, these Portuguese settlers and the indigenous peoples co-existed amicably enough, but when what had been a minor timber operation began to escalate into a mass export operation, the natives began to withdraw their labour. They were even less enthusiastic about working on the many sugar plantations that had been established from the middle of the 16th century onwards. The Portuguese settlers tried to force the native South Americans by enslaving them, but so many died from exhaustion or disease that the plantation owners began to import African slaves instead.

SUGAR AND THE SLAVE TRADE

By the time slavery was finally abolished in Brazil towards the end of the 19th century, around four million African slaves had made the terrible journey from their native land to Brazil. Many did not even survive the long crossing, and many others died shortly after their arrival on the plantations (*engenhos*) where sugar was grown and processed.

A few successfully escaped to form their own secret communities, known as *quilombos*, while others survived their bondage by focusing on keeping alive their music, culture and religion, and cooking food similar to that which they enjoyed at home. It was the Africans who originally introduced ingredients such as black-eyed beans (peas), okra and yams to Latin America, and these thrived in a climate that was quite similar to that of West Africa. Food was used for purposes of ritual as well as sustenance, and some of the recipes cooked throughout Brazil today evolved from the foods prepared by African priestesses to offer to their gods.

Dendê oil

African slaves transported to Brazil initially missed one of their favourite ingredients, dendê oil, which comes from the fruit of the African oil palm and is valued for its rich orange-red colour. Fortunately, they soon discovered that a similar colour could be obtained by adding crushed annatto (achiote) seeds to ordinary oil. Dendê oil is now widely used in Brazilian cooking, especially in Bahia, where the African influence is strongest.

Above: In more cosmopolitan cities such as Rio, every imaginable cuisine from around the world is available.

GOLD RUSH

In the late 17th century, Brazilian explorers, known as *bandeirantes*, began to find gold in the mountain streams to the north of Rio de Janeiro. The ensuing gold rush led to a boom time in Brazil. Despite the relative inaccessibility of the main goldfields, new towns quickly began to spring up in the area that would later come to be known as Minas Gerais (which translates as "general mines").

Prospectors travelled to this area from all over Europe, hoping to make their fortune. Many of the country's sugar-cane planters also joined the gold rush, taking their slaves with them.

Several years later, around 1720, diamonds were also discovered in the region, and for about a century, Brazil became the world's major supplier of both gold and diamonds. To this day, Minas Gerais remains one of the richest areas in the country.

THE ROYAL COURT

In 1808, after the occupation of Portugal by the French, the Portuguese royal court decamped to Rio de Janeiro, making the city the new capital of their empire. When King Dom João VI finally returned to Spain in 1821, he left his son Dom Pedro I behind to rule Brazil. Dom Pedro I was subsequently recalled to Portugal, but he defied his father and the Portuguese government and declared Brazil's independence in 1822, with himself as Emperor.

GERMAN FARMERS

Dom Pedro's wife, Empress Dona Leopoldina, conceived the idea of peopling the vast area of southern Brazil with European farmers to work the land. Thousands of German colonists arrived and settled in the state of Rio Grande do Sul. In places such as Novo Hamburgo and Blumenau, their culinary contribution is evident and remains today, with sauerkraut, sausages, spätzle and delicious sweet pastries.

COFFEE – THE NEW CROP

In the century following independence, coffee replaced sugar as Brazil's premier export product. Further foreign immigration was encouraged for the purpose of having enough labour to work on the coffee plantations. Immigrants, especially Italians, quickly followed by Japanese, Spanish and Portuguese, flocked to cities such as Sao Paulo. Coffee was the major source of income for Brazil in the 1870s and the 1880s, and in 1889 the powerful coffee producers helped to bring about a military coup after which Brazil became a republic.

Below: Large freshwater catfish are displayed for sale at the busy Ver o Peso *market in the Amazon.*

FOOD AND DRINK

There is a wide variety of food on offer throughout Brazil. In the coastal belt, where the majority of the population lives, cosmopolitan cities such as Rio de Janeiro, Salvador and Sao Paulo have every type of restaurant imaginable to choose from, including those that specialize in regional cuisine.

Among the specialities is *feijoada completa*, not so much a dish as a lavish feast. A huge platter of fresh and smoked meats, including pig's tongue, is flanked by black beans, rice, spring greens, farofa (flavoured toasted cassava flour), orange slices and several sauces, all washed down with *caipirinha*, which is a mixture of *cachaça*, sugar and lime. Although they have a burgeoning wine industry in the temperate south, Brazilians prefer to drink iced beer or *cachaça*, which is often mixed with fruit juice or milk.

Rice is grown in Brazil and is the most widely used accompaniment, along with the ubiquitous farofa. In coastal areas, fine seafood is on offer.

REGIONAL CUISINES

There are four main regional cuisines in Brazil, plus the cooking of the Amazon region, where roasted game, exotic freshwater fish and unusual fruits can be encountered.

Above: The traditional Brazilian Saturday lunch is feijoada completa, *a meal of meats, rice, beans, greens and farofa.*

Comida Mineira is the cuisine of Minas Gerais. For over a century Minas Gerais was the wealthiest part of Brazil, and it is still rich in minerals. Farming is also important there. Crops include corn, beans, coffee and fruit, and there are large herds of beef and dairy cattle. Pork is the favourite meat, especially *lombo*, pork fillet or tenderloin. Bean dishes are also typical of the region, a favourite being *tutu*, which consists of black beans cooked with cubes of bacon and cassava flour and served with meat. Minas Gerais is also well known for its cheeses.

The well-travelled chilli

When African slaves introduced the malagueta chilli to Brazil, few people realized it was a returning immigrant. It originated in Central America, was taken to the northern hemisphere by the Spanish and eventually found its way to West Africa, finally returning to the continent of its birth in the baggage of slaves bound for Brazil.

Comida Baiana is perhaps the best known style of cooking in Brazil, celebrating that province's connection with Africa. Popular ingredients here include okra, dendê oil, dried shrimp, coriander (cilantro), coconut milk and lots of fresh seafood. A popular snack is *acarajés*, tasty bean patties or fritters, split and filled with various sauces. *Moqueca* is an aromatic dish of seafood, tomatoes, (bell) peppers, fresh coriander (cilantro) and dendê oil, invariably served with farofa to soak up the delicious coconut sauce. Brazilians like to finish a meal with fresh fruit. Desserts tend to be very sweet and are often based on custards in the Portuguese style. Avocado is often served as a mousse or ice cream.
Comida do Sertão is the cuisine of the vast plateau in the north-east of Brazil and can be sampled in the country's capital, the purpose-built city of Brasília. Dried salted meat – *carne seca* – comes from this region and beans are used in hearty meat dishes. Pumpkins, peppers and corn also feature, along with exotic fruits such as guavas, mangoes and carambolas. Favourite sweetmeats of the region include candied orange peel and candied figs.

Comida Gaúcha means meat and plenty of it. This describes the cooking style of the vast Brazilian cattle country down south. A big feature of this area are the popular *churrascarias* – restaurants where you can sample almost every cut of meat imaginable, including all types of offal and a wide variety of delicious sausages.

Above: Brazil is renowned for its spectacular Mardi Gras carnival, when everyone takes to the streets to party.

Below: A Bahiana street vendor prepares local delicacies for passers-by, including acarajés, *delicious fried bean fritters.*

STREET FOOD AND SNACKS

Brazilians like to be able to eat wherever and whenever the whim takes them, so street food is always on offer. This ranges from simple hot dogs, hamburgers and toasted cheese sandwiches to the filled bean or cheese patties known as *acarajés*. Pastries on offer include *pastels*, *esfihas* and *empadinhas*, which are baby empanadas stuffed with a variety of delectable fillings, such as fresh palm hearts in a tasty savoury sauce.

FEASTS AND FESTIVALS

The main celebration of the year throughout Brazil is *Carnaval*. Rio de Janeiro is the city usually associated with this extravaganza, but Brazilians often prefer to celebrate by taking part in the less touristy but equally electric spectacles in cities such as Salvador, Recife and Olinda. The build-up to *Carnaval* begins soon after Christmas and reaches its peak as Lent begins.

ARGENTINA, URUGUAY AND PARAGUAY

The cuisines of these three countries have one major ingredient in common – beef. Argentines eat a great deal of it and Uruguayans eat even more. It is less popular in Paraguay, but even there you will often find barbecues piled high with tender steaks, ribs and parts of animals that you never knew existed. Few ethnic dishes survive in these countries, except in Paraguay, where the indigenous Guaraní once lived. Their traditional crops – cassava, corn and sweet potatoes – are still staples.

EARLY HISTORY

Although this part of South America was claimed by Spain in the early part of the 16th century, there was no rush to colonize the territory. The first of the explorers to come ashore, Juan Días de Solís, was attacked by hostile natives and – according to some records – eaten. This was a powerful deterrent, although it did not prevent one of the survivors of the expedition from pressing on to Paraguay and then Bolivia. Here he acquired some silver, which was discovered after his death on the return journey. This sparked a rumour that Spain's recent acquisition might hold riches. The country was christened Argentina, meaning "place of silver", but when reality failed to match rumour the Spanish lost interest. In any event, by 1531 they were preoccupied with Peru, where gold and silver was being "liberated" from the Inca Empire by Francisco Pizarro.

The first permanent settlements in Argentina were in the Andean valleys close to the border. Santiago del Estero, Tucumán and Córdoba were established in 1535. A year later, Pedro de Mendoza set up camp close to the Rio de la Plata, on a site that would one day become Buenos Aires. His hopes of founding a city were dashed, however, when natives attacked and he was forced to decamp to Uruguay.

Until the arrival of the Spanish, this part of South America was peopled by various tribes of hunter-gatherers turned farmers, growing crops such as corn, cassava, sweet potatoes, beans and peppers. Coastal peoples supplemented their diet with food from the sea – fish, shellfish and even seals. There were no great civilizations in this area, like those that existed in Peru or Central America. Pottery, stone carvings and rock paintings survive, but few of the inhabitants themselves withstood the arrival of the Europeans. War and disease quickly decimated their numbers, and by the end of the 19th century, very few of the early people remained.

Above: The different varieties of corn display many striking colours – here they have been left to dry in the sun.

THE PAMPAS

In 1581 the Spanish made a second attempt to establish a settlement on the banks of the Rio de la Plata in Argentina, and this time they succeeded. The extensive plains, or pampas, surrounding the place they called Buenos Aires proved to be incredibly fertile, and agriculture was rapidly established.

Cattle and horses that had escaped the original settlement had bred freely, and vast herds of animals now roamed across the pampas. This unexpected bounty was exploited by gauchos, or cowboys, who broke the horses and corralled the cattle. At first the animals were mainly killed for their hides, but when large salting plants were established in the early 19th century, the beef industry burgeoned. The pampas were fenced off and huge estates, *estancias*, were quickly established. Only the very rich could afford to buy these estates and soon the landed class became the most powerful people in Argentina.

Below: Gauchos on an Argentine cattle ranch demonstrate their riding skills for Dia de la Tradicion.

In 1816 the country, for the first time, became independent. During the second half of the 19th century, demand for cheap food in Europe led to further expansion of the beef industry and immigrants poured in. Meat processing factories, including the famous Fray Bentos plant just across the river in Uruguay, were built. At the same time sheep farming was becoming established in Patagonia and by the early part of the 20th century, Argentina was a major exporter of beef and lamb, wheat and wool. These remain important today, although now much of the pampas is given over to grain and oil seed farming.

AN ARGENTINE ASADO

The traditional way of cooking meat in Argentina is *al asador* – on the spit. The meat is impaled on metal rods, which are stuck into the ground at an angle to prevent the meat juices from dripping on to the fire. Whole carcasses or sections of carcasses are cooked this way, and the meat is sliced off and served after guests have enjoyed the traditional appetizers – kidneys, morcilla and chorizo sausages, livers and *chinchulin* (loops of stuffed intestine).

Below: The herbal tea drink, yerba maté, *is drunk throughout Argentina, and is often served in a dried, decorated gourd.*

Above: In Buenos Aires, Argentina, a chef prepares large pieces of meat to be grilled at a traditional asado.

FOOD AND DRINK

With so much good quality beef at their disposal, it is not surprising that meals revolve mainly around meat, which is usually served with a piquant sauce, *chimichurri*. Fish is not as popular as meat, despite being in plentiful supply, and vegetables are not much in evidence either. Meat consumption is lower in Paraguay, which, along with northern Argentina, is the only area where ethnic cuisine is still widely served. Corn meal is used to make delicious spoonbreads and puddings. Cassava, which Paraguayans call *mandioca*, is baked with cheese and eggs or transformed into flat breads that resemble tortillas. The influence of indigenous cooks is also evident in Argentine dishes such as *carbonada criolla*, a stew served in a pumpkin; and *humitas*, a puréed corn mixture which is often steamed in corn husks.

Immigrants have exerted considerable influence on the food of Argentina and Uruguay. The pasta and pizzas in Buenos Aires and Montevideo are said to be as good as any in Italy, and the Italians also inspired an Argentine dish in which pork is baked in milk. The Spanish influence remains strong, but Middle Eastern, Chinese, Japanese and Korean settlers have also made their mark. In the beautiful Lake District, where the Andes provide a towering backdrop to towns that look more European than South American, visitors can sample delicious fondues, sweet pastries or the local chocolate.

Yerba maté, a type of herbal tea, is the drink of choice in Argentina, Uruguay and Paraguay, along with wine, beer and *caña*, a cane spirit.

STREET FOOD AND SNACKS

Empanadas with various fillings are popular, as are tiny cheese and ham sandwiches. Pastries are often very sweet, especially the ones that incorporate *dulce de leche* (caramelized milk). Churros, the Spanish answer to doughnuts, are enjoyed with hot drinks.

FEASTS AND FESTIVALS

The most interesting festivals in this area are those that focus on the gaucho tradition. These include demonstrations of riding skills and the opportunity to sample a traditional *asado*. In Montevideo, the summer *Carnaval* is famous for the African drumming that accompanies *candombe* dance troupes.

PERU, BOLIVIA AND ECUADOR

Many of the world's most popular foods come from the arable Andean highlands of Peru, Bolivia and Ecuador. Potatoes originated in this region, as did tomatoes, squashes, pine nuts, quinoa, tamarillos, sweet potatoes and several types of bean. All of these foods were cultivated by some of the most fascinating civilizations the world has ever seen.

EARLY HISTORY

Unlike Brazil and Argentina, where no major civilizations were based, this part of South America has been home to a succession of highly developed cultures. Among these were the Nasca of Southern Peru, who etched the soil with elaborate geoglyphs so large that their shapes – patterns, birds and animals – can only be fully appreciated from the air. In the north of the country, the Mochica people built impressive pyramids, while the Tiahuanuco established an empire that ruled Peru, Bolivia, Chile and Argentina for over 1,000 years. Shortly after their collapse towards the end of the 12th century, a Quechua tribe, one of many in the mountains, began to establish a power base in the area around Cuzco. Their leader, known as the Inca, was Manco Capac. Within 300 years the Inca empire stretched from Colombia to northern Chile and ruled over more than 15 million subjects. Aside from their military might, skilled governance and prodigious building skills, the Incas also improved farming by introducing terracing and irrigation, cultivating new crops such as cassava and peanuts, and elevating the already high status of corn by declaring that only the Supreme Inca himself could plant the first seed of the new season.

The Inca civilization endured until 1533, when Cuzco fell to the Spanish conquistador, Francisco Pizarro. Along with Ecuador and Bolivia, Peru (which at that time included the northern part of present-day Chile) became part of the Viceroyalty of Peru, administered first from Lima and then from Quito. A period of Spanish colonial rule followed, coming to an end when Peru declared its independence in 1821. Ecuador did the same thing a year later, and Bolivia followed in 1825.

Below: Corn grows in abundance on the Incan agricultural terraces in the Peruvian highlands.

FOOD AND DRINK

Their shared history, first as part of the great Inca empire and later under Spain, means that the countries of Peru, Ecuador and Bolivia share similar cuisines, though each country has its own specialities. The Spanish influence is most noticeable on the coast, while in the high Andes, Quechua people fought to preserve their customs, eschewing Spanish ingredients and cooking methods. Away from the big cities it is still possible to come across dishes that have changed little for centuries.

Potatoes are eaten extensively throughout this region. Cooks are fortunate in having a wide variety of potatoes to choose from, and they take great care in selecting the right type for the dish. The yellow Papa Amarilla, for instance, tastes great in *causa*, a Peruvian speciality, which has an infinite number of variations. One way of preparing it is to layer cooked potatoes with flaked fish, chopped tomatoes and avocado; another variation tops the potato with an onion sauce before garnishing it with hard-boiled eggs, lettuce, peppers and olives. Equally delicious is *ocopa arequipena*, in which cooked potatoes are covered in a spicy cheese and walnut sauce.

A typical Peruvian dish is *carapulcra*. Dried potatoes, a throwback to Inca days when potatoes were freeze-dried on top of the high mountains, then squeezed dry and placed in the sun until hard, are traditionally used for this dish, although fresh potatoes can be substituted if the dried variety are unavailable. Potato and cheese rissoles are extremely popular in Ecuador, while in Bolivia potatoes are often simply mashed with a little oil and lemon juice, then served with chopped cassava, locally known as *yuca*, and corn, both of which are staple foods.

One of the most fascinating Peruvian ingredients is quinoa, known as the "mother grain" by the Incas. The tiny grains have a mild, slightly bitter taste and firm texture, and should be cooked in the same way as rice. Quinoa is an excellent source of protein and can be added to stews, bakes or salads.

Above: At an Ecuadorian market in Otavalo, women in traditional costume buy fresh fruit and vegetables.

FISH AND MEAT

Bolivia is one of only two landlocked countries in Latin America. As a result, the inhabitants do not eat as much sea fish as their neighbours, but fresh fish in the form of trout from Lake Titicaca is very popular. Peruvians enjoy a wide variety of fish and are especially fond of corvina or striped bass. They also have access to excellent seafood. The Pacific seaboard is noted for its delicious ceviche, the dish famous for "cooking" the fish by marinating it in fresh citrus juices. Lime juice is usually used in ceviche but in Ecuador the juice of bitter oranges is preferred.

Although Peruvians produce beef and pork and enjoy both, they are particularly partial to duck and chicken and also like to eat *cuyes* (guinea pigs). These vegetarian animals are raised in much the same way as rabbits or hens, and smallholders will often let them range freely around their homes. *Cuyes* are also raised commercially, on farms. Popular ways of cooking *cuyes* include stewing in a rich sauce and grilling over an open fire. Other exotic meats can be sampled in the jungles of Ecuador, where animals such as wild boar and monkey are often eaten.

Because mountain-bred animals are often tough, their meat is usually chopped into very small pieces, then stewed with corn and the rocoto or mirasol chillies that are widely used in this part of Latin America. This helps to tenderize the meat.

Many fruits are grown in this region, including pineapples, cherimoyas, mangoes, guavas and passion fruit. Bananas and plantains are also widely cultivated, especially in Ecuador. Other important ingredients are walnuts, pine nuts and peanuts, which are often ground to make rich sauces.

A favourite drink is *pisco*, a grape brandy that is common to Peru and Chile. *Chicha*, a type of beer made from fermented corn, is also drunk.

STREET FOOD AND SNACKS

A popular snack is *anticuchos* (ox heart kebabs). The meat is trimmed, marinated in spiced vinegar and speared on lengths of sugar cane before being grilled with a spicy basting sauce. Other street foods include empanadas or *pastelos* (pastries stuffed with a variety of tasty fillings) and *humitas* (fresh corn dough with a savoury or sweet filling, steamed in a corn husk parcel). Crisp plantain chips are an Ecuadorian speciality, while Bolivians like to snack on caramel-coated popcorn called *pasacaya*.

FEASTS AND FESTIVALS

Easter is celebrated in style in all three countries. The best-known Quechua festival is Inti Raymi (the festival of the sun), which celebrates the winter solstice on 24 June each year. This huge celebration often continues for days. In Ecuador, the self-proclaimed banana capital of the world, there is a banana festival every September.

Below: In La Paz, Bolivia, a market trader displays just some of the many varieties of potato grown in the region.

CHILE

A slender ribbon of a country, Chile is dominated by the Andes mountain range and measures some 4,830km/3,000 miles from north to south, but is never much more than 160km/100 miles wide. In the north is the strangely beautiful Atacama Desert; in the south, beyond the Continental ice field, lies a rugged land of glaciers and fjords. Between these extremes is a temperate, fertile zone where fruits and vegetables grow abundantly. The waters off the coast of Chile provide superb seafood.

EARLY HISTORY

The north of Chile was once ruled by the Incas, but before they came to prominence in the early 13th century, the land played host to a succession of tribal groups. The first of these is believed to have settled in the south of the country as early as 14,000 years ago. More recent inhabitants were the Aymara, who cultivated corn and potatoes in the far north, trading these foods for guano, a rich fertilizer gathered by coastal tribes. Also occupying the northern region were the Atacameño, whose descendants still uphold some of their tribal traditions. Another important group, the Mapuche, were fierce warriors who successfully kept the Inca and Spanish invaders at bay for centuries.

The Spanish finally gained a foothold in Chile in 1541, when Pedro de Valdivia founded Santiago. The town was almost lost six months later when natives attacked, but the community survived and less than 20 years later the Spanish were firmly entrenched.

The colonists quickly began to establish large estates or haciendas over much of the country. These were initially worked by native South Americans who were little more than slaves, but when the spread of European diseases virtually annihilated the native population, tenant farmers of mixed blood (*mestizos*) took their place.

Until the 18th century, Chile remained a largely agrarian country. As the Audiencia de Chile, linked for administrative purposes to the Vice-royalty of Peru, it was ruled from Lima, and was only permitted to trade with the mother country. All goods destined for Spain therefore had to go via Lima.

Chile was ripe for change when Napoleon's invasion of Spain in the early 19th century signalled the beginning of the end of that country's dominance in Latin America. When Napoleon placed his brother on the Spanish throne, the citizens of Santiago who were loyal to the deposed King Ferdinand VII refused to acknowledge the usurper, and declared on 18 September 1810 that they would rule Chile themselves until the French were ousted from Spain. This independence was short-lived, however, as troops from Peru soon re-established control. Independence would only be formally declared in 1818, after José de San Martin's liberation army had crossed from Argentina into Chile.

Below: Chile's ice fields, such as Torres del Paine, Patagonia, lie to the south of a more temperate, fertile area.

Above: Garlands of dried shellfish hang from market stalls in Puerto Montt, Chile, a town known for its seafood.

After initial turmoil, the country became relatively stable. Agriculture and mining prospered, and were bolstered by the arrival of settlers from Ireland, England, Germany, France, Italy, Croatia and the Middle East. All of these immigrants had an influence on the Chilean cuisine, but the national diet still has strong links with its origins, and traditional ingredients such as corn, squash, beans and potatoes are widely used.

FOOD AND DRINK

Any discussion about food in Chile inevitably centres on the extent, excellence and variety of seafood available. The plankton-rich Humboldt current is responsible for the largesse, which includes crabs, clams, mussels, abalone, razor clams, sea urchins, squid, octopus, scallops and lobsters. Some or all of these types of seafood, plus less identifiable specialities such as *picorocco* (giant barnacles), are likely to be among the treats on offer at that most Chilean of feasts, the *curanto*, a massive cookout that involves a carefully constructed pit, hot rocks and leaves to seal in the steam.

Fish is equally abundant. Popular varieties include congrio, a slender fish that resembles an eel; corvina, a type of bass; swordfish and the Patagonian toothfish. Chile is also one of the world's biggest exporters of salmon.

Corn features widely in many recipes, from soups and breads to the delicious *pastel de choclo*, which is a traditional stew topped with a corn crust. Meat is not as central to the diet as it is in neighbouring Argentina, but Chile produces some fine beef, pork and lamb nevertheless.

Chilean desserts are similar to those served elsewhere on the continent, mainly taking their inspiration from Spain and making great use of the thick, sweet caramelized milk called *dulce de leche*. The central valleys produce excellent fresh fruit throughout the year, and deliciously sweet cakes and pastries are also available, courtesy of German settlers.

Chileans enjoy a good bottle of wine and are extremely proud of their vineyards, which are rapidly gaining worldwide recognition. Also popular is draft beer, known locally as *schop*, and the delicious grape brandy, *pisco*.

A curanto on Chiloé

The beautiful archipelago of Chiloé, situated off Puerto Montt, is famous for its fine seafood, wooden churches and laid-back atmosphere. This is a great place to sample the *curanto* – a full-scale Chilean seafood feast.

STREET FOOD AND SNACKS

For munching on the move, Chileans tuck into meat, seafood, empanadas, *humitas* and sandwiches, from steak with all the trimmings to *ave-palta* (chicken and avocado).

FEASTS AND FESTIVALS

Independence Day on 18 September is celebrated with music, dancing, eating and drinking, and marks the start of summer. The rodeo season also starts in September, with the major event, the National Rodeo, taking place in March. Ngillatun is an ancient Mapuche festival celebrating harvest and fertility.

Below: An impressive array of fresh fruit and vegetables are on offer at a market in Valdivia in Chile's Lake District.

COLOMBIA AND VENEZUELA

At the upper end of South America lie two countries that are as mysterious as they are magnificent. Colombia and Venezuela have some of the most rugged terrain on the continent. From the tropical rainforest of the coast, the land rises to range after range of high mountains, the cordilleras of the Andes. Ravines, mighty rivers and dense vegetation make exploration difficult, and communities have historically been isolated. Until the first settlers arrived there was, therefore, no universal style of eating, and the Spanish were able to establish theirs as the core cuisine in both countries.

Above: Roadside vendors are a common sight in Colombia, selling fruits such as bananas, melons and pineapples.

EARLY HISTORY

Columbus discovered the mouth of the Orinoco River in 1498. The first Spanish settlement in Venezuela was established in 1521 and in Colombia four years later. In the early 19th century both countries united with Ecuador and Panama to form the union of Gran Colombia, after their independence was won by Simon Bolivar. Venezuela left the union to become a separate state in 1830, as did Ecuador, and Panama eventually left the union in 1903.

FOOD AND DRINK

Both Colombia and Venezuela have lowland plains, temperate zones above 900m/3,000ft and highlands leading to alpine-style meadows. At sea level, sugar, cacao, coconuts, bananas and rice are cultivated. Higher up are the coffee plantations and corn fields, and above these cereal crops, potatoes and temperate fruits are all grown. This huge diversity of landscape means that both countries have a wide range of foods available to them, from the traditional ingredients such as cassava, squash, beans and corn to a dazzling array of fruits.

Favourite Venezuelan dishes include delicacies such as *mondongo* (tripe with vegetables, corn and potatoes), *sancocho* (fish stew) and *parrillado* (barbecued meats), while Colombian specialities include rabbit in coconut milk, chicken hotpot with three different types of potato, and a delicious pineapple custard. Colombia has the benefit of a coastline on both the Caribbean Sea and the Pacific Ocean, so it has a wonderful selection of fish and seafood readily available. *Arepas* (flat corn breads) are a very popular snack. Both countries produce lots of coffee and it is one of their major exports; Colombian coffee is reckoned to be among the finest in the world.

A seasonal speciality and a great delicacy in the lowland regions are flying ants, which are toasted and served like peanuts. In Venezuela a delicious spicy sauce, *katara*, is made from the heads of leaf-cutter ants.

The lure of El Dorado

The rumour of a land where gold was so plentiful that people powdered themselves with gold dust lured many 16th-century adventurers to the countries now known as Guyana, Surinam and French Guiana. The glut of gold never materialized but the Spanish, Dutch, English and French all thought that the land was worth fighting for.

The English eventually triumphed in Guyana, but only after many years of Dutch settlement. Surinam went to the Dutch and French Guiana became first a French penal colony and then an overseas department of France. Still heavily subsidized by France, French Guiana has a distinctly Gallic atmosphere, with pavement cafes and food with a distinctly French flavour. In Guyana and Surinam, where African slaves and indentured labourers from India, China and the East Indies were imported to work the sugar plantations, the cooking is more eclectic. Javanese noodle dishes and Chinese stir-fries are sold alongside native South American Indian dishes like pepperpot – a stew with meat tenderized by cassareep (cassava extract). Seafood is popular, especially prawns (shrimp), and plantains, bananas, cassava, beans, peanuts and squash are also widely used. The area is famous for its superb fruit, and for unusual vegetables like *pom*, a large yellow root that closely resembles cassava.

CENTRAL AMERICA

The land that connects Mexico with the rest of South America consists of seven countries, Guatemala, Belize, El Salvador, Honduras, Nicaragua, Costa Rica and Panama. Beans and rice are the staple foods in all these countries, but there is also fine fish to be had, thanks to the proximity of the Pacific Ocean and the Caribbean Sea.

EARLY HISTORY

The empire of the Maya extended to Honduras. When they disappeared from Central America around AD900 they not only left behind ruined cities like Tikal in Guatemala, but also new foods and sophisticated farming techniques, some of which were adopted by natives.

Columbus reached the shores of Honduras and then Costa Rica in 1502, but the area was not settled until some 20 years later, after troops led by Pedro de Alvarado came south from Mexico. Alvarado took Guatemala, Honduras and El Salvador. By 1530 there were Spanish colonists in most of Central America. Government was a haphazard affair, but in 1535 Guatemala, Honduras, El Salvador, Nicaragua and Costa Rica were incorporated into the Viceroyalty of New Spain, headquartered in Mexico City.

In 1821, the quintet opted out and two years later formed a federal republic, known as the United Provinces of Central America. The states were all autonomous, however. Belize became British, largely by default. Although the area was technically Spanish, British buccaneers established bases there and were later joined by British soldiers from Jamaica. In 1798 the British connection was formalized, and the link was only broken in 1981 when Belize became independent. Panama, meanwhile, looked to the south and was part of the Union of Gran Colombia until 1903. The building of the Panama Canal brought affluence to the area, and Panama is still one of the wealthier countries in Central America.

FOOD AND DRINK

The food of Central America is not as exciting as the surroundings, but competing against orchid-clad forests, volcanoes, waterfalls, barrier reefs and beautiful beaches would be a tall order. Dishes based on rice and beans are everywhere, but there are plenty of alternatives. Fish is universally popular. Varieties include tuna, mackerel, snapper, pompano, swordfish and mahi-mahi. The fish is often cooked simply and served whole, but there are also plenty of rich fish soups and stews. Lobsters, clams, prawns (shrimp) and other types of seafood are also widely available. Chicken is always on the menu, alongside specialities such as *mondongo* (tripe stew) and *cecina* (beef marinated in citrus juices). There is a strong Mexican influence in Guatemala and Belize; Panama takes inspiration from Colombia; and Creole dishes are found on the Caribbean coast. Coffee is grown in Costa Rica, El Salvador and Guatemala and is enjoyed by everyone, from the very young to the very old.

Above: In Costa Rica, a worker spreads out coffee beans to dry in the sun.

Below: Corn fields flourish alongside impressive mountains at the south-east tip of Lake Atitlan in Guatemala.

Fabulous fruits

Central America is blessed with bountiful fruit. Markets throughout the region are filled with bananas, cherimoyas, mangoes, papayas, pineapples and guavas, plus many more varieties that are local to each country. Delicious fruit drinks are a popular choice. *Refrescos* or *frescos* are milk- or water-based, while *batidas* sometimes contain rum or a similar spirit. Also refreshing are *pipas*, large green coconuts that stallholders cut open on request so that thirsty purchasers can sip the cool liquid inside.

MEXICO

Most people tend to see typical Mexican cuisine as tortillas, tamales and tequila, but that is not strictly true. Mexico is a vast country, with an enormous range of unusual and delicious regional recipes, only some of which are represented in that synthesis of styles commonly known as Tex-Mex cooking. Many of the essential ingredients are only gradually becoming known outside the country, and the careful blending of flavours that is the mark of authentic Mexican cooking often comes as a delightful surprise to the uninitiated.

EARLY HISTORY

In ancient times, many different tribal groups occupied the area now known as Mexico. Most of these existed in isolation, hemmed in by lofty mountains or separated from each other by natural barriers such as deserts, jungles and canyons. On the central plateau and in Yucatan, two indigenous civilizations emerged that would have a considerable impact on the future of the country. The first was the Maya, whose empire stretched from Guatemala and Honduras to Yucatan, Chiapas and Campeche. The Maya had a complex society. They used their knowledge of astronomy and mathematics to chart the heavens and built impressive stepped pyramids to their gods. They were also farmers, cultivating corn, beans, squash and chillies, including the bitingly hot habañero, which they used to make a sauce called *ixni-pec* (pronounced schneepeck) which is still popular today. A favourite flavouring was annatto (achiote) and they loved to drink chocolate. The Maya reached their zenith between AD600 and AD800, and by AD900 many of their ceremonial sites had been abandoned.

Not long after this, a tribe called the Mexica – better known as the Aztecs – began to emerge. By the beginning of the 14th century they had built a vast empire, with its capital at Tenochtitlán, where Mexico City is now. The city was magnificent, with gardens irrigated by water brought by an aqueduct from springs some distance away. Here successive emperors dined in splendour while their armies waged war on the surrounding tribes. Believing that the sun would only rise if regularly appeased with offerings of human hearts, the Aztecs sacrificed thousands of captives and earned a reputation for extreme cruelty. Their belief in the gods was to be their downfall, however, for when the Spaniard Hernán Cortes reached their shores in 1519, they believed him to be the god Quetzalcoatl. When Cortes and his party reached Tenochtitlán, the Emperor Montezuma welcomed them, discovering too late that this was not a social visit. Within two years, the Spanish had totally subjugated the Aztecs.

Above: Cocoa beans were used to make chocolate, which was a popular drink among the ancient Aztecs.

For the next 300 years, Spain ruled Mexico, losing control only after Napoleon Bonaparte overran Spain in 1808. Mexico became an independent country in 1821, and a republic was set up in 1824, but this did not spell stability. In 1836 the state of Texas, which had been part of Mexico, declared itself an independent republic. When Texas joined the USA nine years later, the Mexican Civil War began, as a result of which Mexico ceded to the USA all territories south of the Rio Grande. The country has remained a republic ever since, apart from a brief period of French occupation between 1864 and 1867.

FOOD AND DRINK

The Spanish who invaded Mexico found a country filled with foods they had never seen before. Aside from corn, squash and unfamiliar beans, there were tomatoes, chillies, cactus paddles, tomatillos, avocados, jicamas, guavas

Below: Workers sort through piles of newly picked avocados, a popular fruit used in many Mexican dishes.

and pineapples. Turkeys, ducks and small hairless dogs were raised for the table, and runners brought fresh fish from the Gulf of Mexico every day, for Montezuma to feast upon. Corn was cooked in dozens of different ways. The common people consumed it as *atole*, which resembled porridge, or as tortillas, while the ruling class feasted on tamales. At the court of Montezuma, the emperor took his pick of hundreds of different dishes served at elaborate feasts. Although *pulque*, made from the fermented sap of the maguey cactus, was readily available, chocolate was the drink of choice for the Aztec elite.

The livestock that the Spanish brought with them revolutionized Mexican cooking. Cattle, goats, pigs and sheep were introduced. Milk, cheese, butter and eggs entered the diet, although they would never achieve the same importance in Mexico as they had in Europe. Pigs were used for lard, and lard made frying possible, which was a major step. Wheat, barley, citrus, olives, walnuts and grapes were planted, and other fruits and vegetables were introduced. Gradually, an entirely new style of cooking emerged.

Below: Small sugar skulls go on sale in early November to mark The Day of the Dead, a traditional Mexican festival.

Above: A typical Mexican street vendor sells fresh tortillas filled with beans, chillies, cheese and a variety of meats.

The French occupation of Mexico left a legacy in the shape of delicious breads, crêpes, cakes and pastries. German settlers introduced brewing and expanded the local cheese-making, while recent immigrants from Asia and the Middle East have also had an impact on Mexican cuisine.

TYPICAL DISHES

Corn dishes are still hugely important in all but the north of the country, where wheat is more dominant. Tortillas form the basis of many *antojitos* (snack meals), but Mexican food has much more to offer. One example is *sopa seca*, the aptly named "dry soup" in which some of the moisture is soaked up by rice, vermicelli or strips of dry tortilla. On Pacific and Gulf shores, the seafood is outstanding, with sea bass, mackerel, swordfish and large prawns (shrimp) among the delights on offer.

Bean dishes have been popular in Mexico for millennia and *frijoles de olla*, pinto beans cooked slowly with water and a little lard, is not to be missed, especially if served with guacamole. Among the many meat and poultry dishes, *albondigas* (spicy meatballs) should be sampled, as should *chile verde*, pork in a green sauce with cactus paddles. Chillies are a central ingredient in the cuisine, and fresh and dried chillies are frequently blended to create dishes of great complexity.

Custards and rice puddings, which are often very sweet, are the classic desserts. In contrast, fresh fruits are often served with salt, a sprinkling of chilli powder and fresh lime juice. Alcoholic drinks include locally produced wine and beer, tequila and mescal, and there is a wide selection of fruit drinks.

STREET FOOD AND SNACKS

Mexico has a handle on finger food. Neatly packaged burritos, tacos, tamales and *tortas* are all available from street vendors, as are *carnitas* – succulent pieces of pork cooked in orange-flavoured lard with garlic until the outside turns crisp.

FEASTS AND FESTIVALS

Most Mexican festivals have special foods associated with them. Epiphany, on 6 January, is celebrated with Kings' Day Bread, while The Day of the Dead at the start of November, when Mexicans honour their deceased relations, is marked by the eating of tamales, followed by a sweet pumpkin dessert and little sugar skulls. The traditional Christmas centrepiece is *mole poblano*, a rich turkey dish that brings together chilli and chocolate.

THE LATIN AMERICAN KITCHEN

Latin American cuisine is founded on simple ingredients of excellent quality. Fresh fish and shellfish, quality cuts of meat and locally grown exotic fruits and vegetables are abundant. Inevitably, each country has developed its own specialities, but there are common flavourings and techniques that are used throughout Latin America, creating a wonderfully varied cuisine.

EQUIPMENT

Latin American cooks are endlessly inventive, not only in the way they cook, but also in their approach to kitchen equipment. While the items featured here could give your cooking a more authentic touch, few are essential. If you intend making your own tortillas, a press and *comal* will be extremely useful, but for most purposes, it is perfectly possible to improvise.

METATE

Made from a sloping piece of volcanic rock and looking rather like a three-legged stone stool, this grinding stone is used to make *masa* dough from skinned, cooked corn kernels. It can also be used to grind cocoa and *piloncillo* (unrefined cane sugar). The grinding is done with the aid of a stone roller, a *muller*, which is made from the same stone as the *metate*. Before a new *metate* can be used, it must be tempered. A mixture of dry rice and salt is placed on the grinding surface, and the *muller* is rocked back and forth to press the mixture into the surface and remove any loose pieces of sand or grit. These are fairly difficult to obtain outside South America, but they are available by mail order.

Below: A metate *is a traditional grinding stone made from volcanic rock. The design has not changed for many centuries.*

MOLCAJETE AND TEJOLOTE

The Mexican mortar, the *molcajete*, is traditionally made from volcanic rock and must be tempered in the same way as the *metate*. The short, stubby pestle used to grind ingredients is called a *tejolote*. The best *molcajetes* are heavy and not too porous. Before purchasing, grind the *molcajete* briefly with the *tejolote*. If the stone seems soft and a lot of dust is formed, it is probably too porous. Similar to the Thai equivalent, which it closely resembles, it is ideal for grinding herbs, garlic, chillies and other spices such as achiote (annatto), as well as nuts and seeds for making *mole poblano*, for example. Fresh salsas, such as guacamole, are often made with a *molcajete* and *tejolote*. The flavours of the ingredients are crushed out, which gives a rustic texture and flavour. However, grinding spices or pounding chillies with a *molcajete* and *tejolote* is hard work so many Mexican cooks use a food processor or a blender instead.

Above: A mortar and pestle, or molcajete e tejolote, *is an essential tool for grinding spices and chillies.*

TORTILLA PRESS

In Mexico and other parts of Latin America where tortillas and similar griddle cakes are made, the *masa* dough was traditionally shaped by hand. Skilled women were able to make an astonishing number of perfectly shaped tortillas in a very short time, but this is something of a dying art. Today, most people use tortilla presses, and in tortilla bakeries or *tortillerias* the whole process is mechanized. The most effective tortilla presses are made from cast iron, but because these must be seasoned (oiled) before use, and carefully maintained, many people prefer steel presses. Tortilla presses consist of two round metal plates, hinged together. They come in various sizes and are heavy, in order to limit the leverage needed to work them. The dough is placed between the plates, which are then squeezed together with the aid of a lever. Placing thin sheets of plastic on the plates or covering them with plastic bags before making the tortillas will ensure that they are easy to remove once they are pressed. Tortilla presses are sold in good speciality kitchen shops and are also widely available by mail order.

Left: Perfect tortillas can be easily pressed with a heavy steel or cast-iron tortilla press.

CUSCUZEIRO

This looks a bit like a metal colander supported on a frame, and it is used as a mould for the popular Brazilian dish *cuscuz paulista*. The *cuscuzeiro* is lined with a variety of foods that will look decorative when the dish is turned out, for example, slices of tomato, hard-boiled eggs or slices of pepper, with perhaps a few fresh prawns (shrimp). A moist corn meal mixture is then packed on top of these ingredients. More layers are added until the container is full, and it is then covered and steamed. When turned out the layers of the *cuscuz* look pretty and it tastes delicious. The name suggests that *cuscuz* evolved from couscous, and the method of preparation certainly calls to mind the North African dish.

EARTHENWARE DISHES

The Spanish influence on the region's cuisine is clearly visible in the clay pots (*ollas*) that are traditionally used for cooking stews and sauces throughout Latin America. Often beautifully hand-painted and decorated, they give food a unique earthy flavour, but are seldom found outside the region, as their fragility means that they do not travel well and are rarely exported. Sadly, modern materials and designs have made them relatively rare in Latin America itself. Flat earthenware dishes decorated around the edge are more easily found, and these are often used as serving dishes. Traditional Spanish *cazuelas* (shallow terracotta dishes) and casseroles also make excellent alternatives.

COMAL

This is a thin circular griddle, traditionally used over an open fire to cook tortillas. They were placed among the hot coals and pulled out with long sticks. Clay *comals* take longer to heat up, but they do not require oiling before use, unlike metal ones. If you cannot find a *comal*, a cast-iron griddle or large frying pan will do the job equally well.

FARINHERRA

This is a traditional shaker used mainly in Brazil for sprinkling *farinha de mandioca* (cassava flour) over meat or fish dishes, such as *feijoada*, to mop up the sauce and juices.

Above: For slow-cooking rich stews and sauces, Latin American cooks often use ollas, *traditional hand-decorated Spanish clay pots, which give an authentic flavour.*

Left: Available as metal or clay varieties, a comal *is the traditional griddle pan used for cooking tortillas.*

CORN

The Aztecs called it "first mother and father, the source of life". Corn was equally highly revered in Peru, first by the indigenous South Americans, who worshipped the corn goddess, and then by the Incas, who decreed that corn could only be planted after the Supreme Inca had turned the first sod with a golden plough reserved for this purpose.

Corn was a sacred food, of huge significance. Not only was it a vital source of sustenance, but it also provided shelter, fencing and even clothing. Every part of the plant was used, even the silks surrounding the kernels, which became ties for tamales. When corn was cooked, whoever added it to the pot had first to breathe on it to rid it of its fear of dying and accustom it to the heat.

Some corn was eaten fresh, but most was dried and stored, then processed to make a type of porridge called *atole*. This was a lengthy chore, made easier by the discovery that the skins came off much more easily if the kernels were heated in a lime solution. When boiled in fresh water, the skinned kernels made a mash (*pozole*), versions of which were eaten by the indigenous peoples of Central and South America.

The cooked skinned kernels were also the basis for *masa*, a dough made by crushing the corn. The dough was then transformed into tortillas or similar flat breads, using techniques that are much the same today.

Corn is a valuable carbohydrate food but it is deficient in the amino acids lysine and tryptophan. If corn is the sole food source, as in some parts of Africa, diseases such as kwashiorkor and pellagra result. The problem has not arisen in South America or the Caribbean, however, because the basic diet also includes beans and squash, which compensate for the nutritional deficiencies of corn.

History

Corn evolved in Central America but its precise origin is not known. No wild forms have ever been found, and its ancestor may have been a type of grass with tiny kernels, each embedded in a cob no bigger than a haricot bean. How the grass evolved into the much larger plant with rows of kernels growing side by side on a substantial cob is not known, but the indigenous farmers were highly efficient plant breeders.

Corn was already widely grown throughout South America when Columbus first encountered it on the island of Cuba. The tall, leafy plant was called *maïs*, and in many parts of the globe it is still known as maize. The alternative name arose because Columbus and his crew saw it as a staple food equivalent to the corn they grew back home, and dubbed it native corn.

Above: White Andean corn is ground and used to make masa *dough.*

Below: South American corn comes in many colours, including vibrant red.

Above: Corn, known as maïs, *is a native South American crop.*

Varieties

There are five main varieties of corn. Dent corn is the most widely grown globally, and is mainly used for animal feeds and oil. Other varieties are popcorn, flint corn, flour corn and sweet corn, which is the type used in cooking. Baby sweet corn cobs are often picked before they are mature, then cooked and eaten whole. Yellow corn kernels are the most common, but the corn grown in South America comes in other colours too, including red, blue, purple and the pale white that is typical of the Andean region. There are even variegated types available, which have sweet white, red and purple kernels on the same cob. For flavour, one of the most highly prized varieties is Peru's purple corn, *maiz morado*, which has a subtle citrus flavour and is used to make *mazamorra*, a delicious pudding, or the unusual drink, *chicha morrada*.

Buying and storing

If possible, corn should be cooked within 24 hours of being picked. This is because the sugar in the kernels starts to turn into starch as soon as the cobs are cut. Look for husks that are clean, shiny and well filled. If you are not sure whether the corn is ripe or not, take a look at the tassels, which should be golden brown. Unless you are planning to cook the corn the minute you get home, do not part the green husks to check out the contents; once the kernels have been exposed to the air, they will quickly begin to dry out.

Preparing corn

Corn can be cooked in many different ways, but when served as an accompaniment is usually simply boiled.

1 Strip off the green husks surrounding the cobs.

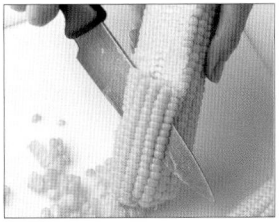

2 If only the kernels are required, lift the cob slightly and slice downwards using a sharp knife to remove a few rows at a time.

3 Whether using whole cobs, slices or just the kernels, plunge the corn into lightly salted boiling water for 4–5 minutes, until tender. Drain and serve with a knob of butter.

Huitlacoche

During times of drought, corn kernels are sometimes infected by a fungus, which turns them grey and causes them to swell to many times their original size. Far from being a disaster, this is seen as a boon, because the "corn truffles" as they are sometimes known, have a delicious, earthy flavour when cooked and are regarded as a delicacy around the world.

Cooking

Corn remains a staple ingredient in modern Latin America. Young, tender corn cobs are first stripped of their husks and then either steamed or cooked whole on a brazier or barbecue as a delicious fast-food snack. The puréed kernels also make an excellent soup. In Argentina, corn is often added to stews, such as the popular meat stew, *carbonada criolla*, while in Ecuador the kernels are mixed with salt cod and other vegetables to make the traditional dish, *fanesca*.

CORN MEAL

Also known as maize flour, corn meal remains slightly gritty when cooked, giving a characteristic texture to the flat breads for which it is most often used. The product known as cornflour in the UK and cornstarch in the US is a pure starch extracted from the grain. When mixed with regular wheat flour in a cake, it produces a lighter result. *Masa harina* is sometimes known as tortilla flour, which indicates its purpose. Although Latin cooks will often make *masa* (tortilla dough) from cooked corn kernels, the flour is an easier option. It comes in various grades, depending on what sort of corn it is made from. *Masarepa* is a similar product, used for making *arepas*, the flat griddle cakes that are popular in Venezuela and Colombia.

Right: Wet corn is ground to make masa harina, *which can then be used to make corn tortillas.*

Above: Dried corn husks should be soaked in cold water before use.

DRIED CORN HUSKS

These make handy wrappers for Mexican tamales and Peruvian *humitas*. They are fairly brittle, so should be soaked in water for about 30 minutes before being used to wrap ingredients. Dried corn husks are not always easy to obtain outside Latin America, so baking parchment can be used instead.

RICE

After its introduction to Latin America and the Caribbean by the Spanish in the 16th century, rice rapidly became a staple food crop. Large tracts of wetlands are given over to rice production, especially in Brazil, which grows as much rice as Japan. Rice is an important source of protein and carbohydrates for the poorest sector of the population, especially in urban areas where individuals spend 15 per cent of their income on white rice.

In Brazil, rice is an essential accompaniment to almost all main meals, particularly the national dish, *feijoada*, and is often layered in a mould with many other ingredients. Rice is also an extremely important ingredient in Caribbean cooking. In Peru, Colombia and Ecuador, where cooked rice is served quite dry, its granular texture earns it the name *arroz graneado*. Rice is also used to make drinks, such as the Mexican *horchata* and Ecuador's fermented rice drink, *arroz fermentado*.

Varieties

White long-grain rice is the variety grown throughout the region, although the influence of immigrants means that other varieties are imported. White rice has been fully milled to remove the outer husk from the inner kernel, leaving a white grain with a delicate fragrance and slightly nutty flavour.

Left: White long-grain rice is served as an accompaniment throughout Latin America and the Caribbean.

Buying and storing

Buy good quality rice in packets and store it in a cool, dry place. Rice keeps well, but once opened, it should be transferred to an airtight container. If cooked rice is cooled quickly, it can be stored for up to 24 hours in the refrigerator. Make sure it is piping hot before it is served next time. Don't reheat rice more than once, and never keep it warm for long periods because there is a risk of food poisoning.

Quinoa

Indigenous to Peru, quinoa is a complete protein, possessing all eight essential amino acids. Low in saturated fat and high in fibre, it is a good source of calcium, potassium, zinc, iron, magnesium and B vitamins. Cooked like rice, the grain becomes soft and creamy, but the germ stays crunchy.

Preparing rice

White long grain rice is fluffy and absorbent when cooked, and makes the perfect accompaniment to soups, stews and sauces. It may also be cooked with other ingredients to make a composite dish. If serving rice as an accompaniment:

1 Add 15ml/1 tbsp oil to a pan, heat gently, then add 1 clove of crushed garlic.

2 Add the rice to the pan and roast the grains for a few minutes until they begin to turn golden.

3 Transfer the rice to a pan full of lightly salted water. Bring to the boil, then add a tight-fitting lid and simmer gently until all of the liquid has been absorbed.

If the rice is to be mixed with other ingredients, for example in the Mexican dish, *sopa seca*, try the following method. It encourages the rice to absorb other flavours and reduces the final cooking time.

1 In a pan or heatproof bowl, soak the rice in freshly boiled water for 10 minutes.

2 Drain thoroughly before adding the other ingredients.

This fairly unusual method of cooking rice is very popular throughout the region, especially in Colombia, and is particularly delicious served with seafood.

1 Add 50ml/2fl oz/¼ cup coconut milk to a pan with a pinch of brown sugar.

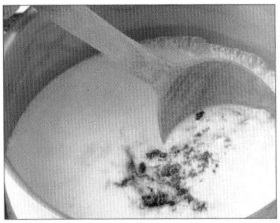

2 Add the rice, bring to the boil and simmer gently for 10–15 minutes, or until tender.

POTATOES

The potato is native to South America and was discovered by pre-Inca peoples in the foothills of the Andes. Archaeological digs in Peru and Bolivia have uncovered evidence that it was used as a food as long ago as 400BC. In Peru, the potato had religious significance, and the potato goddess was depicted with a potato plant in either hand. Potato designs were found in Nazca and Chimu pottery. One of the ways the South American Indians had of measuring time was to gauge how long it took to cook potatoes to certain consistencies. The Incas perfected the art of freeze-drying potatoes 2,000 years ago by leaving them out on lofty mountain tops to produce the early convenience food, *chuno*. In an entirely natural process, the night air froze the potatoes and the sun completed the lengthy dehydration process.

When the Inca empire was invaded by Francisco Pizarro in the 16th century, potatoes were among the plunder that the Conquistadors took back to Spain with them. Cultivation quickly spread throughout Europe via explorers such as Sir Francis Drake. Today there are up to 4,000 varieties worldwide. The potato is the staple food for two-thirds of the world's population and our third most important food crop.

Under the skin

Most of the nutrients in potatoes are either in or just beneath the skin, so it is best to avoid peeling potatoes if at all possible.

If you need to peel them, use a potato peeler that removes only the very top surface.

Potatoes are one of the best all-round sources of nutrition known to man. A valuable carbohydrate food, they also contain fairly high levels of protein. They are a very good source of vitamin C, a fact that was of huge value to early seafarers, who discovered that feeding potatoes to their crews helped to prevent scurvy. Potatoes also contain potassium, iron and vitamin B.

Above: Grown in Uruguay and Venezuela, the Red Pontiac has dark red skin and white waxy flesh.

Varieties

In the UK, only about 15 varieties of potato are on general sale, but in Peruvian markets it is claimed that you can buy up to 100 different types, ranging in size from tiny potatoes to large ovals. Worldwide there are thought to be around 4,000 varieties. The colours are equally diverse, including red, black, yellow, brown, purple and black. Most are known only by their local names, but some are beginning to reach markets in the northern hemisphere. Look out for the Purple Peruvian, with its earthy, slightly nutty-tasting lavender flesh. Also prized, particularly for mashing, is the buttery Papa Amarilla, or yellow potato. Among the varieties with dark skins and dazzling white flesh are the Yanaimilla and the Compis. Potatoes will grow anywhere from sea level to 4,300m/14,000ft, so it is not surprising that so many different varieties continue to be cultivated in their place of origin.

Buying and storing

When buying potatoes, it is important to choose a variety that will give you the right results for the cooking method you intend to use. Check the labels or ask for advice from the seller. Store potatoes in a dark, cool, dry place. Paper sacks are better than plastic bags, which create humid conditions and hasten deterioration.

Preparing and cooking

In Latin America, potatoes are usually either boiled in the minimum of water, as in the Peruvian speciality, *ocopa arequipena*, or diced and fried, which is a popular method in Mexico. Chillies are frequently added. Purple Peruvian potatoes are excellent in salads and they require less cooking than white or yellow potatoes.

Below: With striking dark skin and white flesh, Compis potatoes are grown by farmers in the Andean highlands.

BEANS

Along with corn and rice, beans are an extremely important food throughout the Caribbean and Latin America. The inhabitants of Mexico and Central America eat around six times as many beans as are consumed in Britain every year, and in Chile, where meat can be relatively scarce, they are a vital source of protein. Beans are served, in one form or another, at most meals.

Several varieties of bean are indigenous to this part of the world. They were traditionally planted with corn and squash, the idea being that the corn stalks would support the growing beans, while the squash plants spread out to suffocate encroaching weeds. This ancient method of cultivation also ensured that the beans enriched the soil depleted by the corn. The beans were served fresh in season, but vast amounts were dried to furnish versatile and nutritious dishes all year round. In the Caribbean, beans are often referred to as "peas".

Beans are a good source of protein and carbohydrate and supply vitamins A, B_1 and B_2. They also contribute valuable amounts of minerals, such as potassium and iron, to the diet.

Below: Black beans are an essential ingredient in the extravagant Brazilian national dish, feijoada.

Above: Versatile white beans, a type of haricot (navy) bean, are plump and soft with a delicious floury texture.

Varieties

Black beans These small, shiny, kidney-shaped beans, sometimes known as black turtle beans, are particularly popular in Mexico, the Caribbean and Brazil. They are highly valued for their creamy white flesh and delicate earthy flavour, reminiscent of mushrooms. Their skins remain bright and shiny after cooking, so they look dramatic when combined with rice or other ingredients. Black beans are often used in salsas and soups, and are eaten as an accompaniment to Brazil's national dish, *feijoada*. In Costa Rica they are often fried with white rice to make the traditional breakfast dish, *gallo pinto*.

White beans A type of haricot (navy) bean, these vary in size but are always the same plump oval shape. When cooked, they have an earthy, rather floury flavour, and a fairly soft texture, but they retain their shape well. White beans are an extremely versatile ingredient and can be substituted for most other varieties when a recipe calls for dried beans.

Pinto beans A smaller, paler version of the borlotti bean, the pinto has an attractive orange-pink skin speckled with rust-coloured flecks. One of the many relatives of the kidney bean, pinto beans are native to Latin America. They feature extensively in Mexican cooking as well as the cuisines of most other Spanish-speaking countries. The skins soften on cooking, which makes them easy to mash, so they are the perfect ingredient for the popular Mexican dish, *frijoles refritos* (refried beans).

Right: Native to Latin America, pinto beans are traditionally used to make refritos, *the Mexican speciality.*

Red kidney beans The shiny, dark red skin of these beans hides a pale interior. They retain their shape and colour when cooked and have a soft, mealy texture. Red kidney beans are particularly popular in Brazil, Mexico and some parts of the Caribbean, where they are used to make a delicious red bean chilli and the Jamaican speciality, rice and peas. They can also be used instead of the traditional pinto beans to make a variation on refried beans.

Lima beans These beans originated in Peru and are named after that country's capital city. Cream-coloured and tender, with soft flesh, these hold their shape well when cooked. Lima beans have a delicate flavour, similar to that of walnuts. Fresh lima beans are delicious. One variety of lima bean is the large white butter bean, which is familiar throughout Europe. Be careful not to overcook lima beans as they become pulpy and mushy in texture.

Black-eyed beans/peas Small and white, with a distinctive black mark, these beans were introduced to the Caribbean from West Africa. They need not be soaked before use because they rapidly become tender when cooked. They taste slightly sweet and readily absorb other flavours, especially in stews and curries. Add black-eyed beans to soups and salads for extra flavour.

Gungo peas Also known as pigeon peas, these are approximately the size of a garden pea. They have a sweetish, slightly acrid flavour, and are used fresh, canned or dried.

Chickpeas Also known as garbanzo beans, robust and hearty chickpeas resemble shelled hazelnuts and have a delicious nutty flavour and creamy texture, although they require lengthy cooking. Spanish migrants first introduced chickpeas to Latin America, and although they have never been as important or popular as native beans, they are now naturalized throughout the region. When fresh, they can be eaten raw or cooked, but they are more commonly available dried. The skin on chickpeas can be tough and you may like to remove it. Do this once the chickpeas are fully cooked and cooled.

Above: Chickpeas were first introduced to Latin America by Spanish settlers, but quickly became a popular ingredient.

Buying and storing

When buying fresh beans, buy young ones with bright, firm skins because the pods of older beans are likely to be slightly tough. Be sure to use fresh beans as soon as possible after purchase because they do not store well. Most fresh beans need little preparation other than trimming the ends, but older beans may need stringing.

When buying dried beans, look for plump, shiny beans with smooth, unbroken skins. Beans toughen with age and will take longer to cook the older they are, so although they will keep for up to a year in a cool, dark place, it is best to buy them in small quantities from a store with a regular turnover of stock. Avoid beans that look dusty or dirty, and store them in an airtight container in a cool, dark, dry place.

Canned beans are a useful standby as they require no soaking or lengthy cooking. Choose canned beans that do not have any added sugar or salt, and be sure to drain and rinse well before use. Canned beans still contain a reasonable amount of nutrients.

Preparing dried beans

Dried beans must be soaked before cooking.

1 Tip the beans into a colander or sieve (strainer) and pick them over to remove any grit or damaged beans.

2 Rinse the beans under cold running water and then drain.

3 Soak in cold water overnight, changing the water once.

4 Drain the soaked beans, rinse them, then place in a large pan with plenty of cold water.

5 Bring to the boil and boil vigorously for 10 minutes to remove natural toxins (this is particularly important with lima beans or red kidney beans).

6 Reduce the heat and simmer until the beans are tender.

COOK'S TIP

If you don't have time to soak dried beans overnight, put them in a pan with water to cover, bring them to the boil, then remove from the heat and leave to soak for about 1 hour.

CHILLIES AND SWEET PEPPERS

Chillies and their mild-mannered cousins, the sweet (bell) peppers, are without doubt Latin America's greatest contribution to the global kitchen. Full of flavour, colourful, nutritious and versatile, they are now so widely used in many different cuisines that it is difficult to imagine a world without them.

FRESH CHILLIES

The first chillies were tiny wild berries that grew in the South American jungle thousands of years ago. The plants gradually spread northwards from central South America through Central America and the Caribbean to south-western North America, evolving over the centuries into the wide range of shapes and sizes we encounter today.

It was Christopher Columbus who introduced chillies to the rest of the world. When he tasted a highly spiced dish on San Salvador, he assumed that its heat came from black pepper. He named the plant pimiento (pepper), and this name endured long after he realized his mistake. Columbus took chilli plants back with him when he returned to Europe, and by the 16th century they were widely distributed. Today the chilli is the most extensively cultivated and most commonly used spice in the world.

There are as many as 200 different varieties of chilli, varying enormously in shape, size, colour, flavour and, most of all, in the amount of heat they deliver.

Below: Poblanas, popular in Mexico, are often roasted to intensify their flavour.

Above: Scotch bonnet chillies are popular throughout the Caribbean and are used to make hot pepper sauce.

The fiery sensation from chillies is caused by capsaicin, an alkaloid that not only causes a burning sensation in the mouth, but also triggers the brain to release endorphins, natural painkillers that promote a sense of wellbeing and stimulation; this is why eating chillies can become quite addictive. Capsaicin is concentrated in the seeds and membrane of the pods, so removing these parts before eating will reduce the fieriness of a chilli considerably. Chillies are an excellent source of vitamin C and also yield valuable quantities of beta-carotene, folate, potassium and vitamin E. They stimulate the appetite, help improve circulation, and can also be used as a powerful decongestant.

Varieties

Of the vast range of chillies grown in Latin America and the Caribbean, the following are the most popular. They have been rated on a scale of one to ten for heat and are listed in order of potency, mildest first. Be careful: the heat can vary widely, even with chillies from the same plant, so use these ratings as a guide only.

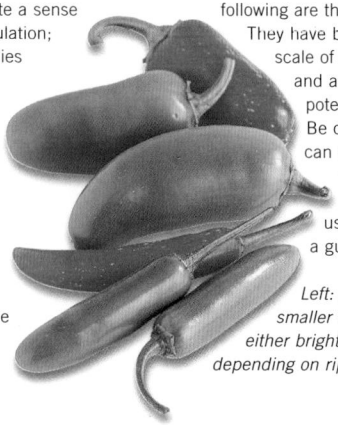

Left: Jalapeños and the smaller serrano chillies are either bright green or red, depending on ripeness.

Poblano These mild to medium-hot chillies (heat scale 3) are very popular in Mexico. Big and beautiful, poblanos are about 7.5cm/3in long, with thick flesh and a rich, earthy flavour. They start off dark green with a purple-black tinge and ripen to dark red. Green poblanos are always used cooked, and roasting gives them a more intense flavour. They are perfect for stuffed dishes such as *chillies rellenos* and taste good in traditional mole sauces. Dried poblanos are called anchos.

Jalapeño Well known and widely used the world over, jalapeños are medium-hot (heat scale 4–7). Plump and glossy, they are used in stews, salsas, breads, sauces and dips. Green jalapeños have a fresh, grassy flavour; red ones are slightly sweeter. Smoke-dried jalapeños are known as chipotle chillies.

Fresno Plump and cylindrical, these chillies are usually sold when red. They have thick flesh and a hot, sweet flavour (heat scale 5). Fresnos are excellent in salsas, ceviche, stuffings, bread and pickles. Roasting brings out their delicious sweetness.

Serrano Thin-skinned and quite slender, serranos are the classic Mexican green chilli (*chiles verdes*) and are always used in guacamole. Although they are quite fiery (heat scale 7), they have a clean, biting heat, matched by a high acidity. Both red and green serranos are frequently added to cooked dishes. They can also be pickled.

Measuring the heat
The heat level of a chilli is often measured in Scoville units on a scale where 0 is the rating for a sweet (bell) pepper and 557,000 relates to the hottest chilli grown in Latin America, the habañero. The simpler system used in this book rates the chillies on a scale of one to ten, with one indicating the mildest and ten the hottest.

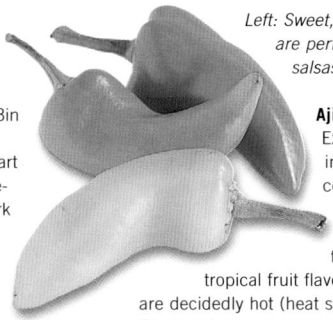

Left: Sweet, juicy fresnos are perfect for fresh salsas or pickles.

Aji mirasol Extensively used in Peruvian cooking, these chillies are narrow and tapered, with a tropical fruit flavour, yet they are decidedly hot (heat scale 6–7). Fresh yellow ones are particularly prized for salsas and ceviche. They are also used in cooked dishes, such as soups or stews, and are sometimes made into a paste, which is mixed with oil to make a hot dipping sauce.

Brazilian malagueta These very hot chillies (heat scale 8) are believed to be a wild form of tabasco. Very small, only about 2cm/¾in long, they have thin flesh and a fresh yet fiery taste. Malaguetas are often added to marinades and vinegars.

Jamaican hot, Scotch bonnet and habañero These chillies are closely related and are all intensely fiery (heat scale 10). The Jamaican hot is bright red and has a sweet hot flavour. It goes well with tropical fruits and is also used in fresh salsas, Caribbean fish stews, curries and spicy chutneys. The Scotch bonnet is an essential ingredient in many Caribbean dishes, especially curries and jerk sauce, and is used to make Jamaican hot pepper sauce.

Below: Chilli powder is a good alternative when fresh chillies are not available.

Preparing Fresh Chillies
Take great care when handling chillies, as the capsaicin they contain is an extremely powerful irritant. Wear rubber gloves while preparing chillies or wash your hands in soapy water afterwards. If you touch your skin by mistake, splash the affected area with cold water. Avoid scratching or rubbing inflamed skin because this could aggravate the problem.

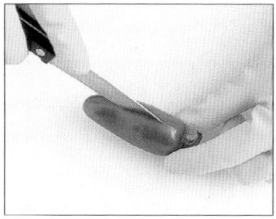

1 Cut the chilli in half lengthways, cut off the stalk and carefully scrape out the seeds (unless you wish to leave them in for extra heat).

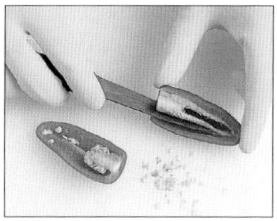

2 Remove the remaining core and any white membrane.

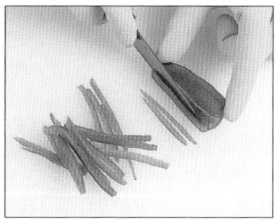

3 Finely slice or chop each piece, depending on use.

SWEET PEPPERS

Sometimes known as capsicums, sweet (bell) peppers are native to Mexico and Central America and were widely grown there in pre-Columbian times. Pepper seeds were carried to Spain in 1493 and from there spread rapidly throughout Europe. They also spread rapidly throughout South America and were a staple food of the Incas in Peru. They contribute colour and flavour to a huge variety of dishes, including salsas, stews and spicy meat fillings, as well as fish dishes, vegetable accompaniments and salads. Sweet peppers come in many unusual shapes and sizes, from chilli-size rounds to slender drops, bells and even hearts. Colours range from bright green, through yellow and orange to vibrant red, and there is even a dark purple variety (but this does turn green when cooked). Mild and sweet in flavour, with crisp, juicy flesh when ripe, they can be eaten either raw in salads or cooked. A popular way of serving peppers is to stuff and bake them.

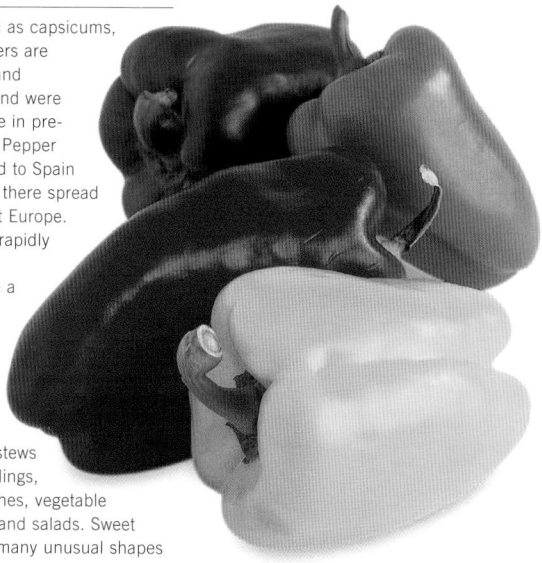

Below: Delicious either cooked or raw, sweet peppers should look glossy, feel firm and have a crisp, juicy bite. Avoid those that are wrinkled.

Preparing sweet peppers

Depending on use, the core and seeds should usually be removed before cooking sweet peppers.

1 Halve or quarter the peppers, then, using a small, sharp knife, carefully cut out the core, any white membrane and the seeds.

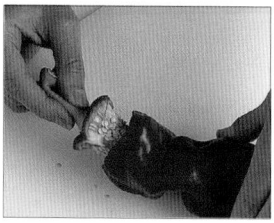

2 If the peppers are being used whole, for example to be stuffed, cut around the stem and pull out the seeds like a plug.

Buying and storing

Whether you are buying hot chillies or mild sweet peppers, look for firm, shiny specimens with unblemished skins. Avoid peppers that are limp, that wrinkle when touched or that have "blistered" areas on the skin. Green peppers should be purchased before they change colour, but should not be too dark as this indicates immaturity and lack of flavour. Avoid red peppers with dark patches on the skin, as this could be a sign that they have begun to rot inside. Store peppers in the vegetable crisper in the refrigerator. Sweet peppers will keep well for up to a week and chillies up to three weeks.

Roasting peppers and chillies

To really bring out the delicious, sweet flavour of fresh peppers and chillies, try roasting them.

1 Place them under a hot grill (broiler) and turn occasionally until the skins blister and char.

2 Alternatively, dry-fry them in a frying pan or griddle until the skins are scorched.

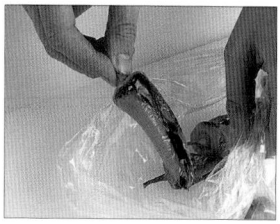

3 Place them in a strong plastic bag and tie the top tightly, or place them in a bowl and cover with cling film (plastic wrap).

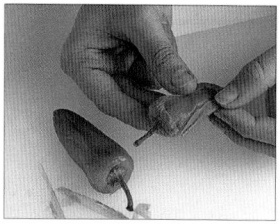

4 After approximately 20 minutes, remove the skins, then slit each pepper or chilli. Remove the seeds and membrane, and tear or slice the flesh into pieces.

DRIED CHILLIES

Travel through Latin America and you will frequently see bunches of colourful chillies dangling from hooks on the walls of houses. In the bright sunshine they soon dehydrate and can be packed away until needed. When rehydrated, the chillies will not taste the same as before. In many cases they will have acquired a new intensity and richness of flavour, which is one of the reasons why Mexicans really value dried chillies and view them as distinct from the fresh, often giving them completely different names. Each variety has unique characteristics, and cooks will often blend several types to get exactly the results they require.

Varieties

The following are the most widely used varieties of dried chilli.

Ancho These dried red poblanos have a rich deep colour and mild fruity flavour (heat scale 3). Anchos can be stuffed and are often used in mole sauces.

Mulato Related to the ancho and with the same level of heat, mulatos taste smoky rather than fruity.

Guajillo These large dried chillies, orange-red in colour, have a slightly acidic flavour (heat scale 3–4).

Right: Habañeros are used for chilli sauces.

Below: Anchos are delicious stuffed or added to stews.

Left: Cascabels have a delicious, slightly nutty flavour.

Pasada Roasted, peeled and dried, these chillies have a toasty flavour (heat scale 3–4), with apple, liquorice and cherry notes.

Cascabel The name means "little rattle" and refers to the sound the seeds make when the chillies are shaken. Thick-skinned and smooth, cascabels have a rich, woody flavour (heat scale 4).

Pasilla Long, slender and very dark, the flavour of pasillas is rich with hints of berries and liquorice (heat scale 4).

Chipotle Smoke-dried jalapeños, these have wrinkled dark red skin and thick flesh. Chipotles need long, slow cooking to soften them and bring out their full, smoky taste (heat scale 6–10).

Aji mirasol The dried version of Peru's favourite chilli is deep yellowish red with a berry-like fruit flavour (heat scale 6–7).

Pequin These small chillies are pale orange-red in colour, with a light, sweet, smoky flavour suggestive of corn and nuts (heat scale 8–9). They are excellent in sauces, salsas and soups and can be crushed over food as a condiment.

Habañero Used in moderation, these have a wonderful tropical fruit flavour (heat scale 10). Like dried Scotch bonnets, they are often used to make classic hot pepper sauces, particularly in the Caribbean, and are also good when added to fish stews and salsas.

Above: Pasadas are often used in sauces for meat or fish, or in rich spicy stews.

Buying and storing

Dried chillies should be flexible. Avoid any that smell musty or have powdery skins, as this could indicate insect infestation. Store for up to 1 year in an airtight container in a cool, dry place.

Preparing dried chillies

To appreciate their full flavour, dried chillies should be soaked before use. Toasting dried chillies before soaking will give a lovely smoky flavour. If the chillies are to be used in a slow-cooked stew, soaking is not necessary.

1 Lightly dry-fry or toast the dried chillies in a frying pan or griddle for a couple of minutes.

2 Seed large chillies and tear into pieces, then soak in warm water until soft. Soak smaller chillies before cutting into pieces.

Caribbean hot sauces

Most islands have their own recipe for hot chilli sauce. Based on the fiery habañero or Scotch bonnet chilli pepper, they should be used sparingly by the uninitiated.

OTHER VEGETABLES

A visit to a market in any Latin American country is a real feast for the eyes. Fruit and vegetables are laid on mats or heaped high on tables, strings of chillies hang overhead and everywhere there are people bustling or bargaining. The colours are glorious, the aromas are unfamiliar and there will usually be several local specialities on sale.

CHAYOTES

Also known as christophenes or chokos these pale green gourds are particularly popular in the Caribbean, where they are used in soups, salads and stews. Raw chayote is crisp and clean-tasting, rather like water chestnut. The cooked vegetable has a rather bland flavour, so needs plenty of seasoning. Cholesterol-free and low in calories, chayotes are a good source of fibre and vitamin C.

Buying and storing

Choose smooth, unwrinkled chayotes and store in the refrigerator. They keep well but are best used as soon as possible after purchase.

Preparing chayotes

Chayotes can be peeled, chopped and cooked in soups or stews, or cut in half and baked.

1 Preheat the oven to 190°C/375°F/Gas 5. Cut the chayotes in half, place them skin-side down on a shallow baking tray and brush with a little olive oil.

2 Bake for approximately 25 minutes or until tender.

Roasting squash

Instead of roasting, pieces of squash could be lightly boiled or steamed and added to stews.

1 Preheat the oven to 190°C/375°F/Gas 5. Cut the squash into wedges, remove the skin and seeds.

2 Place the wedges in a large roasting pan with a little olive oil and roast for approximately 45 minutes or until tender.

SQUASH

Cultivated in Latin America long before Columbus sailed, squash is an important food. Many different types are eaten in Latin America, from courgettes (zucchini) to huge hard-skinned pumpkins. Squash are eaten in both savoury and sweet dishes, often with brown sugar. Pumpkin and prawns (shrimp) is an unusual but delicious combination. A hollowed-out pumpkin makes a good container for cooking and serving, as in the Argentine stew, *carbonada criolla*. A good source of fibre and carbohydrate, pumpkins are low in calories. Varieties with bright flesh are high in vitamin A.

Buying and storing

If buying courgettes or other summer squash, the general rule is that the smaller the specimen the better the flavour. Store courgettes in the refrigerator and use as soon as possible. Thanks to their hard skins, unbruised pumpkins and other winter squash keep well. Cut pumpkin should be wrapped in clear film (plastic wrap) and stored in the refrigerator.

Below: Halved chayotes can be baked for a simple yet delicious side dish.

Below: Pumpkins can be easily stored over the long winter months, making them a popular ingredient all year round in many Latin American countries.

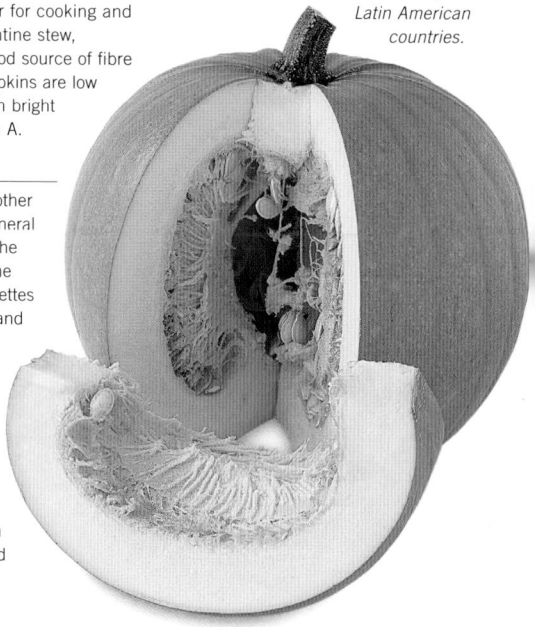

Above: Thin slices of sweet potato are fried to make chips, a popular street snack throughout Latin America.

SWEET POTATOES AND YAMS

These root vegetables are not related, although the American habit of calling red sweet potatoes yams can lead to confusion and the two are sometimes mixed up. Sweet potatoes have been grown in South America for centuries. In pre-Inca times, sun-dried sweet potato slices were a popular treat and Mayan cooks also used the vegetable to provide a sweet note in many savoury meat and fish dishes. Yams were brought to South America by African slaves and are widely used throughout the Caribbean and Brazil. Both of these vegetables provide some vitamin C, while orange-fleshed sweet potatoes also contain beta-carotene.

Varieties

There are hundreds of varieties of both sweet potatoes and yams. In Latin American cooking, the red-skinned sweet potato with white flesh is best known. The most commonly used yam is brown, with moist cream-coloured flesh that becomes dry when cooked.

Buying and storing

Buy vegetables that are firm and dry, with no soft areas. Store loose or in a brown paper bag in a cool, dry place, but do not put them in the refrigerator.

Preparing and cooking

Like regular potatoes, sweet potatoes can be scrubbed and baked in their skins, or peeled and sliced, then boiled or fried. They are delicious mashed or creamed, and make very good chips. Yams must be thickly peeled and should be washed well before and after slicing; this helps to remove any toxins that may be present in the raw tuber. Always cook yams very thoroughly.

CASSAVA

Also known as *manioc*, *mandioc* or *yuca* (in Peru), this starchy tuber looks like a long, fat sausage with dark, rough outer skin. Native to Brazil, it is also a popular ingredient in West Indian cooking. It is important to distinguish between sweet and bitter cassava: the root and leaves of the former can safely be eaten, but bitter cassava contains cyanide. Although bitter cassava is used for making beer, tapioca and cassava flour – *farinha de mandioca* – it must be detoxified first. Sweet cassava is a carbohydrate food with a high fibre content, and the leaves are a valuable source of protein. *Cassareep* is a delicious syrup made from cassava and flavoured with cinnamon and cloves. It is an essential ingredient in the traditional Jamaican pepperpot stew. Cassava is fairly bland so it is best served with a sauce or dressing such as the traditional Cuban *mojo*, which is a mixture of oil, citrus juices and garlic.

Below: Sweet cassava is a versatile tuber and can be cooked in many ways.

Buying and storing

Most cassava that is exported around the world is first coated in a layer of wax to keep it fresh. When buying sweet cassava, look for roots that are fairly firm, dry and odour-free.

Preparing cassava

An extremely versatile vegetable, sweet cassava can be cooked in a number of ways.

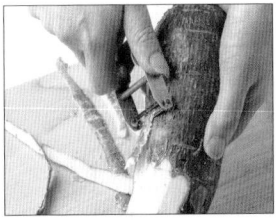

1 Scrub the root, peel, then cut into fairly large pieces, removing the fibrous core.

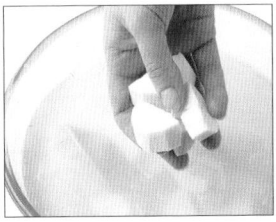

2 Drop the pieces into a bowl of acidulated water to prevent discoloration.

3 Boil, steam, bake or fry the cassava pieces until tender.

PALM HEARTS

The terminal bud of the Acai or cabbage palm has long been considered a regional delicacy. Native to South America, this fast-growing palm is now widely cultivated in vast plantations, mainly in Brazil and Costa Rica. Fresh palm hearts make very good eating, but are rarely available outside the country of origin. Canned palm hearts have a slightly different texture to fresh, but are still delicious and make a good alternative. Low in saturated fat and cholesterol, palm hearts are a valuable source of vitamin C.

Buying and storing

Fresh palm hearts should be pale, moist and evenly coloured. To enjoy them at their best, use as soon as possible after purchase. Canned hearts are much more readily available.

Preparing and cooking

To prepare fresh palm hearts, simply strip off the outer layers. Eat them raw or roast or steam in the same way as asparagus. Canned palm hearts are delicious in soups, salads and pies.

Below: Canned palm hearts make a good alternative if fresh ones are unavailable.

Above: Look for okra pods that are firm, plump and smooth, but not too big.

OKRA

Also known as ladies' fingers, these pods ooze a sticky liquid when cut, which acts as a thickener in sauces. Okra was introduced to Latin America by African slaves and is an important ingredient in Brazilian and Caribbean cooking. A source of vitamin C, fibre-rich okra also contains folate, thiamin and calcium.

Buying and storing

Okra should be a fresh, pale green colour. Buy smaller pods and avoid any that are flabby, shrivelled or bruised. Store in the refrigerator and use as soon as possible after purchase.

Preparing and cooking

If cooking whole, trim the top of each pod. If destined for a composite dish, where the viscous liquid will act as a thickener, cut the pods into slices. Otherwise, leave whole. Okra can be steamed, boiled or fried. Try it Brazilian-style, with chicken and chillies. The Barbadian speciality, Cou-cou, combines okra with corn meal.

LEAFY GREEN VEGETABLES

A number of leafy green vegetables are on sale in Latin American markets, and many are available only in certain areas. The young tops of cassava and sweet potatoes are regularly eaten, as is amaranth, a chard-like vegetable esteemed by the Aztecs. *Callaloo* is the name given to the leaves of two related tubers that are used for a popular Caribbean soup. *Nopales* are the edible leaves of the prickly pear cactus, while bottled *nopales*, commonly known as *nopalitos*, can be found in specialist food stores.

Unusual tubers

Jicama is indigenous to Mexico but has achieved widespread popularity thanks to its crisp, juicy flesh. Also known as yam bean or Chinese turnip, it can be eaten raw with orange juice and chilli powder, or cooked, and is especially good in salsas.

Oca looks like a short, fat wrinkled carrot. There are several varieties available, including white, yellow, red and purple. Its sharp taste is moderated by sun-drying the tubers before cooking.

Yacón, related to the Jerusalem artichoke, is highly valued in Peru and Bolivia for its sweet, crunchy flesh. It can be eaten either raw or cooked.

Añu is a white or yellow tuber from a nasturtium-like plant with edible leaves and flowers. It is an important crop in Ecuador, Peru, Bolivia, Colombia and Venezuela.

Jicama *has crisp, juicy flesh, similar to green apples or water chestnuts.*

FRUIT VEGETABLES

Neither savoury nor sweet, these are popular throughout Latin America.

TOMATOES

Along with chillies and corn, tomatoes are one of Latin America's most important contributions to the global cooking pot. Although they originated in the lands to the west of the Andes, both the Mayas and the Aztecs grew the little cherry-sized fruit vegetables and the Spanish introduced them to Europe. Largely composed of water, tomatoes are a good source of vitamins A and C. Raw ones contain useful amounts of vitamin E. Tomatoes also contribute the powerful antioxidant, lycopene, which may help to lower the risk of cancer.

Varieties

There are hundreds of varieties ot tomato. Cherry tomatoes, the closest in size to their Peruvian ancestors, are delicious in salads, juicy plum tomatoes make excellent sauces and beefsteak tomatoes are great for stuffing. Tomatillos (literally translated as "little tomatoes") are covered in brown papery husks. The fruit itself is green, with a clean, slightly acidic flavour.

Buying and storing

For the best flavour, buy tomatoes straight from the grower and store them at room temperature. Chilling tomatoes dulls their taste. Fresh tomatillos are difficult to obtain outside Latin America, but canned ones make a perfectly acceptable substitute.

Below: Fresh tomatillos are a tasty addition to spicy Mexican salsas.

Above: Tomatoes were enjoyed by the Mayas and Aztecs in ancient times.

Preparing and cooking

When adding to salsas and sauces, tomatoes should ideally have the skin removed. To skin tomatoes, cut a cross on the base, put them in a heatproof bowl and pour over boiling water. Leave for 30–60 seconds, then remove the remaining skin with a sharp knife. In Mexico, tomatillos are used fresh and raw, mostly in salsas, but they also taste great cooked.

AVOCADOS

The most nutritious of all the fruit vegetables, the avocado is native to Mexico, where it is called *acuacate*. In Brazil it is known as *abacate*, and in the US, alligator pear.

Nutrition

Despite the hefty calorie content – half an avocado delivers around 143kcals – the fat they contain is mostly mono-unsaturated and is a valuable source of energy. Avocados are protein-rich and also contain vitamins E, C and B_6, plus copper and iron.

Varieties

Among the many varieties, some with soft, smooth skins, others encased in dark, wrinkled shells, the avocado with the best flavour is the hass, a dark avocado with buttery, golden yellow flesh.

Buying and storing

Obtaining the perfect avocado can be a tricky business. Some supermarkets package the fruits with a "ready to eat" label, which is helpful if the avocados are hard-skinned. To test if a soft-skinned avocado is ripe, press the top end gently – it should just give. Ripe avocados can be stored in the refrigerator; unripe ones should be put in a paper bag with a banana to soften.

Preparation and cooking

Avocados soon discolour when cut, but sprinkling the cut surface with lemon juice will help prevent this. To halve an avocado, run a knife lengthways around the fruit, cutting in to the stone (pit), then ease the halves apart. Remove the stone and peel the halves before chopping the flesh. The most common use for avocados is in guacamole, but they also taste wonderful in soups and mousses. Avocados are seldom cooked, but in Latin America slices are often added to soups or stews just before serving. In Brazil, avocado is served as a creamy dessert, *creme de abacate*.

Below: Although high in calories, avocados contain healthy fats and plenty of vitamins and minerals.

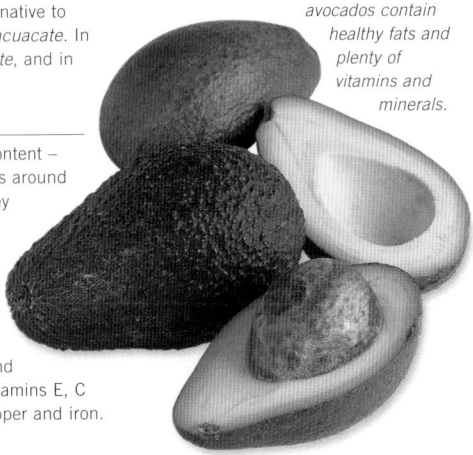

FRUIT

Some of the world's most colourful, exotic and intensely flavoured fruits are to be found throughout Latin America and the Caribbean.

PINEAPPLES

The taste of a freshly picked ripe pineapple is incomparable. Their aroma is so intense that a single pineapple can perfume the entire house, and the flesh is so sweet that it is unnecessary to add sugar or any other sweetener. Cultivated in Central America and the Caribbean long before the arrival of Columbus, this majestic fruit has become popular the world over. Costa Rica and the Dominican Republic are the major producers. Pineapples are used in both sweet and savoury dishes and make refreshing drinks. In Venezuela and Columbia, pineapple is a popular flavouring for sweet custard desserts. Rich in vitamin C and a valuable source of fibre, pineapples also contain bromelain, a protein-digesting enzyme that soothes digestive complaints.

Varieties

There are hundreds of varieties of pineapple, ranging in size from the small "baby pineapples" to specimens 30cm/12in long. Some turn a deep golden yellow as they ripen, while others remain a bronze-green colour. The latest varieties to be cultivated are deliciously sweet and juicy.

Below: Papaya is a popular addition to Latin American fruit salads.

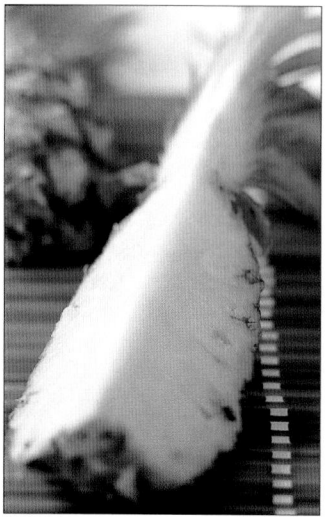

Above: Look for okra pods that are firm, plump and smooth, but not too big.

Buying and storing

Choose firm, ripe fruit with no bruising. The leaves should be glossy and fresh, and there should be a distinctive pineapple aroma. One test of ripeness is to gently pull a leaf from the bottom of the plume; if it comes away easily, the pineapple is ripe. Store whole pineapples in a cool place, but not the refrigerator, and use them as quickly as possible. Slices or cubes of pineapple should be stored in an airtight container and chilled in the refrigerator, where they will keep for up to three days.

Preparing pineapple

The fruit is usually served fresh and raw, but cooking brings out the sweet flavour still more and pineapple tastes particularly good in hot, spicy dishes. Avoid using fresh pineapple in gelatine-based desserts, as the bromelain will prevent it from setting.

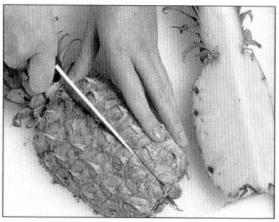

1 To grill (broil) pineapple, cut the fruit into quarters, remove the core from each piece, then loosen the flesh by running a sharp knife between the flesh and the skin, as when preparing melon.

2 Douse liberally with rum, sprinkle with brown sugar and place under a hot grill (broiler) until caramelized.

3 To cube pineapples, quarter the fruit, then remove the core and skin from each quarter, taking care to cut out the peppery "eyes". Cube the wedges or cut them into sticks.

PAPAYAS

These Latin American natives were slow to gain popularity in Europe. Before careful packaging techniques and speedy air travel ensured that the fruit reached its destination in good condition, the papayas on sale throughout Europe were far from their best – hard and unappetizing or soft and squashy. Today, the situation has improved considerably and more and more people are now beginning to appreciate the sweet, scented flesh of this delicious fruit. Papayas are extremely easy to digest, thanks to an enzyme, called papain, which they contain. Papain is a natural tenderizer, a fact that was well known to the pre-Colombian Indians who often marinated their meat in papaya juice to improve the quality. Amply stocked with vitamins A and C, and calcium, papayas are also a valuable source of fibre.

Preparing mangoes

Ripe mangoes are juicy and can be messy to eat. For convenience, cut the fruit into cubes or strips.

1 Cut a broad slice from either side of the mango, removing the "cheeks" or plump sides.

2 For long pieces, peel the skin from each cheek, slice the flesh lengthways, then cut off any flesh still sticking to the stone (pit).

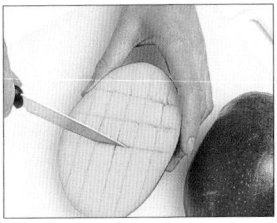

3 To dice mango, leave the flesh on the skin and use a sharp knife to mark it into neat squares.

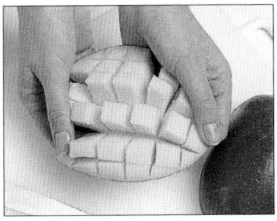

4 Gently press the mango cheek back on itself so that the pieces stand proud. Either eat straight from the skin with a spoon or use a sharp knife to slice off the chunks.

Below: A Caribbean native, Julie, one of more than 300 varieties of mango has sweet, tender flesh and an intense perfumed fragrance.

Varieties

All papayas are pear-shaped, but the size varies considerably, with some weighing up to 5kg/11lb or more. The skin starts off green, before ripening to a bright yellow or red. The sweet, scented flesh can be either pink or yellow. A hybrid form of papaya is the *babaco* from Ecuador, a fruit that can be served fresh or cooked. Stewed *babaco* tastes particularly good with roast meats.

Buying and storing

Look for small, soft papayas with undamaged, yellow skins. Handle them gently and use them as soon as possible. Store ripe papayas in the refrigerator; unripe papayas will continue to ripen at room temperature.

Preparing and serving

Cut the fruit in half and scoop out the seeds. The flavour of papaya is often improved with a squirt of fresh lime juice. Papaya can be combined with coconut milk to make a soothing drink, while in the Caribbean, the unripe fruit is used in savoury dishes.

MANGOES

While many exotic native fruits have been transported from Latin America to European countries, mangoes made the journey in the opposite direction. These delectable fruits originated in Asia, but were enthusiastically embraced by Caribbean and Central American farmers as soon as they were introduced. The meltingly tender flesh, with its unique fragrance and flavour, makes mangoes a popular choice for drinks, desserts and even some savoury dishes. Ripe mangoes are a good source of fibre and they contain generous amounts of vitamin C. The vibrant orange flesh also makes them a valuable source of beta-carotene.

Varieties

Over 300 varieties of mango are commercially cultivated, with many more being grown in tropical gardens. One of the most popular varieties imported into Europe from the Caribbean is Julie. This medium-sized mango, slightly flattened on one side, comes mainly from the islands of Jamaica and Trinidad and Tobago. It contains only a small amount of fibre and is particularly noted for its fine flavour. Two other favourites are the kidney-shaped Madame Francis, which originated in Haiti, and the Brazilian Itamarica. Of the fibreless varieties, the Jamaican Bombay Green is highly regarded, as is Brazil's Mango de Ubá.

Buying and storing

Not all mangoes turn yellow or become rosy-cheeked when ripe, so colour is not necessarily a clear indication of ripeness. Avoid fruit with dark patches on the skin as this is a sign that the fruit is past its best. A perfect mango will have an intense sweet aroma and will yield when lightly pressed. Unripe mangoes will quickly ripen if placed in a paper bag with a banana.

Above: Guavas are used to make the delicious sweetmeat dulce de guayaba.

GUAVAS

Native to Central and Southern America, guavas were introduced to Europe by the Conquistadors. Brazil remains a major producer of these highly perfumed fruit, known as *guayabas* in Mexico. Guavas are usually used in desserts, but their flavour is such that they are equally good in savoury dishes, especially with fish. Guavas are an excellent source of vitamin C, better than most citrus fruits. They also contain vitamins A and B6.

Varieties

The fruits can be oval or round, with shiny skin that turns pale yellow when ripe. Some varieties have creamy white flesh, while others have pink or even purple flesh. Guava flesh has a clean, sweet, slightly acidic flavour, and a rather musky scent, but this disappears when the fruit is cooked.

Buying and storing

Look for firm, fairly small fruit that has ripened to a uniform yellow. Avoid any that are bruised or pockmarked. Wrap them well to avoid contaminating other foods with their musky odour, and store them in the refrigerator.

Preparing and serving

If the guavas are young there is no need to peel them. Just wash the fruit, then slice it, removing the larger seeds. Older fruit will need to be skinned and seeded. Guavas can be eaten raw with a little sugar to bring out their flavour, or cooked. In Latin America, sweetened guava pulp is used to make *dulce de guayaba*, which is similar to *membrillo*, the Spanish quince "cheese".

CITRUS FRUITS

The only citrus fruit that originated in Latin America was the grapefruit. A descendant of the Polynesian pomelo or shaddock, it is said to have been cultivated on Barbados. Grapefruit is thought to be useful in helping to lower cholesterol. Oranges came from China and India, and were introduced to the Caribbean by early traders. Seville oranges are particularly popular in the islands – although too bitter to eat raw, they are widely used in poultry and meat dishes. Limes were also an early import, hugely valued because they helped to prevent scurvy. Limes grow well in Latin America and their juice is widely used. Its most famous function is as a marinade for raw fish; the

Below: Grapefruits are native to Latin America.

Dulce de guayaba

This sweet guava paste, popular throughout Latin America, is delicious served with a hard cheese such as Manchego.

1 Peel 1kg/2¼lb guavas, then half each guava and scoop the seeds into a bowl. Add 200ml/7fl oz/ scant 1 cup water and set aside.

2 Chop the guavas and put them in a large, heavy pan. Pour over water to cover, bring to the boil, then cover and simmer, stirring frequently, for about 2 hours. Strain in the juice from the guava seeds and stir well.

3 Purée the mixture in a food processor, then press through a sieve into a bowl. Using a cup measure, scoop it into a heavy pan, noting the number of cups. Add an equal number of cups of sugar and stir in 30ml/2 tbsp lime juice.

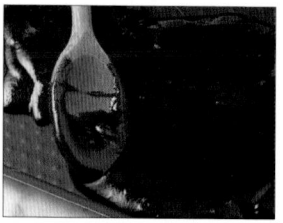

4 Stir over a low heat until the mixture reddens and becomes very thick. Pour into a shallow pan and smooth the surface. Dry out in a barely warm oven and serve in small squares.

Above: Limes are a popular ingredient, especially in Mexican dishes.

action of the acid on the protein cooks the fish. Lemons are used in Latin American cooking, but are secondary to limes. All forms of citrus fruit are low in calories and are good sources of fibre and vitamin C.

Varieties

Grapefruit may be white, pink or ruby. There is also a green-skinned variety with sweet flesh. Oranges are either sweet or bitter. There are many varieties of sweet oranges, including Valencias, which are juicy and seedless. Of the bitter oranges, Sevilles are the best known. In addition to being used in cooking, bitter oranges are the basis for several Caribbean liqueurs, including curaçao. There are three main types of lime – Tahitian, Mexican and Key Limes. Mexican limes are fairly small but have a strong and aromatic flavour.

Buying and storing

The juiciest fruits are those that feel fairly heavy for their size. Choose those with firm skin, avoiding any that are damaged or wrinkled. This advice is especially relevant to limes because they perish more quickly than other forms of citrus fruits. Choose bright green limes with shiny skins that are unmarked by brown patches. Grapefruit, lemons and limes should be stored in a cool place or the refrigerator for up to 1 week; oranges have a slightly longer shelf-life and will keep well for up to 2 weeks at cool room temperature.

BANANAS

Introduced to South America from Portugal in the 16th century, bananas rapidly became naturalized and are today a very important food crop in the region. In some areas, such as the Windward Islands in the Caribbean, they are practically the only crop. A large proportion of the world's organic bananas come from this area, as well as from the Dominican Republic and Mexico. Bananas are convenient, nutritious, tasty and so easy to digest that they can be eaten by everyone, old or young. With high levels of potassium, bananas also contribute vitamins C and B_6. The carbohydrate they contain boosts flagging energy levels. Banana leaves are used as a wrapper for *pastelles*, the corn meal and meat parcels that are a speciality on Trinidad and Tobago, and similar wrapped dishes.

Varieties

There are hundreds of different varieties of banana, though few are identified by name. Most familiar in our stores are the common yellow curved bananas, but it is sometimes possible to buy the tiny Brazilian lady fingers or sugar bananas. Red bananas, which come from Ecuador, have orange flesh and taste particularly good when cooked.

Buying and storing

Bananas are harvested when they are still green. By the time they reach stores in the northern hemisphere they have begun to ripen, and most are at their peak after being allowed to ripen in a warm room for a day or two. The skin of the fruit will become progressively darker, and will acquire brown speckles, but even at this stage, the flesh will probably be perfectly good to eat. Do not throw away very soft bananas; they can be used to make banana bread.

Preparing and serving

There's nothing tricky about preparing a banana – simply peel back the skin and eat. If you want to eat half a banana, fold the skin back across the uneaten piece, wrap the fruit well and it will still be edible the next day. Bananas are delicious fresh but can also be cooked. A popular way of preparing them in the Caribbean is to bake them, or cook them on the barbecue, with plenty of brown sugar and a dash of rum to caramelize.

Above: Bananas are an important crop in Latin America and the Caribbean; much of the world's supply comes from plantations in these areas.

OTHER FRUITS

Latin America and the Caribbean are also home to some more unusual fruits, including the following.

Ackees The only part of this bright red fruit that is edible is the creamy-coloured aril, which looks a bit like scrambled egg. Ackee has an interesting texture and a subtle flavour and is one of the key ingredients of the Jamaican dish, salt fish and ackee. Canned ackees are available from Caribbean food stores.

Breadfruit This large green fruit has very starchy flesh. Although very ripe breadfruit can be eaten raw, they are more often roasted, as a Caribbean speciality, baked, boiled or fried. They are available fresh or canned.

Cherimoyas Indigenous to the region, cherimoyas have delicious creamy flesh that tastes like a cross between banana and pineapple, with a texture similar to papaya. The skin and seeds should not be eaten. Varieties include custard apples and soursops.

Prickly pears These are the fruit of a Central American cactus. Beneath the prickly skin, the flesh is sweet-scented, with a taste similar to melon. Prickly pear flesh can be eaten raw with a squeeze of lime juice and a sprinkling of chilli powder to bring out the flavour.

Right: Beneath the pink skin, the flesh of the prickly pear is vibrant red.

Above: Be sure to remove tamarillo skin before eating or cooking the tangy flesh.

Tamarillos Native to the west coast of South America, these shiny, bright red oval fruits are grown commercially in Argentina, Brazil, Colombia and Venezuela. The skin is very bitter and must be removed before the tangy flesh can be enjoyed. A tamarillo dip is the traditional accompaniment for *arepas*, the flat corn breads that are popular in Venezuela and Colombia.

Passion fruits These fragrant fruits come from Central and South America and the best-tasting variety is round and very dark-skinned. The greenish yellow pulp has an exquisite flavour and the seeds are edible, although some people prefer to remove them. Large yellow passion fruits that look rather like light bulbs are granadillas. These have greyish pulp and are neither as flavoursome nor as highly scented as passion fruits.

Above: Choose passion fruits with extra-dark skin as these are sweetest.

Plantains

These are a type of banana grown as a vegetable, but the name is also used for green sweet bananas. True plantains taste very bitter and must be cooked before being eaten. Treat them like potatoes – they are good when baked in their skins, or they can be boiled, mashed, baked or fried as chips. A popular snack on Spanish-speaking Caribbean islands is *tostones de plátano*, long slices of plantain that are partially fried, squashed flat and fried again until brown and crisp.

Below: Fresh plantains are prepared and cooked more like a vegetable than a fruit.

NUTS

Nutrient-rich nuts are a huge part of the Latin American diet, and they appear in various guises, most commonly as a thickening ingredient in both sweet and savoury sauces.

Coconuts The Latin American cuisine relies heavily on coconuts. The liquid they contain is used to flavour drinks and desserts, while the dense nutmeat is a valuable ingredient in almost everything, including soups, seafood and meat dishes and desserts. It is used fresh, dried or as coconut milk or cream, which can be bought canned.

Cashew nuts These are the fruit of an evergreen tree. Each nut grows out of the bottom of a fleshy bulge, which is called a cashew apple. Although not technically a fruit, it closely resembles one, rewarding the picker with crisp, juicy flesh. The nuts themselves are toxic and shelling is a tortuous business, but when released and detoxified, they make a tasty snack and are also used in drinks and sauces.

Pecan nuts These glossy red-skinned nuts are cultivated in northern Mexico, where they are often used in recipes, that hark back to the French occupation in the 19th century. Pecan nuts have a very high fat content so should be eaten sparingly.

Below: Many Latin American desserts are based on coconut or coconut milk.

Pine nuts The nuts of several native pine trees, including the Chilean araucaria and the Brazilian parana pine, are used in Latin American cooking. All are highly nutritious.

Almonds were introduced to Latin America by the Spanish, who cannily added the caveat that they might not be grown on a large scale, thus ensuring that the trade with their native country continued. They are still largely imported, so are fairly expensive and tend to be saved for more extravagant dishes or special occasions. Almonds are still used to make traditional Mexican chocolate, while almond paste is the basis of the luxurious sweetmeat, *turrón*.

Left: Almonds are mainly imported from Spain, while pecans and walnuts are native.

Below: Peanuts are a popular ingredient in savoury dishes, particularly with poultry.

Below: Cashew nuts are eaten as a snack with a cold beer or caipirinha.

Walnuts are grown in the highlands of central Mexico. Their bitter-sweet flavour makes them a popular ingredient in savoury dishes as well as desserts. They taste delicious when baked with potatoes and chillies.

Brazil nuts are the seeds of towering trees that grow wild in the Amazon rain forest. Inside the large husks are around twenty nuts, packed tightly together. Very high in oil, Brazil nuts go rancid quickly when shelled, so crack them at the last minute.

Peanuts These are actually pulses not nuts, and they grow just beneath the soil. They have been cultivated in Peru for centuries and are a valuable food crop, contributing protein and fat to the diet. Peanut brittle is a popular sweet treat, while savoury dishes include pork and potatoes in peanut sauce. Peanut oil and peanut butter are also used, the latter being the basis for a popular punch, which is often served in Trinidad with a shot of rum.

HERBS, SPICES AND FLAVOURINGS

Many of the herbs and spices used in Latin American cooking will be familiar to the foreign visitor. Bunches of thyme, basil, oregano, mint, parsley and coriander (cilantro) scent the air in city markets, and spices such as nutmeg, allspice and cinnamon add their warm aroma. Asian immigrants have introduced cumin, five-spice power and curry powder, but it is perhaps the local specialities that are of most interest to the food tourist: *epazote*, *palillo*, *guascas* and the fiery chilli sauces developed by Caribbean cooks.

THYME

Widely used, especially in Mexico, Colombia and the Caribbean, this robust herb lends its inimitable flavour to dishes such as rice and peas, okra fried rice, Colombian chicken hot-pot and thyme and lime chicken. The dried herb is included in the dry rub that is used to flavour *carnitas*.

Pebre

This hot coriander and chilli salsa from Chile is delicious with meats.

1 Whisk 15ml/1 tbsp red wine vinegar with 30ml/2 tbsp olive oil.

2 Add 2–3 aji mirasol chillies, seeded and very finely chopped, 1 finely chopped small onion, 2 crushed garlic cloves and 75ml/5 tbsp water.

3 Mix well, then stir in 90ml/6 tbsp chopped fresh coriander (cilantro). Cover and set aside for 2–3 hours at room temperature to allow the flavours to blend.

Below: Thyme is a popular flavouring in many Colombian dishes.

CORIANDER/CILANTRO

Native to Europe, coriander is grown in South America too, and is hugely popular, especially in Mexico and the Bahian cuisine of Brazil. Fresh coriander leaves go particularly well with fish. Chilli clam soup and Cuban seafood rice both owe their distinctive flavouring to this popular herb. It also goes well with avocado and is used in both guacamole and avocado soup. Mexican green tomato dishes inevitably include coriander.

Right: Use mint to make a refreshing mojito.

Below: Coriander is an essential ingredient in the Mexican salsa, guacamole.

MINT

South America cooks delight in using herbs in innovative ways. Mint and seafood is not an obvious combination, but their use of this familiar flavouring in chunky prawn chowder works extremely well. Mint is also used to flavour drinks and salads.

INDIGENOUS HERBS

Annatto/achiote The seeds of a tropical flowering tree, annatto has long been used as a flavouring and natural dye. The dried seeds have a mild flavour, with a hint of orange blossom. Annatto oil, pressed from the hard orange pulp that surrounds the seeds, is a popular flavouring and colouring for meat, fish and vegetable dishes. In the Yucatán peninsula and nearby Cuba, annatto seeds are often ground with cumin and oregano to make an aromatic rub for meats, such as spiced roast leg of lamb.

Epazote

Also known as goose-foot, this herb is as commonplace in South America as oregano is on the islands of Greece. The dried leaves are crumbled and sold in jars. *Epazote* is widely used in central and southern Mexico, especially in bean dishes. The taste has been compared to anis.

Palillo This is an indigenous Peruvian herb. Dried and ground, it has little flavour and is mainly used to give food an attractive golden colour. Turmeric can be substituted, but use only half the amount suggested, as the flavour of turmeric can be overwhelming.

Guascas In Colombia, this herb is so common that it is sometimes viewed as a weed. The essential flavouring of the national dish, *ajiaco*, a delicious chicken soup, it is fairly difficult to obtain outside the country, except in dried and ground form. There is no real substitute as the flavour is unique, although it has been suggested that fennel comes close.

Huacatay comes from a plant that is closely related to the marigold. Pungent, with a rather unpleasant flavour, it is very much an acquired taste.

Left: (From top) Warm spices, such as allspice, cinnamon sticks, ground cinnamon and achiote are popoular throughout Latin America.

Caribbean spice mixes
These seasoning mixes are so frequently used in Caribbean recipes that it is perhaps worth making up a large amount and storing for future use.

Herb seasoning Chop 4 spring onions (scallions) and put them in a mortar. Add 1 chopped garlic clove and 15ml/1 tbsp each fresh coriander (cilantro), thyme and basil. Pound until smooth.

Spice seasoning Put 15ml/1 tbsp garlic granules in a bowl. Add 7.5ml/1½ tsp each of ground black pepper, paprika, celery salt and curry powder. Stir in 5ml/1 tsp caster (superfine) sugar. Mix well and store in a tightly sealed container in a dry, cool place.

SPICES

The most popular spices in Caribbean and Latin American cooking are those with warm flavours, such as cinnamon, cloves, cumin, nutmeg and paprika. Several of these flavours are combined in the aptly named allspice, which comes from a type of tree related to the myrtle. Allspice berries are dark brown. When dried they resemble peppercorns. Both the whole berries and the ground spice are used in Latin American cooking. Ground allspice is one of the main flavourings in the traditional Caribbean speciality, salt fish and ackee, and also appears in the marinade for the popular jerk chicken.

Vanilla is another warm spice. The pods or beans come from a climbing tree orchid, which grows in parts of Central America. Added whole to warm milk or chocolate, they impart a wonderfully sweet and fragrant flavour. If just the seeds are required, slit the bean lengthways and carefully scrape them out with a sharp knife.

SWEET AND SOUR

Ever since sugar was introduced to Latin America in the 16th century, sweetmeats (*dulces*) have been enormously popular. Elaborately shaped and decorated, they are an everyday indulgence, as are caramel desserts, such as the flan, which resembles a caramel custard, but sometimes contains pineapple or coconut. Many cooks use unrefined sugar to make treats like these, selecting either *piloncillo*, the dark-brown Mexican sugar, or *panela*, the Colombian version.

As a contrast to all this sweetness, bitter flavours are also highly valued. Angostura bitters, an infusion of gentian root and herbs on a rum base, is often used to add a tart note to fish and meat dishes as well as drinks.

Below: On the island of Barbados, fresh grapefruit is often served with a dash of herb-flavoured Angostura bitters.

DAIRY PRODUCTS AND EGGS

Dairy products came to Latin America relatively late, and although milk, cheese and eggs are important foodstuffs, they do not have as prominent a role as in Europe or North America.

CHEESE

Before the Spanish conquest in the 16th century, fresh milk was a rarity in Latin America. In Peru, indigenous llamas, vicuñas and alpacas that had been domesticated were occasionally milked, but cheesemaking was unknown until the arrival of Spanish missionaries. Nor did their presence spell instant conversion to cheesemaking, since finding a ready supply of milk would remain problematic for some time. The native animals were deemed unsuitable and goats failed to thrive in the humid lowlands. It was only when dairy cattle were established in more temperature zones that cheesemaking was attempted on anything but a minor scale, and the monks who travelled with the conquerors taught local people.

Cow's milk was used to make *queso blanco* (white cheese) – the simple soft cheese that is now a familiar sight in most Latin American countries. In the upland areas where goats were farmed, some cheese was made, but sheep's milk was not used until fairly recently, when farmers in Chile began producing a sheep's milk cheese similar to that produced in the Pyrenées.

There are plenty of cattle in Argentina and Brazil, but they are mainly beef animals. Most of the cheese eaten in Brazil is imported, as the high humidity makes cheese production difficult. A fresh cheese – Minas Frescal – is made in the Minas Gerais region, north of Rio de Janeiro, together with a stretched curd cheese called Minas Prensado.

The influx of immigrants proved to be a trigger for cheese production in many parts of South America. In 19th century Argentina, homesick Italians developed a cheese that closely resembled Parmesan, Treboligiano, as well as a mozzarella-type cheese called Moliterno. Cheese similar to Edam and Gouda satisfied the longing of Dutch settlers on Aruba for familiar flavours.

Below: Queso anejo *is a firm, dry cheese – use fresh Italian parmesan if unavailable.*

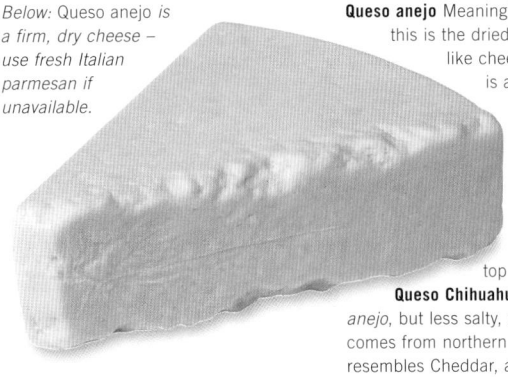

In Mexico, the demand for more European cheeses led to local production of cheeses such as Gruyère, Camembert and Port Salut, as well as a version of the Spanish cheese, Manchego. However, soft white cheeses remain the mainstay of the industry.

Queso blanco Made in most Latin American countries and eaten throughout the region, this white cow's milk cheese is traditionally produced from skimmed milk coagulated with lemon juice. Soft and crumbly, it is often used on enchiladas.

Queso fresco As the name, which means "fresh cheese" suggests, this is not a cheese for keeping. Young and unripened, it is usually eaten within a day or two of being made. It is mild and light, with a grainy, slightly crumbly texture. *Queso fresco* is actually the generic name for a number of cheeses, all of which share several common characteristics. It is often used for crumbling on top of finished dishes such as scrambled eggs, cooked *nopales* or other vegetables or bean dishes as a tasty garnish. *Queso fresco* has a fairly clean, sharp taste and is a good melting cheese so it is often used in tacos and on other tortilla-based snacks. If you can't find it in your local supermarket, substitute a good-quality mozzarella or ricotta.

Queso anejo Meaning"aged cheese", this is the dried version of a feta-like cheese. *Queso anejo* is a sharp, salty and fairly firm grating cheese similar to Parmesan, which makes a good substitute. It is often used for sprinkling on top of enchiladas

Queso Chihuahua Similar to *queso anejo*, but less salty, this originally comes from northern Mexico. It resembles Cheddar, and medium Cheddar can be used as a substitute. Alternatively, use the popular American cheese, Monterey Jack, which originated as *queso del pais* (country cheese) and was introduced to California by Spanish missionaries in the 18th century.

Asadero This slightly tart-tasting cheese is sometimes called *queso Oaxaca*, after the place in Mexico where it was originally made. The name *asadero* means "roasting cheese". It is a fairly stringy, supple cheese that is at its best when melted. It is ideal for stuffing fresh chillies, sweet (bell) peppers or other vegetables or meats, as it is unlikely to leak out during cooking. If *asadero* is unavailable, the closest equivalent is Italian mozzarella.

Above: Asadero *melts very well and is perfect for stuffing vegetables and meat.*

Above: When chickens were introduced to Latin America by the Spanish, hen's eggs quickly became popular and were added to many dishes.

MILK

As is the case in Spain, fresh milk is quite difficult to come by in this part of the world because of the heat and humidity. As a result, long-life, evaporated (unsweetened condensed) and condensed milks have become more popular. The use of these treated milks is simply a practical solution to the problem of keeping milk fresh in the heat, but several delicious dishes have evolved that make the most of these treated milks as ingredients. The most famous of these is *dulce de leche*, an incredibly sweet, caramel-flavoured concoctionthat is so thick and creamy it can be spread on bread like butter or jam. *Dulce de leche* is enomously popular among Latin American children. A rich bread and butter pudding from Barbados also makes the most of evaporated milk as one of its main ingredients.

Milk and cream are also used throughout the region in a similar way to in Europe – they are often combined with fruit to make refreshing drinks, added to rich desserts and used in many savoury sauces, stews and soups. Canned evaporated or condensed milk is nearly always used instead of fresh cream or milk in hot drinks, such as coffee and hot chocolate, adding a distinctive rich, thick sweetness.

EGGS

Until the Spanish arrived in Latin America, the only eggs eaten were those from game birds, ducks, wild geese, reptiles and insects. The Aztecs farmed wild turkeys, but although there is evidence of turkey eggs being used in religious festivals, the birds appeared to have been prized more for their plumage and meat. When chickens arrived on the scene, however, hen's eggs rapidly became a valued food, and today it would be hard to imagine Mexico without *huevos rancheros*, a complete egg-based breakfast, and *rompope*, a cinnamon eggnog; Brazil without *quindao*; or anywhere in Latin America without the traditional flan (caramel custard). Throughout the region, eggs are used in both sweet and savoury dishes. Hard-boiled eggs are often used as a garnish on top of stews or vegetable dishes.

Below: Milk and cream are often added to fresh fruit to make refreshing drinks.

Bajan bread and butter custard

This Caribbean variation of bread and butter pudding relies on evaporated milk for its rich flavour.

SERVES 4

3 thin slices buttered bread, crusts removed, plus extra butter
400g/14oz can evaporated milk
150ml/¼ pint/⅔ cup fresh milk
2.5ml/½ tsp mixed spice (pumpkin pie spice)
40g/1½oz/3 tbsp brown sugar
2 eggs
75g/3oz/½ cup sultanas (golden raisins)
30ml/2 tbsp rum
nutmeg

1 Lightly grease a baking dish with butter. Quarter each slice of bread and layer the pieces in the dish.

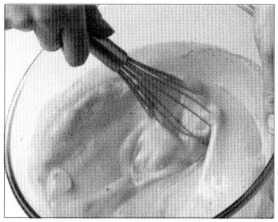

2 Whisk the milks, spice, sugar and eggs in a bowl. Pour over the bread and leave to stand for 30 minutes.

3 Meanwhile, soak the sultanas in the rum. Preheat the oven to 180°C/350°F/Gas 4.

4 Sprinkle the sultanas over the pudding, grate over a little nutmeg and bake for 30–45 minutes.

FISH AND SHELLFISH

When it comes to fish and shellfish, citizens of Latin America and the Caribbean are spoilt for choice. Every country except Bolivia and Paraguay has a coastline. You might expect the widest selection of fish to be available to the island dwellers of the Caribbean, but the finest seafood actually comes from the coastlines of Chile and Peru, where plankton brought up from the Antarctic by the icy Humboldt current provides a rich diet for the abundant sea life. The rivers and lakes teem with fresh fish, and both trout and salmon are farmed. The following list introduces just some of the fish available in Latin America, chosen either because they are particularly abundant or make a significant culinary contribution.

FRESH FISH

Snapper Two varieties of red snapper are to be found in the tropical waters of Central and South America. The American red snapper, which has lean white flesh with a very good flavour, is bright red all over, even including the eyes and fins. Its relative, the Caribbean red snapper, tends to be slightly smaller and is distinguished by its yellow eyes and paler belly. All snappers are very good to eat, whether baked, grilled (broiled), poached, steamed or pan-fried. The sweet, delicate flesh goes well with many types of fruit and fruit vegetables, such as mango or avocado. Caribbean snapper is often simply stuffed and baked, and sometimes wrapped in strips of bacon to keep the flesh juicy and tender.

Above: A large Caribbean red snapper can be stuffed and simply baked or grilled for a delicious meal.

Mahi mahi/dolphinfish/dorade Of all the many names for this flavoursome fish, dolphinfish is perhaps the most unfortunate, since it leads people to imagine, quite wrongly, that it is related to the dolphin. The mahi mahi looks like no other fish. It has an unusual square head and a long, tapering body, which makes it look somewhat like a baseball bat. The firm white flesh of mahi mahi has a delicious sweet flavour.

Mackerel Several varieties of king mackerel are fished off the coast of Latin America, including the *cero*, which is fairly abundant in the Gulf of Mexico, and the *sierra*, which frequents Pacific waters. Mackerel are at their most delicious when eaten extremely fresh, and are a popular choice to be "cooked" with lime juice and eaten as *escabeche*. When cooking mackerel, team it with robust or sharp flavours, to offset the richness.

Below: Found in the Caribbean seas, warm-water groupers have fairly firm flesh that can be cooked and served in many ways.

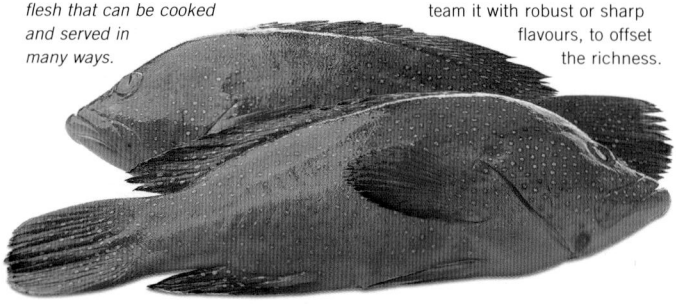

Sea bass These look rather like salmon, with elegant, slim bodies and silvery scales. Various species are found in the Caribbean Sea and the Pacific Ocean. Sea bass can be grilled (broiled), baked, braised, poached, fried or steamed, and they taste particularly good when combined with spicy flavours. In Peru, where the striped bass or corvina is preferred, the fish is cooked with chillies, while in Argentina it is often stuffed and baked.

Grouper These rather glum-looking fish, with their characteristic pouty lips, are members of the sea bass family. The warm-water groupers, such as those that are found in the Caribbean Sea, tend to have firmer flesh than delicate sea bass, and are good for poaching as well as frying, baking or cooking on the barbecue.

Patagonian toothfish This large fish is commonly known as the Chilean sea bass. It does come from Chilean waters, but the sea bass label is not accurate because it belongs to a separate species. Famed for its fine flavour, the Patagonian toothfish is popular in the US and Asia. There have been concerns about overfishing in recent years.

Buying fish

When buying fish, make sure that it is as fresh as possible. This is particularly important if you are intending to serve it as ceviche. Here's what to look for:

- There should be no apparent odour, other than a pleasant, faint smell of the sea.
- The eyes should be clear, bright and slightly bulging.
- The flesh should be firm and elastic; if you press it lightly with your finger it should spring back.
- The gills should gape, revealing a red or rosy interior.
- The scales should be firmly attached, not flaking off.

Left: Fresh trout are plentiful in Lake Titicaca, and are commonly eaten in the highlands of Peru and Bolivia.

Swordfish are landed in the Gulf of Mexico and off the coast of Costa Rica from June to January and in Chile in late spring. The meaty flesh is low in fat and dries out quickly, so must be basted frequently if barbecued, or cooked in a sauce for the best results. Swordfish goes well with spicy flavours and Latin American cooks like to cook it with chillies and tomatoes. When buying swordfish, which is usually sold as steaks, check that the flesh is slightly translucent. It should be creamy white or pale pink, with the darker areas shading to a reddish-brown colour. Avoid steaks that look grey.

Pompano These are oily fish that taste similar to mackerel. They are available all year round, sometimes whole, but more often as fillets. There are several varieties in the warm seas off the coast of Central America, but the most common is the African pompano. This silvery, grey-finned fish has meaty flesh with a good, strong flavour. It is ideal for spicy dishes and goes well with chillies, coriander, red (bell) peppers and citrus fruit.

Congrio Found off the coasts of Chile and Peru, congrios resemble eels but are actually members of a distinctly separate species – *genypterus chilensis*. There are three types, all with firm, flavoursome flesh that flakes beautifully when cooked. This is one of the few fish to find its way into a poem. The Nobel prize-winning poet Pablo Neruda was so impressed with a bowl of congrio soup supped in his native Chile that he wrote an ode to the delicious fish.

Flying fish Also known as exocets, from which the name of the missile derives, these small fish really do look as if they are flying when you glimpse them leaping from the sea. Their propulsion comes from the tail and they stay in the air for several seconds, their large pectoral fins giving them lift. When freshly caught and pan-fried, flying fish taste delicious. Caribbean cooks like to rub them with a spicy mixture of garlic, herbs and hot pepper sauce before coating them in seasoned flour and frying them.

Above: Fresh swordfish steaks are delicious barbecued with a lime and chilli marinade.

Salt cod

Among the rations given to African slaves shipped over to work the sugar plantations was salt cod. They developed a taste for the rather unprepossessing looking food, and invented many recipes to make the most of its flavour. Some of these were based on those cooked by their Spanish or Portuguese masters, but they were often new. In Brazil, salt cod is served as a topping for baked eggs, while a Caribbean speciality is salt cod with scrambled eggs, spinach and bacon.

Below: Salt cod is used in many traditional Caribbean dishes.

Trout There are plenty of trout in the cooler regions of Latin America. Rainbow, brown and brook trout are found in the Patagonian lakes close to Bariloche, and the icy rivers that flow from the Andes to the sea in Peru are also a magnet for trout fishermen. Lake Titicaca, on the Andean highlands between Peru and Bolivia, also has a plentiful supply of trout. Trout has a fresh, clean flavour and, although it is often cooked very simply – either fried or grilled (broiled) – more inventive chefs delight in introducing unusual flavour combinations. One particularly tasty Caribbean dish combines spiced trout fillets with a rich wine and plantain sauce in a tasty Caribbean dish. The rosy flesh also looks lovely and tastes delicious when paired with fresh prawns (shrimp).

SHELLFISH

Latin America is a great place for shellfish. In the markets you'll not only come across familiar varieties, such as crabs and lobsters, but also rare and remarkable shellfish that look like algae-encrusted rocks, and sea urchins so large that their nickname – sea hedgehogs – seems entirely appropriate. In the Caribbean you can feast on conch, and in Brazil you can dine on some of the biggest prawns (shrimp) you are ever likely to encounter.

Crabs Both sea and land crabs are a delicacy in Latin America. There are many different varieties, from the soft-shelled blue crabs of the Atlantic and Gulf coasts to the mighty Patagonian king crabs. In Brazil, mangrove crabs are a great favourite, while Mexicans are partial to the California or Dungeness crab. Sweet and succulent, crab meat can be used in a wide variety of dishes. When carefully cooked, crab tastes good just as it is, but it also makes a great gumbo. Crab cakes are delicious. In Trinidad and Tobago, a favourite dish is a mixture of onion and crab meat in a rum sauce, served in crab shells.

Below: Crab meat is a Latin American delicacy, which can be added to soups or stews, alongside other seafood.

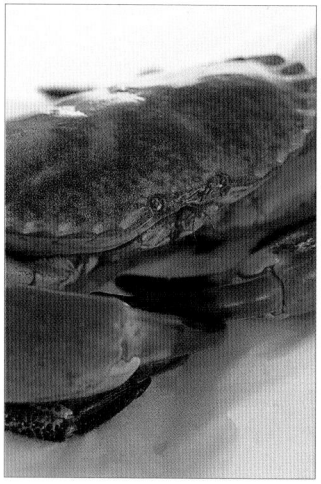

Above: Tender king prawns are often grilled with fresh coconut for a popular Brazilian street snack.

Prawns and shrimp Several different types of prawns and shrimp are found in the oceans surrounding the continent. The biggest and best are probably the Gulf shrimp, which are found in warm waters. Sometimes pinky grey in colour but more often brilliant scarlet, these are big and succulent. Prawns are always included on a cold mixed fish and shellfish platter but also feature in cooked dishes. They are often cooked with fresh coconut or coconut milk, an unusual combination but one that works extremely well.

Dried shrimp Tiny shrimp, tossed in dendê oil and dried in the sun until crunchy, are popular throughout Latin America, but particularly in Brazil's coastal Bahia region. They give flavour and texture to soups, stews and salads, and are an essential ingredient in the Brazilian dipping sauce, *vatapá*. To prepare dried shrimp, rinse them under cold running water, then soak in hot water for about 35 minutes. They are often ground before being used.

Mussels On the west coast of the continent, where the sea is often turbulent, mussels cling tenaciously to the rocks until prised off by chefs or diners. They inevitably form part of the pit-cooked seafood extravaganza, the Chilean *curanto*, and are also used in a variety of soups and stews. Their sweet, tender flesh is nutritious and they taste best when lightly steamed. Before cooking mussels, it is important to discard any that are not tightly closed, or which do not close when tapped. The opposite applies after cooking, when it is those mussels that have failed to open that must be discarded.

Clams Among the hundreds of different clams found in Latin America and the Caribbean, perhaps the most delicious are the *navajuelas* (razorshells) found off the coast of Chile and Peru. These clams have tubular brown shells. When packed in bundles, they look like bamboo sticks, with the soft creamy flesh of the animal protruding from one end. Razorshells are often served raw, but can be cooked. More familiar hard shell clams include quahogs and littlenecks, which are often used in *chupes* (chowders) and angelwing clams, which are harvested in Mexico, Cuba, Puerto Rico and Chile.

Below: Fresh mussels are abundant in Chile, where seafood is plentiful.

Above: Razorshell clams, also known as navajuelas, *can be cooked but are more often served raw.*

Scallops Easily identified by their fan-shaped shells, scallops are a source of two delectable treats: the sweet, tender white meat and the bright orange roe or "coral". In Latin America, scallops are widely enjoyed, especially on the western seaboard. Black scallops, which are found off the coast of Ecuador, are especially sought after. Scallops are often eaten raw, with just a squeeze of lime, but they can be cooked. Keep the cooking time short, however – a couple of minutes at most.

A Chilean extravaganza
The ultimate South American seafood experience has to be the Chilean *curanto*, a sort of clambake but with a much wider selection of fish and shellfish, including squid, mussels and scallops. A fire is made in a large stone-lined pit. When the stones are hot, the fish and shellfish are placed on top and covered with leaves. The pit is then sealed and only opened hours later when everything is cooked to perfection. One of the best places to sample a real *curanto* is on the island of Chiloe, otherwise, try the one-pot version called *curanto en olla*.

Right: Really fresh king scallops have the best flavour.

Conch Pronounced "konk", this is the animal that lives inside those big, beautiful pink-lined shells that many people display in their bathrooms. A large relative of the whelk, conches are found in the warm, shallow waters of the Caribbean. The pink flesh is tasty and chewy and good to eat, whether raw or cooked, but it must be beaten to tenderize it first. The meat is often used in chowders, but is also good delicately fried. In Barbados, fresh conch fritters are a great favourite, and are often served as a quick bar snack, alongside an ice-cold beer.

Abalone Like the conch, this is a gastropod, a sea creature with a single large foot for locomotion. Abalone feed exclusively on seaweed. They thrive in the cold waters off southern Chile, which are close to the world's largest kelp forests. Abalone are extremely difficult to prise from the rocks that they cling to, which helps to explain why they are fairly expensive. They are highly prized not only for their flesh, but also for their beautiful shells, which are lined with iridescent mother-of-pearl. Abalone has a delicious flavour but must be carefully prepared. Like conch, it needs to be tenderized carefully. Cynics sometimes suggest that the only way to do this successfully is to run it over with a truck, but beating with a wooden mallet usually does the trick.

Sea urchins There are over 800 species of sea urchin found all over the world, but only a few are edible. The ones found in Chile – called *erizos* – are unusually large, up to 10cm/4in across. Regarded as a gourmet delicacy, they are generally eaten raw. A tasty vinaigrette dressing may be offered, but lovers of sea urchins generally prefer them completely unadorned.

Squid
This is a very popular ingredient, especially in Mexico, Central America and the islands of the Caribbean. Squid has firm, lean, white flesh that can be tender and delicious when properly cooked. In Cuba, it forms part of a classic fish and shellfish rice dish, while in Chile it is combined with fresh chillies, potatoes and tomatoes to make a rich, warming stew. Small pan-fried squid can be found for sale along the coasts of South America as a delicious beach snack.

Below: Squid is a popular ingredient in Latin American cooking, with squid casserole a common dish in many areas.

MEAT

Visit Argentina, and you could easily imagine that South America was some kind of monument to meat, yet it was not always so. Before the 16th century, cattle, sheep and pigs were unknown on the continent and the only meat that was consumed came from wild boar, game birds, including the wild turkey, cameloids, small mammals, iguanas, snakes and some other reptiles.

BEEF

Fanning out from either side of the Rio de la Plata are the pampas, large grassy plains that are home to some of the finest beef cattle in the world. Stretching for thousands of miles, the pampas cover the temperate zones of Argentina and Uruguay.

It was the early colonists who introduced beef cattle to the region, along with the European grasses that soon supplanted native varieties. Those first cattle, with horses and other farm animals, were kept in compounds, but inevitably many escaped and, finding the pampas very much to their liking, multiplied to form the nucleus of what would eventually become vast wild herds. With both wild horses and cattle at large, it was only a matter of time before gauchos, the South American cowboys, tamed the one and set about capturing the other. Such private enterprise could not continue indefinitely, however. By the end of the 19th century, much of this cattle country was in the hands of private ranchers, and the gauchos had to work for them if they wanted to maintain their chosen way of life. Cattle farming became big business and today much of the world's supply of beef comes not only from Argentina but also from Brazil, Peru and Colombia. Large tracts of rainforest have been cleared to make way for new cattle stations; something that is of considerable and rising concern to environmentalists.

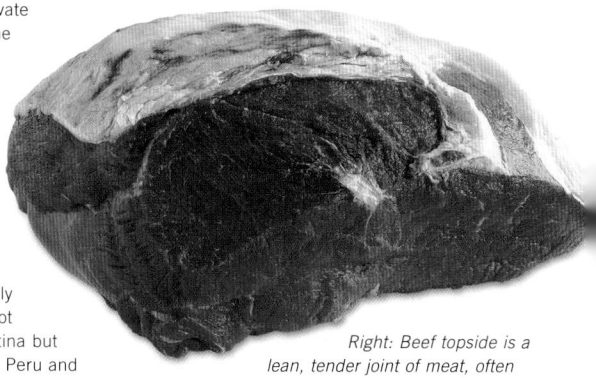

Right: Beef topside is a lean, tender joint of meat, often used for braising or pot-roasting.

In Latin America, and especially in Argentina and Brazil, beef consumption is high. Argentines eat around one and a half times as much beef as Americans, with much of it cooked over coals, whether in restaurants or at outdoor *asados*. That the meat should be cooked to perfection is a matter of pride. Whole rib sections or flanks of beef are cooked vertically, speared on iron rods that are set at an angle to prevent the juices from dripping on to the fire. Smaller portions are laid out on barbecue grills, some of which are as big as table tennis tables.

A Brazilian speciality is the *churrasco* or mixed grill, which includes excellent beef steaks. Variations on this traditional dish are a feature of special restaurants called *churrascarias* that also specialize in spit-roasts. Pot roasts are a popular choice too, and there are scores of different recipes for rich beef stews, often incorporating chillies, chorizo or other sausages, fresh or dried fruit or even fish and shellfish. Vegetables that cook down to a purée, like potatoes and pumpkin, are often used for thickening sauces, or the delicious juices are mopped up with farofa, a form of toasted cassava flour. Beef is also used to make meatballs or as a tasty and often spicy filling for empanadas, *humitas* or tamales.

Below: Succulent thick rib joints are ideal for barbecuing.

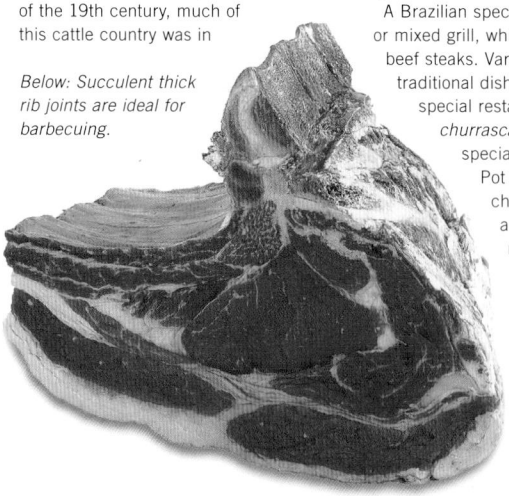

Dried meat

In the heat of Latin America, meat tends to go off fairly quickly, so before refrigeration was an option it was necessary to find ways of preserving it. Chief among these was drying, a method that remains popular to this day. To make *cecina*, beef or pork is salted and partially dried, then treated with fresh lemon juice before being briefly air-dried again. During the process the meat acquires a robust flavour, and when it is tenderized it makes extremely good eating. *Cecina* is used to add a rich flavour to stews or as fillings for tortillas and tamales. More thoroughly dehydrated meat is *charqui* or *jerky*, which is produced by air-drying strips of meat in the icy Andean winds. Also available is *carne seca*, the traditional sun-dried salt beef of Brazil, a version of which is also produced in Colombia.

Carnitas
These crisp morsels of marinated meat, usually pork, are a popular Mexican snack, especially in Bajio, to the north of Mexico City.

The meat is cooked in lard, with garlic and oranges, and has a delicious flavour. *Carnitas* are served with salsa as an appetizer or used as a delicious filling for tacos or burritos.

LAMB

The main sheep-farming areas of Latin America are Patagonia, in the south of Argentina, and Uruguay. Sheep are also to be found on the Paramos, the high plateaux between the tree line and the snow line in Chile and Peru. Although lamb and mutton have historically been less popular than beef in Argentina, lamb is now gaining ground. Mutton and lamb are popular in Mexico and the islands of the Caribbean, featuring in dishes such as lamb pelau, lamb and lentil soup and "seasoned-up" lamb in spinach sauce. A favourite way of cooking lamb is to marinate it in a mixture of garlic and warm spices, including ground annatto (achiote) seeds, then roast it with sweet (bell) peppers and beans. The annatto gives the meat a rich red colour.

Below: Lamb is becoming more popular in South America and is often rubbed with a mixture of spices.

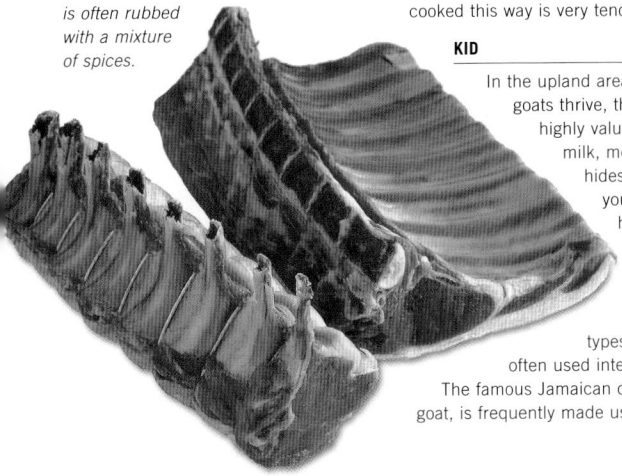

PORK

When Spanish and Portuguese colonists introduced pigs to Mexico and other parts of Latin America, there was jubilation, not just because the meat tasted so good, but also because the lard was such a valuable ingredient for frying and baking. Pork hasn't got the high profile that beef enjoys, but it is a popular meat, especially in Mexico, the Caribbean and Brazil, where pork ribs, smoked tongue and pork sausage feature in the national dish, *feijoada*. A favourite Caribbean treatment is to roast pork with rum, while in Argentina and Peru, meat is cooked in milk. Pork cooked this way is very tender.

KID

In the upland areas where goats thrive, they are highly valued for their milk, meat and hides. Kid – young goat – has a slighlty more gamey flavour than lamb, but the two types of meat are often used interchangeably. The famous Jamaican dish, curry goat, is frequently made using lamb instead, although the title makes it obvious that this wasn't always the case. As well as a slightly stronger flavour, kid is a little tougher than lamb, and therefore needs a longer cooking time for the best results.

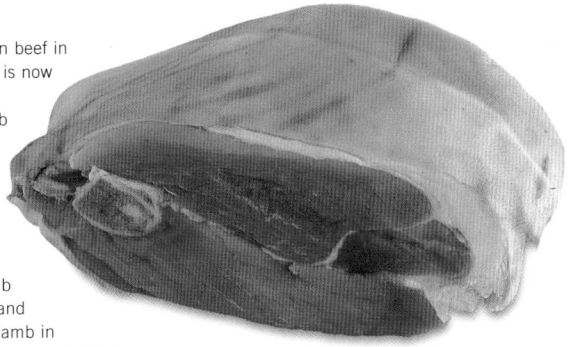

Above: The top end of a pork leg is excellent as a joint for roasting.

Offal
Latin American cooks don't just eat offal, they celebrate it. Intestines, hearts, kidneys, tripe, pigs' feet – in fact all the animal parts eschewed in many other places around the world – are elevated to gourmet status by careful cooking with herbs, spices and sauces. Sausages of all types are also widely eaten, with chorizo being a particular favourite.

Below: Spanish-style chorizo and other dried sausages are often eaten in Latin America.

POULTRY

Although turkeys are native to Latin America and were first domesticated by the Aztecs, along with ducks, chickens were unknown until they were introduced by the Spanish and Portuguese colonists.

CHICKEN

As in many other places throughout the world, chickens can be found absolutely everywhere in Latin America: scratching in backyards, on sale at busy markets and on the menu at home and in restaurants. In the Caribbean, where there is seldom enough land to raise large food animals, chickens are a practical source of protein. Chicken is often grilled (broiled); cut into strips and simmered in soups; roasted for traditional Sunday lunch; rubbed with jerk seasoning and cooked over the coals; or stewed in delicious hot-pots thickened with okra, squash, cassava or peanut-based sauces. All over Latin America, and especially in Peru, you can find simple spit-roasted chickens – *pollos a la brasa* – on sale.

Jointing a duck

When preparing a duck, it is important to remember that there is not a great deal of meat on these birds. The simplest and fairest way of serving it is in four equal-sized portions, so the duck must be jointed before cooking.

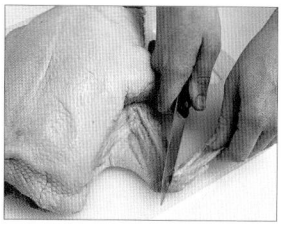

1 Place the whole bird, breast-up, on a chopping board. Remove the wing tips with poultry shears or a sharp knife and then cut the breast in half, working from the tail towards the neck.

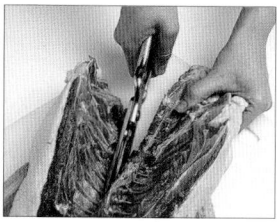

2 Continue cutting the bird in half, along either side of the backbone.

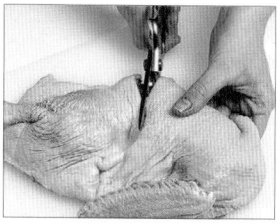

3 Cut each piece of duck roughly in half, cutting diagonally.

Below: Every part of Latin America and the Caribbean has its own favourite chicken recipe.

DUCK

The wild ducks that wintered in Mexico were hunted for food long before the arrival of the Spanish, and muscovy duck was just one of the more than 300 dishes on the menu when the renowned Aztec emperor, Montezuma, sat down to dine. Duck is also extremely popular in Peru, where it is often cooked with fresh coriander (cilantro) leaves. For lovers of duck, Latin America provides some delicious and unusual recipes, such as duck roasted with sweet potatoes and red wine, or cooked with rum.

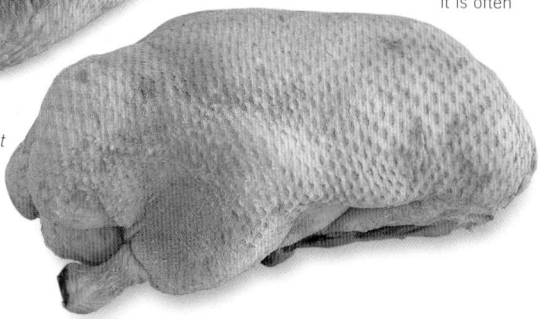

Right: Duck is eaten throughout the region – a tasty Caribbean speciality is duck in rum.

TURKEY

Two types of turkey are native to Latin America, one emerging in Yucatán and Guatemala and the other in Mexico. Turkeys were introduced to Europe by the Spanish and they soon became a popular choice in France, Italy and Britain. The wild birds were fast runners and strong fliers, and their bright feathers were highly prized for ceremonial head-dresses and jewellery, and to provide flights for arrows. The Aztecs were the first to domesticate wild turkeys, which they called *huexolotlin*. Aside from being a valuable food source, turkeys also had a strong religious significance, and two festivals were held every year in their honour. Probably the most famous Latin American dish involving turkey is the

Above: Quails are very small birds – for a main course, serve two per person.

Mexican *poblano mole*. There are many versions of this, all of which involve the bird being cooked in a thick, rich sauce, which contains numerous fresh or dried chillies and several pieces of rich, dark chocolate or cocoa powder. Turkey is often cooked with fresh fruit and tastes especially good with sweet, juicy mango in a traditional Caribbean dish.

GAME BIRDS

Wild birds were a vital part of the South American diet in the pre-Colombian era, and they are still hunted in many places today. Pheasant, partridge, quail and pigeon are all regularly eaten, along with several types of jungle bird, including some breeds of parrot. Pheasant is particularly good for roasting or stewing, young partridge is best simply roasted and served in their own cooking juices, while pigeon is delicious braised or cooked in a pigeon pie. The *curassow*, a large black bird with a distinctive crest of curved feathers, can be found from Mexico to Brazil. It is widely regarded as being the best game bird in Latin America, and is therefore in high demand, a fact that has led to over-hunting. Sadly, it has become an endangered species in some areas.

EXOTIC AND UNUSUAL MEATS

In Peru, guinea pigs (*cuyes*) have long been a favourite food. Domesticated in much the same way as chickens, roaming around backyards, they are cooked by similar methods. The vegetarian diet of *cuyes*, like rabbits, gives their meat a fairly light, delicate flavour. Roast *cuy* is sometimes on the menu at out-of-town restaurants and is readily available roasted at many Peruvian markets and on street stalls, but it is more often eaten at home.

Deer are hunted in forest regions, as are *moufflon*, a type of wild sheep, *peccaries*, which are similar to pigs, and wild goats. Llamas and other large cameloids were often cooked and eaten many centuries ago. In certain areas, they occasionally still are, but they tend to be more highly valued as pack animals. Subsistence hunters catch agoutis, tapirs, armadillos, capybara, monkeys, snakes, iguanas and even tortoises. Turtles are also considered a delicacy and are occasionally eaten, although some countries have made their capture and trade illegal.

Above: Turkeys are native to Latin America and were bred by the Aztecs centuries ago.

Pheasant in green pipian sauce
This delicious recipe from the Yucatán peninsula can be used for almost any game bird.

SERVES 4

INGREDIENTS
30ml/2 tbsp oil
2 oven-ready pheasants, halved lengthways
1 onion, finely chopped
2 garlic cloves, crushed
275g/10oz can tomatillos
175g/6oz/generous 1 cup pepitas (pumpkin seeds), ground
15ml/1 tbsp annatto (achiote) seeds, ground
475ml/16fl oz/2 cups chicken stock
salt and ground black pepper
fresh coriander (cilantro), to garnish

1 Heat the oil in a frying pan and sauté the pheasant halves until lightly browned. Place them in a large roasting pan.

2 Purée the onion, garlic and tomatillos, with their juice, in a food processor or blender. Scrape the purée into a pan and add the pepitas and annatto seeds.

3 Stir in the stock and cook gently for 10 minutes, taking care not to burn. Leave to cool.

4 Preheat the oven to 180°C/350°F/Gas 4. Pour the sauce over the pheasant and bake for about 40 minutes, basting occasionally. Garnish with fresh coriander (cilantro) and serve immediately.

DRINKS

There are some delightful ways of slaking your thirst in Latin America, from sipping cool coconut juice or a refreshing fruit drink to sampling local wines and spirits. If the latter makes you sleepy, there is always strong coffee to wake you up, or a cup of chocolate to help you relax.

ALCOHOL-FREE DRINKS

Fruit drinks These are something of a speciality in many parts of Latin America and the Caribbean. *Sugos* and *refrescos* or *frescas* are always worth sampling and are particularly popular with children. Made while you wait, from whatever local fruit is available, these fruit drinks tend to be on the sweet side. Ice helps to take the edge off, but they can be served without sugar if preferred. One unusual drink, which is very popular in Brazil, is *guaraná*. Made from the berries of a tree sacred to Amazonian tribes, the drink is sold in both still and carbonated forms and is credited with a vast range of health-giving properties. In the English-speaking islands of the Caribbean, ginger beer is a popular drink, especially around Christmas time, as is *agua de Jamaica*, a refreshing drink made from the bright red sepals of a tropical plant.

Below: Ginger beer is a popular drink in some parts of the Caribbean.

The perfect cup
In Latin America, any time is the right time for full-bodied coffee, and visitors are often staggered by the strength of the brew and the amount consumed. To make a perfect cup, follow these directions:
- Use fresh, cold water that has not been chemically softened.
- Use 60–75ml/4–5 tbsp per 600ml/1 pint/2½ cups.
- Boil the water, then let it cool slightly before pouring it on to the ground coffee.
- If you are using a jug or cafetière (plunge pot) let the coffee stand for 3–4 minutes before pouring or plunging.
- Do not reheat coffee or keep it warm for long periods.

Coffee Two-thirds of the world's supply of coffee comes from Latin America and the Caribbean. Brazil is the leading grower and exporter, with Colombia second. Other important producers are Mexico, El Salvador, Guatemala, Costa Rica, Ecuador and Peru. Coffee is not native to Latin America, however. It was introduced, so the story goes, by a young naval officer called Gabriel de Clieu, who carried a small sapling with him when he sailed to the Caribbean from Europe in 1723. On the voyage, the ship was becalmed, but De Clieu used part of his own water ration to keep the sapling alive until he could plant it on his estate in Martinique. It was clearly a robust specimen, however, because in fewer than 60 years there

Below: Coffee beans must first be roasted before they can be ground.

were 18 million coffee trees on Martinique and production had spread to Central and South America.

There are about 50 species of coffee, but the only ones that are commercially significant are *Coffea arabica* and *Coffea canephora (robusta). Robusta* likes humid, tropical conditions and grows well below 600m/1,900ft, while *arabica* prefers the heights and is cultivated between 600 and 2000m/1,900 and 6,500ft. The young trees do best in well-drained volcanic soil. They need plenty of sun, but cannot tolerate excessively high temperatures, so shade trees are planted between the rows.

Coffee trees are beautiful. They bear jasmine-scented white flowers up to three times a year, and these are followed by the berry-like fruit. These start off green, but gradually ripen to red, when the cherries, as they are called, are harvested. After picking, which must be done by hand for coffee of the highest quality, the cherries go through lengthy processing to release the pair of beans hidden inside each. Before the beans can be ground to make coffee, they must be roasted. Coffee connoisseurs in Latin America like to roast and grind their own beans at home every day, but most of us buy our beans ready-roasted. In some countries, a light roast is preferred, while in others a dark roast is favoured.

Discriminating drinkers demand specific types of coffee, such as Colombian Medellin, but most of what is exported has been blended, either to appeal to the majority or to persuade us to buy coffee tailored to a time of day: light for breakfast and full-bodied for after dinner, for instance.

Yerba maté
This herbal tea, made from the leaves of a plant that resembles holly, is popular in Argentina, Uruguay, Paraguay and Southern Brazil. It is traditionally sipped through a silver straw from a hollow gourd, the *maté*, from which it takes its name.

Above: Good-quality chocolate is still produced in Bariloche, Patagonia.

Above: Hot chocolate is the perfect end to a meal, according to Montezuma.

Chocolate The cacao tree is indigenous to Latin America. One fifth of the world's production now comes from Brazil, with Ecuador only 2 per cent behind. The Olmecs, who inhabited Central America around 1200BC, are credited with discovering that the cacao bean could be transformed into a delicious drink, but it was the Maya and later the Aztecs who perfected the art. For the emperor Montezuma, the perfect end to one of his legendary feasts was a gold cup full of the frothy beverage.

The Aztecs credited cocoa with medicinal powers, and used the drink to treat all sorts of ailments. In this they were ahead of their time, for cocoa has been proven to be high in antioxidants, the natural compounds that are widely believed to reduce cholesterol levels, fight cancer and heart disease and delay signs of ageing. The drink the Aztecs enjoyed was not sweetened, but the natural bitterness of the chocolate was often offset by adding chillies and other warm spices, such as vanilla.

The Spanish first introduced chocolate to the rest of the world and the beverage was soon being drunk in sophisticated resorts and cities all over Europe. Although it is now as a form of confectionery that chocolate is best known and loved in Europe and the US, its main use in Latin America continues to be as a drink. Mexican chocolate is a delicate mixture of dark and bitter chocolate, sugar, ground almonds and cinnamon, and it tastes incredibly rich.

Swiss chocolate, Argentine-style
Although chocolate is more likely to be a drink than a sweet treat in Latin America, there is one place where bars of very good chocolate are regularly produced, and that is the beautiful Lake District of Patagonia. Descendants of Swiss, German and Northern Italian immigrants have established a thriving chocolate industry in Bariloche, with many locals hand-making their own chocolates. This Andean village is a visual delight, known for its mountains, its lakes and the European look of its streets. The thriving chocolate industry helps to reinforce the town's decidedly Swiss character.

WINE

Much of South America is too hot for successful wine production. However, in Argentina and Chile, in the cool valleys on either side of the Andes, grapes flourish and wine is produced widely.

Argentina is the world's leading wine producer outside of Europe and the US, coming fifth in the global line-up. Until recently, Argentines drank most of the wine they produced themselves, but this is gradually changing. Despite producing less wine than Argentina, Chile has a bigger bite of the international market, and produces some highly regarded wines. Wine is also produced on a smaller scale in Uruguay, Brazil and Mexico.

Argentina

The first vines were planted in Argentina in the middle of the 16th century by Jesuit priests eager to ensure a steady supply of communion wine, Gradually the vineyards became established, and the industry gained a useful boost in the 18th and 19th centuries with the arrival of European viticulturists. They introduced many of the varieties that continue to dominate: Merlot, Cabernet Sauvignon, Chardonnay, Chenin and Pinot Noir.

Below: Parts of South America, particularly Chile and Argentina, are well known for both their red and white wines.

Most of Argentina's wine comes from the western part of the country, in an area stretching from Rio Negro in the south to La Rioja and Salta in the north. By far the most productive region is Mendoza, which has well over a thousand wineries, despite having very low rainfall. This is because the whole area lies in the rain shadow of the Andes. Paradoxically, however, it is thanks to the Andes that the grapes flourish, as the vines are fed by irrigation from snow and ice-melt.

It is for red wines that Argentina is best known. These include Cabernet Sauvignon, Syrah, Merlot, Malbec, Bonarda, Pinot Noir, Tempranillo and Sangiovese. Malbec is of particular interest. This black grape originated in France, but never fully realized its potential until it was introduced to South America. A wine with an intense, vibrant colour, Malbec has been described as having distinctive berry flavours, with hints of damson, liquorice and even chocolate.

Among the white wines produced are Chenin Blanc, Sauvignon Blanc, Chardonnay and Semillon, From the northern provinces of Salta and La Rioja comes Torrontés, a varietal that is believed to have Spanish antecedents, but which is now strongly established in its adoptive country. Fresh, fruity and deliciously dry, it is extremely popular.

Chile

Roughly one-third of the length of this slender ribbon of a country is given over to the growing of grapes. Although the northern part of the country is desert and the southern tip is too cold for wine production, the central temperate valleys have ideal conditions. The main wine-producing area stretches for just under 900km/550 miles from north of Santiago to Concepción. This part of the country has a Mediterranean climate similar to that enjoyed in South Africa's Western Cape, and because the moisture-laden clouds that roll in from the ocean drop their rain in winter on the Chilean side of the Andes, irrigation is not the problem it is on the other side of the mountains in Argentina.

Right: Red Stripe lager is one of Jamaica's most famous exports, and is popular throughout Europe and the USA.

Wine production began with the introduction of the rustic Pais grape to Chile in 1548, and owes its present character to the introduction of French vines in the middle of the 19th century. Established varieties like Cabernet Sauvignon, Cabernet Franc, Merlot, Malbec and Sauvignon Blanc soon flourished, and when European vineyards were devastated by a small insect – phylloxera – Chile was fortunately spared and made the most of this opportunity.

The Maipo Valley is the most famous wine-growing area of Chile and the site of some of the oldest established vineyards. It is well-known for producing excellent Cabernet Sauvignon. Also well known for reds are the Curicó and Colchagua Valleys, while some of the finest white wines come from the Aconcagua and Casablanca Valleys in the north. Mulchen, which is at the southern tip of the wine-producing region, is another white wine area, known especially for Sauvignon Blanc and Chardonnay wines.

Thanks to the huge north-south spread and a variety of microclimates, Chile has a wide range of both red and white wines, including several organic varieties. Aside from those varieties already mentioned, Merlot, Carmenère, Malbec, Syrah, Pinot Noir and Viognier are also successfully produced.

BEER

Best known for light, thin lager drunk straight from the bottle with a wedge of lime, Central and South American beer actually has a much richer tradition than is widely appreciated. The Mayans were brewing beer from fermented corn stalks long before Spanish conquistadors invaded, while, in northern Mexico, the Aztecs enjoyed a fermented drink made with sprouted maize. The Spanish settlers set up small breweries from the 16th century onwards, but beer came a poor second to distilled spirits, until German immigrants introduced lager to Mexico. Many of the brewing companies in existence today have German roots. Mexico remains the leading beer producer, followed by Brazil. Lager is the drink of choice and well-known brands include Corona Extra, Cuzco, Dos Equis, Sol and Tecate. These lagers go well with spicy Latin American food.
The Caribbean also has a strong beer culture and one of Jamaica's most famous exports is Red Stripe lager, now a familiar sight in the US and the UK.

SPIRITS

Latin America has given the world some fine spirits, including rum and tequila.
Rum Legend has it that rum was discovered after sugar-cane mash was left to ferment in the Caribbean sun soon after the first sugar plantations were established on the islands in the 16th century. In the early 18th century, it became standard practice for the British Navy to issue sailors with a daily ration of rum, largely because the spirit endured extremes of weather so much better than beer. At the same time, rum was becoming popular in Britain. Over the centuries, the spirit has been refined, and aged rums now have the same sort of prestige as that accorded to single malt whiskies. Rum is still largely produced in the Caribbean, and some of the world's finest rums come from Jamaica, Cuba, the Dominican Republic, Martinique, Barbados, Haiti and the British Virgin Islands. Rum is also produced in some parts of South America.
Cachaça Another cane spirit, *cachaça* is distilled from the first crush of the sugar cane. Also called *pinga* or *aguardente*, it is the national drink of Brazil and is often mixed with freshly squeezed lime juice and sugar to make the delicious and popular *caipirinha* cocktail, which is often enjoyed with meals.
Pisco A grape brandy, the birthplace of *pisco* is in some doubt. It originated either in Peru or Chile, depending on which of those countries your informant favours. Its one-time reputation for rough fieriness does not apply to the top grades of *pisco*, which have a delicate, fruity flavour.
Mescal and tequila A distillate made from the juice of the agave cactus, *mescal* is that pale yellow spirit that traditionally comes with a worm in the bottle, and many Mexicans appreciate its fiery qualities. Tequila, of which there are many varieties, is produced by putting the spirit through a second distillation process.

Liqueurs

Some of the world's most popular liqueurs originated in parts of Central America and the islands of the Caribbean. Curaçao, the bitter orange liqueur invented by Dutch settlers on the island of the same name, was the forerunner of Grand Marnier and Cointreau. All are still made using Caribbean oranges. Tia Maria is a popular coffee liqueur from Jamaica. It is slightly sweeter than its Mexican rival, Kahlúa, while Toussaint, a coffee liqueur from Haiti, has a delectable strong espresso flavour that makes it extremely good for cooking as well as drinking.

Above: The best rum in the world is still produced in the Caribbean.

Below: Mexico's finest exports include mescal *(left) and* tequila blanco *(right).*

Street Food and Snacks

Throughout the Caribbean and Latin America there is a tradition of street food. Market stalls, beach huts, bars and snack houses all offer sweet or savoury snacks, which make perfect accompaniments to fruit juice, cold beer or cocktails.

CASSAVA CHIPS

FOR A PERFECT SUNDOWNER, THERE'S NOTHING QUITE LIKE ENJOYING AN ICE-COLD BEER WITH SOME FRESHLY COOKED, GOLDEN CASSAVA CHIPS. DON'T WORRY ABOUT CUTTING PERFECT-SIZED CHIPS; THEY SHOULD BE CHUNKY AND IRREGULAR, AND EXTRA CRISP.

SERVES FOUR

INGREDIENTS
- 800g/1¾lb cassava
- vegetable oil, for frying
- salt

1 Peel the cassava and cut it lengthways into 5cm/2in-wide pieces. Then cut these pieces into slices, about 2cm/¾in thick.

2 Place the slices in a large pan of salted water and bring to the boil. Lower the heat until the water simmers and cover the pan.

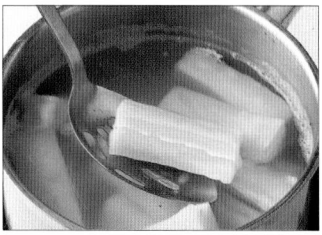

3 Cook the cassava for approximately 15 minutes, or until the slices are tender and just beginning to break up. Drain the cassava thoroughly and pat dry with kitchen paper.

4 Pour vegetable oil to a depth of 5cm/2in in a deep wide pan. Heat the oil, then add the cassava pieces. Fry for 3–4 minutes, turning occasionally, until the chips are golden and crisp all over. You may need to do this in batches.

5 Lift the chips from the pan with a slotted spoon and drain on kitchen paper. Season with salt and serve warm or at room temperature.

VARIATION

The chips are sometimes served with a sprinkling of grated Parmesan, in which case they will not need as much salt.

CHEESE TAMALES

CORN MEAL DUMPLINGS STEAMED IN CORN HUSKS ARE TO BE FOUND THROUGHOUT SOUTH AMERICA. THE RECIPE VARIES, WITH FRESH CORN KERNELS BEING USED INSTEAD OF CORN MEAL ON SOME OCCASIONS. THERE ARE MANY POSSIBLE FILLINGS; THIS RECIPE HAS ONE OF THE SIMPLEST.

MAKES TEN

INGREDIENTS
- 10 large dried corn husks or greaseproof (waxed) paper
- 75g/3oz/6 tbsp lard or white cooking fat, at room temperature
- 225g/8oz/2 cups *masa harina*
- 5ml/1 tsp salt
- 5ml/1 tsp baking powder
- 250–300ml/8–10fl oz/1–1¼ cups warm light vegetable stock
- 200g/7oz fresh white cheese, such as feta, roughly chopped

1 Place the corn husks in a bowl and pour over boiling water to cover. Soak for 30 minutes, until the husks become soft and pliable. Remove from the water and pat dry with a clean dishtowel.

2 Meanwhile put the lard or white cooking fat in a mixing bowl and beat with an electric whisk until light and fluffy. Test by dropping a small amount of the whipped lard into a cup of water. If it floats, it is ready to use.

3 Combine the *masa harina*, salt and baking powder in a separate bowl. Gradually add to the lard, beating in 45ml/3 tbsp at a time. As the mixture begins to thicken, start adding the stock, alternating the dry mixture and the stock until both have been used and the mixture is light and spreadable. If it feels tough, or dry to the touch, beat in a little more warm water, but don't add more stock, as the dough will already be flavoursome enough.

4 To assemble, lay the prepared corn husks on a board and spread about one-tenth of the *masa* mixture in the centre of each, leaving a small border at either side, with a larger border at the top and bottom.

5 Place a piece of cheese in the centre of the *masa* mixture. Fold one of the longer lengths of husk over, so that it covers the filling, then repeat with the opposite end. Close the package by folding over the two remaining sides, to make a neat parcel. Secure the tamales by tying each one with a piece of string or strip of corn husk.

6 Pile the tamales in a steamer basket placed over simmering water. Cover and steam for 1 hour. Check the level of the water occasionally, topping up if necessary. The tamales are ready when the dough comes away from the corn husk cleanly. Allow to stand for 10 minutes, then serve.

COOK'S TIP

Masa harina is a flour made with finely ground dried white corn kernels. It is most famously used to make corn tortillas, to which it imparts a nutty flavour. *Masa harina* can be found in Latin food stores and markets.

PLANTAIN AND SWEET-POTATO CHIPS

SALTY YET SWEET, THESE CRISP CHIPS ARE A CARIBBEAN SPECIALITY AND MAKE A DELICIOUS SNACK.

SERVES FOUR

INGREDIENTS
- 2 green plantains
- 1 small sweet potato
- oil, for deep-frying
- salt

VARIATIONS
For maximum crispness, it is important to use green plantains. If these are not available, substitute green bananas. Yam can be used instead of sweet potatoes. The vegetables must be soaked in cold salted water to prevent discoloration.

1 Using a small sharp knife, trim the plantains and cut them in half widthways. Peel by slitting the skin with a knife, following the natural ridges, then lifting it off. Place the peeled plantains in a bowl of cold, salted water.

2 Peel the sweet potato under cold running water, and add it to the plantains in the bowl.

3 Heat the oil in a large pan or deep-fryer. Remove the vegetables from the salted water, pat dry on kitchen paper and slice into thin rounds.

4 Fry the plantains and sweet potatoes in batches for about 2 minutes until crisp, then remove with a slotted spoon and drain on kitchen paper. Sprinkle with salt and serve when cool.

COCONUT KING PRAWNS

POPULAR THROUGHOUT THE CARIBBEAN ISLANDS, THESE BUTTERFLIED PRAWNS LOOK VERY PRETTY AND THEY TASTE WONDERFUL WHEN PARTNERED WITH A CRISP COCONUT AND CHIVE COATING.

SERVES FOUR

INGREDIENTS
- 12 raw king prawns (jumbo shrimp)
- 2 garlic cloves, crushed
- 15ml/1 tbsp lemon juice
- 50g/2oz/4 tbsp fine desiccated (dry unsweetened shredded) coconut
- 25g/1oz/⅔ cup chopped fresh chives
- 150ml/¼ pint/⅔ cup milk
- 2 eggs, beaten
- salt and ground black pepper
- oil, for deep-frying
- lime or lemon wedges and fresh flat leaf parsley, to garnish

COOK'S TIP
If raw king prawns (jumbo shrimp) are difficult to obtain, substitute cooked prawns. However, the raw prawns will absorb more flavour from the marinade, so they are the ideal choice.

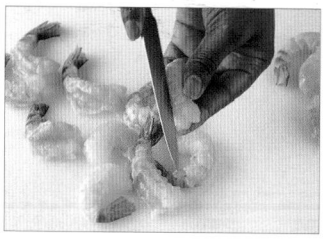

1 Peel and de-vein the prawns, leaving the tails intact, then deepen the incision made when de-veining the prawns, cutting from the back almost to the belly so that they can be opened out. Rinse the prawns under cold water and pat dry.

2 Mix the garlic and lemon juice with a little seasoning in a shallow dish, then add the prawns. Toss to coat, cover and marinate for about 1 hour.

3 Mix the coconut and chives in a separate shallow dish, and put the milk and eggs in two small bowls. Dip each prawn into the milk, then into the beaten egg and finally into the coconut and chive mixture.

4 Heat the oil in a large pan or deep-fryer and fry the prawns for about 1 minute, until golden. Lift out and drain on kitchen paper. Serve hot, garnished with lime or lemon wedges and parsley.

TAMALES DE PICADILLO

IN ANCIENT TIMES THESE LITTLE PARCELS MADE FROM CORN HUSKS, POPULAR THROUGHOUT THE WHOLE OF MEXICO, WERE COOKED IN THE HOT ASHES OF A CAMP FIRE.

MAKES TWELVE

INGREDIENTS

12 dried corn husks
50g/2oz/¼ cup lard or white cooking fat
150g/5oz/1 cup *masa harina*
2.5ml/½ tsp salt
5ml/1tsp baking powder
175ml/6fl oz/¾ cup chicken stock

For the picadillo

15ml/1 tbsp olive or corn oil
450g/1lb minced (ground) beef
½ onion, finely chopped
1 garlic clove, chopped
1 eating apple
225g/½lb tomatoes, peeled, seeded and chopped
1 or 2 drained pickled jalapeño chillies, seeded and chopped
25g/1oz raisins
1.5ml/¼ tsp ground cinnamon
1.5ml/¼ tsp ground cumin
salt and ground black pepper

1 Soak the corn husks in warm water for about 30 minutes until pliable.

2 Meanwhile, make the picadillo. Heat the oil in a frying pan. Add the beef, chopped onion and garlic, and cook, stirring, until the beef is brown and the onion is tender.

2 Peel, core and chop the apple. Add the pieces to the pan with all of the remaining picadillo ingredients. Cook, uncovered, for about 20–25 minutes, stirring occasionally to prevent sticking.

4 In a bowl, cream the lard until it is light and fluffy. Mix the *masa harina* with the salt and baking powder, then gradually beat it into the lard, taking care not to add too much at once.

5 Warm the chicken stock slowly. It should not be hot or it will melt the lard.

6 Gradually beat enough of the chicken stock into the *masa* mixture to make a mushy dough. To see if the dough is ready, carefully place a small piece on top of a bowl of water. If it floats, the dough is ready; if it sinks, continue to beat the dough until the texture is light enough for it to float.

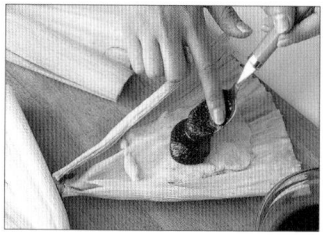

7 Drain a corn husk and lay it flat on a board. Spread about 30ml/2 tbsp of the dough down the centre part of the husk, leaving plenty of room all round for folding. Spoon 30ml/2 tbsp of the picadillo on to the centre of the dough.

8 Roll up the husk from one long side, so that the filling is completely enclosed, then fold the ends of the husks under. Make more tamales in the same way.

9 Prepare a steamer or use a metal colander and a deep pan into which the colander will fit with about 2.5cm/1in space all around.

10 Put the tamales in the steamer, folded ends under. Alternatively, place them in the colander and pour boiling water into the pan to within 2.5cm/1in of the bottom of the colander. Steam the tamales for about 1 hour, or until the dough comes away from the husk. Top up the water as required to prevent the tamales from drying.

11 Serve the tamales immediately, in the husk, leaving guests to open them at the table to reveal the delicious picadillo filling inside.

MIXED TOSTADAS

LIKE LITTLE EDIBLE PLATES, THESE TRADITIONAL MEXICAN FRIED TORTILLAS CAN SUPPORT ALMOST ANY INGREDIENTS YOU LIKE, SO LONG AS THEY ARE NOT TOO JUICY.

MAKES FOURTEEN

INGREDIENTS

- oil, for shallow frying
- 14 freshly prepared unbaked corn tortillas
- 225g/8oz/1 cup mashed red kidney or pinto beans
- 1 iceberg lettuce, shredded
- olive oil and vinegar dressing (optional)
- 2 cooked chicken breast portions, skinned and thinly sliced
- 225g/8oz guacamole
- 115g/4oz/1 cup coarsely grated mature (sharp) Cheddar cheese
- pickled jalapeño chillies, seeded and sliced, to taste

1 Heat the oil in a shallow frying pan and fry the corn tortillas one by one, until golden brown on both sides and crisp but not hard.

2 Spread each tortilla with a layer of mashed pinto or kidney beans. Put a layer of shredded lettuce (which can either be left plain or lightly tossed with a little dressing) over the beans.

3 Arrange chicken slices on top of the lettuce. Carefully spread over a layer of the guacamole and finally sprinkle over the grated cheese.

4 Arrange the mixed tostadas on a large platter and serve immediately, while still warm. Use your hands to eat tostadas as they are extremely messy.

VARIATIONS

- Instead of chicken, try using shredded pork, minced (ground) beef or turkey, or sliced chorizo.
- For a more authentic taste use *queso fresco* or feta cheese instead of Cheddar.

CHEESY EGGS

THESE DELICIOUS CARIBBEAN STUFFED EGGS ARE SIMPLE TO MAKE AND IDEAL FOR LAST-MINUTE PARTY SNACKS. SERVE THEM WITH A CRISP SALAD GARNISH AND DHAL PURI.

SERVES SIX

INGREDIENTS
- 6 eggs
- 15ml/1 tbsp mayonnaise
- 30ml/2 tbsp grated Cheddar cheese
- 2.5ml/½ tsp ground white pepper
- 10ml/2 tsp chopped fresh chives
- 2 radishes, thinly sliced, to garnish
- lettuce leaves, to serve

VARIATION
A variety of fillings can be used instead of Cheddar cheese. Canned sardines or tuna mayonnaise make a tasty alternative.

1 Cook the eggs in boiling water for about 10 minutes until hard-boiled. Lift out the eggs and place them in cold water. When cool, remove the shells.

2 Put the mayonnaise, Cheddar cheese, pepper and chives into a small bowl. Cut the hard-boiled eggs in half lengthways and carefully scoop out the yolks without breaking the whites, Add the yolks to the bowl.

3 Mash all the ingredients with a fork until well blended.

4 Fill each egg white with the egg yolk and cheese mixture, and arrange on a plate. Garnish with thinly sliced radishes and serve with crisp green lettuce leaves.

CRAB CAKES

SERVED WITH A HOT AND SPICY TOMATO DIP, THESE CARIBBEAN CRAB CAKES ARE QUITE DELICIOUS. USE THE FRESHEST CRAB MEAT AVAILABLE AND SERVE AS A SNACK AT ANY TIME OF DAY.

MAKES ABOUT FIFTEEN

INGREDIENTS
- 225g/8oz white crab meat
- 115g/4oz cooked potatoes, mashed
- 30ml/2 tbsp fresh herb seasoning
- 2.5ml/½ tsp prepared mild mustard
- 2.5ml/½ tsp ground black pepper
- ½ fresh hot chilli, seeded and chopped
- 2.5ml/½ tsp dried oregano, crushed
- 1 egg, beaten
- 15ml/1 tbsp shrimp paste (optional)
- flour, for dusting
- oil, for frying
- lime wedges and fresh basil leaves, to garnish

For the tomato dip
- 15ml/1 tbsp butter or margarine
- ½ onion, finely chopped
- 2 canned plum tomatoes, drained and chopped
- 1 garlic clove, crushed
- 150ml/¼ pint/⅔ cup water
- 5–10ml/1–2 tsp malt vinegar
- 15ml/1 tbsp chopped fresh coriander (cilantro)
- ½ chilli, seeded and chopped

1 To make the crab cakes, combine the crab meat, mashed potato, herb seasoning, mustard, black pepper, chilli, oregano and egg in a large bowl. Add the shrimp paste, if using, and mix well. Cover and chill for 30 minutes.

VARIATION

If you cannot get hold of fresh crab meat, these taste just as good made with canned tuna.

2 Make the tomato dip. Melt the butter or margarine in a small pan. Add the onion, chopped tomato and garlic and sauté for about 5 minutes until the onion is soft.

3 Add the water, vinegar, coriander and chilli. Simmer for 10 minutes, then blend to a smooth purée in a food processor or blender. Pour into a bowl. Keep warm or chill, as required.

4 Using a spoon, shape the crab mixture into rounds and dust with flour. Heat a little oil in a large frying pan and fry the crab cakes, a few at a time, for 2–3 minutes on each side until golden brown. Remove with a fish slice, drain on kitchen paper and keep hot while cooking the remaining cakes. Serve with the tomato dip and garnish with lime wedges and basil leaves.

PAN-FRIED SQUID

VISIT A BEACH BAR ANYWHERE ALONG THE COAST OF SOUTH AMERICA AND THIS IS PRECISELY THE TYPE OF SNACK YOU ARE LIKELY TO FIND ON SALE.

SERVES FOUR

INGREDIENTS
- 1kg/2¼lb fresh small squid
- 30ml/2 tbsp olive oil
- 2 garlic cloves, crushed
- 1 fresh red chilli, seeded and finely chopped
- 45ml/3 tbsp *cachaça*
- juice of 1 lime
- salt
- chunks of bread, to serve

1 Clean the squid under cold water. Pull the tentacles away from the body. The squid's entrails will come out easily. Remove the piece of cartilage from inside the body cavity and discard it.

VARIATION
If you cannot find *cachaça*, replace it with white rum or vodka.

2 Wash the body and peel away the membrane that covers it. Cut between the tentacles and head, discarding the head and entrails. Leave the tentacles whole, but discard the hard beak in the middle. Cut the body into small pieces.

3 Heat the oil over a high heat. Add the garlic, chilli and squid. Season with salt and cook for 2–3 minutes, until the squid is opaque and lightly charred.

4 Pour in the *cachaça* and continue cooking the squid until most of the liquid has evaporated. Remove the pan from the heat and then stir in the lime juice.

5 Tip the squid on to a plate and serve with chunks of bread to soak up the delicious cooking juices. Offer cocktail sticks (toothpicks) for picking up the pieces of squid.

FRIED WHITEBAIT WITH CAYENNE PEPPER

FOR THE PERFECT BEACH SNACK, TRY THESE CRISP, SPICY, BITESIZE FISH WITH A SQUEEZE OF LIME.

SERVES FOUR

INGREDIENTS
- 50g/2oz/½ cup plain (all-purpose) flour
- 1.5ml/¼ tsp cayenne pepper
- 250g/9oz whitebait
- vegetable oil, for deep-frying
- salt and ground black pepper
- lime wedges, to serve

VARIATIONS
Small fresh anchovies are also delicious cooked whole in this way. Alternatively, make up a mixed platter using whitebait, squid and prawns (shrimp).

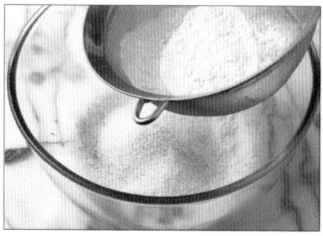

1 Sift the flour and cayenne pepper into a deep bowl or large shallow dish. Season with plenty of salt and ground black pepper.

2 Thoroughly coat the whitebait in the seasoned flour, then shake off any excess flour and make sure the whitebait are separate. Do this in batches, placing the coated fish on a plate ready for frying.

3 Pour oil to a depth of 5cm/2in into a deep wide pan. Heat the oil until very hot, then add a batch of whitebait and fry for 2–3 minutes until golden. Remove from the pan with a slotted spoon and drain on kitchen paper. Repeat with the remaining whitebait.

4 Pile the fried whitebait on a plate, season with salt and serve immediately with the lime wedges.

BLACK-EYED BEAN AND SHRIMP FRITTERS

THIS BRAZILIAN SNACK, LOCALLY KNOWN AS ACARAJÉ, IS FROM BAHIA, A REGION HIGHLY INFLUENCED BY ITS AFRICAN SLAVE HERITAGE. WOMEN FRY THESE PATTIES TO ORDER. THEY ARE THEN CUT OPEN AND FILLED WITH VARIOUS SAUCES, ALL DELECTABLE BUT VERY MESSY TO EAT.

MAKES TEN

INGREDIENTS

- 250g/9oz/1¼ cups black-eyed beans (peas)
- 40g/1½oz/¼ cup dried shrimp
- 1 onion, roughly chopped
- palm oil and vegetable oil, for frying
- salt
- chilli oil, to serve

For the filling

- 30ml/2 tbsp palm oil
- 115g/4oz/⅔ cup dried shrimp
- 1 large onion, thinly sliced
- 2 fresh hot red chillies, seeded and finely chopped

1 Put the black-eyed beans in a large bowl and cover with plenty of water. Soak overnight to loosen the skins. Drain, then soak for a further 30 minutes in hot (but not boiling) water.

2 Drain the beans and tip them on to a board. Rub them between your hands to separate them from their skins. The patties will be very dry if the skins are not removed.

3 Transfer the beans to a bowl and pour over cold water to cover. The loose skins will begin to rise to the surface. Remove them with a slotted spoon and throw them away. Stir the beans to encourage more skins to float to the surface, continuing until all the skins have been removed. You'll be able to chart your progress easily, as the beans lose their distinctive "eye" when peeled. Drain.

4 Blend the dried shrimp and onion in a food processor until smooth. Add the beans and blend to a thick purée. Season with salt.

5 Mix equal quantities of palm oil and vegetable oil to a depth of about 5cm/2in in a deep pan. Form the *acarajé* mixture into 10 oval shapes. Heat the oil and fry half of the fritters for 5 minutes or until golden. Lift out with a slotted spoon and drain on kitchen paper. Between batches, skim the oil to remove any burnt bits.

6 Make the filling. Heat the oil in a frying pan. When hot, add the dried shrimp and sauté for 2–3 minutes until golden. Lift out with a slotted spoon and drain on kitchen paper. Lower the heat and stir in the onion slices. Cook for 5 minutes until soft, then add the chilli. Sauté for 1 minute and set aside.

7 Cut each fritter open lengthways and fill with the onion mixture. Add a couple of dried shrimp and drizzle with chilli oil.

BEEF EMPANADAS

YOU'LL FIND THESE PASTRY TURNOVERS THROUGHOUT LATIN AMERICA, WITH COLOMBIA'S BEING PERHAPS THE MOST FAMOUS. THEY COME WITH A VARIETY OF FILLINGS, INCLUDING BEEF, PORK, VEGETABLES AND CHEESE. WHAT BETTER WAY FOR USING UP LEFTOVERS?

MAKES TWENTY

INGREDIENTS
- 225g/8oz/2 cups plain (all-purpose) flour
- 2.5ml/½ tsp salt
- 90g/3½oz/scant ½ cup cold butter, cut into small chunks
- juice of ½ lime
- 50ml/2fl oz/¼ cup lukewarm water
- vegetable oil, for deep-frying
- chilli salsa, to serve (optional)

For the filling
- 450g/1lb beef shin or leg (shank)
- 60ml/4 tbsp olive oil
- 1.5ml/¼ tsp ground cumin
- 1 garlic clove, crushed
- 10ml/2 tsp paprika
- 250ml/8fl oz/1 cup light beef stock
- 450g/1lb potatoes, peeled and cubed
- 2 tomatoes, finely chopped
- 3 spring onions (scallions), finely chopped
- salt and ground black pepper

1 Make the filling. Cut the beef into large chunks and chop in a food processor until finely diced, but not minced (ground). This will tenderize the meat, cutting the cooking time.

2 Heat 30ml/2 tbsp of the olive oil in a wide, heavy pan over a high heat. Add the beef chunks and sauté until golden brown. Push the beef to the side and add the cumin, crushed garlic and paprika to the pan. Reduce the heat and cook, stirring gently, for around 2 minutes, until the spices begin to release their delicious aroma.

3 Stir in the stock and bring to the boil. Cover and cook over a low heat for 30 minutes. Stir in the potatoes, tomatoes and spring onions. Cook for 15 minutes more, or until the beef and potatoes are tender. Season with salt and pepper to taste, then leave to cool.

4 Meanwhile, place the flour and salt in a food processor. Add the small chunks of butter and pulse until the mixture resembles fine breadcrumbs. Combine the lime juice and water and slowly pour into the food processor, with the motor still running. As soon as the pastry comes together, tip it on to a floured surface and gently knead to a soft dough. Shape into a ball, wrap in clear film (plastic wrap) and chill for at least 20 minutes.

5 On a floured surface roll out the pastry until it is very thin. Cut out 6cm/2½in circles, using a pastry (cookie) cutter.

6 Spoon about 7.5ml/1½ tsp of the filling into the centre of a pastry circle, then brush the edges with water. Fold the pastry over to form a half-moon, then press around the edges to seal. Repeat with the rest of the pastry.

7 Pour vegetable oil to a depth of 5cm/2in into a deep frying pan. Heat the oil, then add five or six empanadas. Fry for 5 minutes until golden brown, turning halfway through cooking. Remove from the pan with a slotted spoon and drain. Repeat with the remaining empanadas. Serve with a little chilli salsa, if using.

NUT BRITTLE

NUTS ARE VERY POPULAR IN SOUTH AMERICA AND VARIATIONS OF THIS SNACK ARE TO BE FOUND THROUGHOUT THE CONTINENT. IN BRAZIL IT'S CALLED PE-DE-MOLEQUE *(KID'S FEET).*

MAKES ABOUT TEN

INGREDIENTS
- vegetable oil, for greasing
- 250g/9oz/2¼ cups unsalted peanuts
- 250g/9oz/generous 1 cup granulated sugar

COOK'S TIP
Act quickly once the sugar has reached the ideal colour, otherwise the caramel could burn and become bitter. Don't worry if the pieces of brittle don't snap evenly when cooled – they'll be just as delicious if irregular.

1 Using vegetable oil, grease a shallow 30 x 20cm/12 x 8in baking tin (pan). Tip the sugar and peanuts into a heavy pan and place over a low heat.

2 As the sugar begins to melt, start stirring the nuts with a wooden spoon, bringing the sugar that is beginning to caramelize around the edges of the pan into the centre.

3 When all the mixture has caramelized and has taken on a deep brown colour, remove the pan from the heat and quickly pour the mixture into the prepared baking tin. Leave it to cool.

4 When the brittle has almost set, use a knife to mark it into regular squares or rectangles. This will make it easier to snap the cold brittle into pieces.

COCONUT SWEETS

THESE CHEWY SWEETS (CANDIES) ARE A FAVOURITE WITH CHILDREN. THEY CAN BE MADE PLAIN, BUT THE LIME JUICE AND CLOVES ADD AN INTERESTING TWIST THAT ADULTS CANNOT RESIST EITHER.

MAKES TWENTY-FIVE

INGREDIENTS
- 50g/2oz/⅔ cup desiccated (dry unsweetened shredded) coconut
- 105ml/7 tbsp water
- 175g/6oz/¾ cup light muscovado (brown) sugar
- large pinch ground cloves
- juice of ½ lime

1 Line a baking tray with baking parchment. Place the coconut in a pan with the water and sugar. Heat gently until the sugar dissolves.

2 Stir in the ground cloves and lime juice and increase the heat. Cook, stirring with a wooden spoon, until the mixture has thickened and become dark golden brown.

3 Drop spoonfuls of the mixture on to the lined tray, pressing the mixture down with the back of the spoon to flatten it lightly into chunky, irregular pieces. Leave to cool before eating.

VARIATION
Equal quantities of grated fresh coconut and grated raw pumpkin can be used instead of the desiccated coconut.

SOUPS

The colonizers of Latin America and the Caribbean introduced soup to the region, transforming their original recipes by using local ingredients. Light soups, such as heart of palm soup, are ideal as an appetizer, while heartier soups, such as chilli clam broth, make excellent light meals.

VERMICELLI SOUP

THIS POPULAR MEXICAN SOUP, DELICIOUS AS AN APPETIZER, DRAWS INSPIRATION FROM TRADITIONAL ITALIAN CUISINE, USING INGREDIENTS SUCH AS VERMICELLI, GARLIC AND PARMESAN CHEESE.

SERVES FOUR

INGREDIENTS
- 30ml/2 tbsp olive or corn oil
- 50g/2oz/⅓ cup vermicelli
- 1 onion, roughly chopped
- 1 garlic clove, chopped
- 450g/1lb tomatoes, peeled, seeded and roughly chopped
- 1 litre/1¾ pints/4 cups chicken stock
- 1.5ml/¼ tsp sugar
- 15ml/1 tbsp finely chopped fresh coriander (cilantro)
- salt and ground black pepper
- chopped fresh coriander, to garnish
- 25g/1oz/¼ cup freshly grated Parmesan cheese, to serve

COOK'S TIP
Vermicelli burns easily, so move it about in the frying pan and remove from the heat as soon as it is brown.

1 Heat the olive or corn oil in a shallow frying pan and gently sauté the vermicelli over a moderate heat until golden brown. Take care not to let the strands burn. Remove the vermicelli with a slotted spoon and drain thoroughly on kitchen paper.

2 Purée the chopped onion, garlic and tomatoes in a food processor until smooth. Return the frying pan to the heat. When the oil is hot, add the purée.

3 Cook the tomato purée, stirring constantly, for about 5 minutes.

4 Transfer the purée to a pan. Add the vermicelli and pour in the stock. Season to taste. Stir in the coriander, bring to the boil, then lower the heat, cover the pan and simmer until the vermicelli is tender.

5 Serve sprinkled with chopped coriander, with the Parmesan on the side.

TOMATO SOUP

THE TASTE OF FRESH CORIANDER ADDS A MEXICAN FLAVOUR TO THIS CLASSIC TOMATO SOUP RECIPE. SPRINKLE GENEROUSLY WITH BLACK PEPPER AND SERVE WITH CRUSTY BREAD FOR A SATISFYING LUNCH.

SERVES FOUR

INGREDIENTS
- 15ml/1 tbsp corn or peanut oil
- 1 onion, finely chopped
- 900g/2lb tomatoes, peeled, seeded and chopped
- 475ml/16fl oz/2 cups chicken stock
- 2 large fresh coriander (cilantro) sprigs
- salt and ground black pepper

1 Heat the oil in a pan and gently fry the finely chopped onion, stirring frequently, for about 5 minutes, or until it is soft and translucent but not brown.

2 Add the chopped tomatoes, chicken stock and coriander sprigs to the pan. Bring to the boil, then lower the heat, cover the pan and simmer gently for about 15 minutes.

3 Remove and discard the coriander. Press the soup through a sieve and return it to the clean pan. Season and heat through. Serve sprinkled with ground black pepper.

CREAMY HEART OF PALM SOUP

THIS DELICATE SOUP HAS A LUXURIOUS, CREAMY, ALMOST VELVETY TEXTURE. THE SUBTLE YET DISTINCTIVE FLAVOUR OF THE PALM HEARTS IS LIKE NO OTHER, ALTHOUGH IT IS MILDLY REMINISCENT OF ARTICHOKES AND ASPARAGUS. SERVE WITH FRESH BREAD FOR A SATISFYING LUNCH.

SERVES FOUR

INGREDIENTS
- 25g/1oz/2 tbsp butter
- 10ml/2 tsp olive oil
- 1 onion, finely chopped
- 1 large leek, finely sliced
- 15ml/1 tbsp plain (all-purpose) flour
- 1 litre/1¾ pints/4 cups well-flavoured chicken stock
- 350g/12oz potatoes, peeled and cubed
- 2 x 400g/14oz cans hearts of palm, drained and sliced
- 250ml/8fl oz/1 cup double (heavy) cream
- salt and ground black pepper
- cayenne pepper and chopped fresh chives, to garnish

1 Heat the butter and oil in a large pan over a low heat. Add the onion and leek and stir well until coated in butter. Cover and cook for 5 minutes until softened and translucent.

2 Sprinkle over the flour. Cook, stirring, for 1 minute.

3 Pour in the stock and add the potatoes. Bring to the boil, then lower the heat and simmer for 10 minutes. Stir in the hearts of palm and the cream, and simmer gently for 10 minutes.

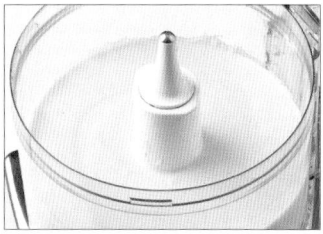

4 Process in a blender or food processor until smooth. Return the soup to the pan and heat gently, adding a little water if necessary. The consistency should be thick but not too heavy. Season with salt and ground black pepper.

5 Ladle the soup into heated bowls and garnish each with a pinch of cayenne pepper and a scattering of fresh chives. Serve immediately.

VARIATION

For a richer, buttery flavour, add the flesh of a ripe avocado when blending.

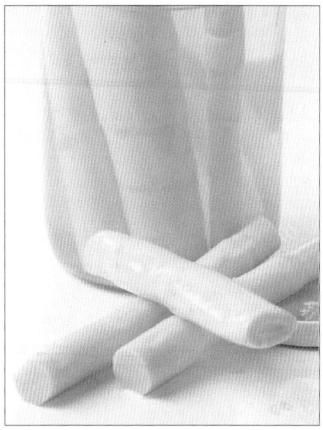

PEANUT AND POTATO SOUP WITH CORIANDER

PEANUT SOUP IS A FIRM FAVOURITE THROUGHOUT CENTRAL AND SOUTH AMERICA, AND IS PARTICULARLY POPULAR IN BOLIVIA AND ECUADOR. AS IN MANY LATIN AMERICAN RECIPES, THE GROUND NUTS ARE USED AS A THICKENING AGENT, WITH UNEXPECTEDLY DELICIOUS RESULTS.

SERVES SIX

INGREDIENTS

- 60ml/4 tbsp peanut oil
- 1 onion, finely chopped
- 2 garlic cloves, crushed
- 1 red (bell) pepper, seeded and chopped
- 250g/9oz potatoes, peeled and diced
- 2 fresh red chillies, seeded and chopped
- 200g/7oz canned chopped tomatoes
- 150g/5oz/1¼ cups unsalted peanuts
- 1.5 litres/2½ pints/6¼ cups beef stock
- salt and ground black pepper
- 30ml/2 tbsp chopped fresh coriander (cilantro), to garnish

1 Heat the oil in a large heavy pan over a low heat. Stir in the onion and cook for 5 minutes, until beginning to soften. Add the garlic, pepper, potatoes, chillies and tomatoes. Stir well to coat the vegetables evenly in the oil, cover and cook for 5 minutes, until softened.

2 Meanwhile, toast the peanuts by gently cooking them in a large dry frying pan over a medium heat. Keep a close eye on them, moving the peanuts around the pan until they are evenly golden. Take care not to burn them.

COOK'S TIP

Replace the unsalted peanuts with peanut butter if you like. Use equal quantities of chunky and smooth peanut butter for the ideal texture.

3 Set 30ml/2 tbsp of the peanuts aside, to use as garnish. Transfer the remaining peanuts to a food processor and process until finely ground. Add the vegetables and process again until smooth.

4 Return the mixture to the pan and stir in the beef stock. Bring to the boil, then lower the heat and simmer for 10 minutes.

5 Pour the soup into heated bowls. Garnish with a generous scattering of coriander and the remaining peanuts.

FISH AND SWEET POTATO SOUP

THE SUBTLE SWEETNESS OF THE POTATO COMBINES WITH THE STRONGER FLAVOURS OF FISH AND OREGANO TO MAKE THIS AN APPETIZING SOUP, POPULAR THROUGHOUT THE CARIBBEAN.

SERVES FOUR

INGREDIENTS
- 175g/6oz white fish fillet, skinned
- ½ onion, chopped
- 1 sweet potato, about 175g/6oz, peeled and diced
- 1 small carrot, about 50g/2oz, chopped
- 5ml/1 tsp chopped fresh oregano or 2.5ml/½ tsp dried oregano
- 2.5ml/½ tsp ground cinnamon
- 1.35 litres/2¼ pints/5½ cups fish stock
- 75ml/5 tbsp single (light) cream
- chopped fresh parsley, to garnish

1 Remove any bones from the fish and put it in a pan. Add the onion, sweet potato, carrot, oregano, cinnamon and half of the stock. Bring to the boil, then simmer for 20 minutes or until the potatoes are cooked.

2 Leave to cool, then pour into a food processor and blend until smooth.

3 Return the soup to the pan, stir in the remaining fish stock and gently bring to the boil. Reduce the heat.

4 Stir the cream into the soup, then gently heat it through without boiling. If the soup boils the cream will curdle. Serve hot, garnished with the chopped parsley.

CARIBBEAN VEGETABLE SOUP

THIS HEARTY VEGETABLE SOUP IS FILLING ENOUGH TO BE SERVED ON ITS OWN FOR LUNCH, BUT STRIPS OF COOKED MEAT, POULTRY OR FISH CAN ALSO BE ADDED.

SERVES FOUR

INGREDIENTS
- 25g/1oz/2 tbsp butter or margarine
- 1 onion, chopped
- 1 garlic clove, crushed
- 2 carrots, sliced
- 1.5 litres/2½ pints/6¼ cups vegetable stock
- 2 bay leaves
- 2 fresh thyme sprigs
- 1 celery stick, finely chopped
- 2 green bananas, peeled and quartered
- 175g/6oz white yam or eddoe, peeled and cubed
- 25g/1oz/2 tbsp red lentils
- 1 chayote (christophene), peeled and chopped
- 25g/1oz/2 tbsp macaroni (optional)
- salt and ground black pepper
- chopped spring onion (scallion), to garnish

1 Melt the butter or margarine in a pan and fry the onion, garlic and carrots for a few minutes, stirring occasionally. Add the stock, bay leaves and thyme, and bring to the boil.

2 Add the celery, green bananas, white yam or eddoe, lentils, chayote and macaroni, if using. Season with salt and ground black pepper and simmer for 25 minutes or until the vegetables are cooked through. Serve garnished with chopped spring onion.

VARIATION

Use other root vegetables, such as potatoes or sweet potatoes, if yam or eddoes are not available.

CRAB, COCONUT AND CORIANDER SOUP

QUICK AND EASY TO PREPARE, THIS SOUP HAS ALL THE FLAVOURS ASSOCIATED WITH THE BAHIA REGION OF BRAZIL: CREAMY COCONUT, PALM OIL, FRAGRANT CORIANDER AND, OF COURSE, CHILLI.

SERVES FOUR

INGREDIENTS

- 30ml/2 tbsp olive oil
- 1 onion, finely chopped
- 1 celery stick, finely chopped
- 2 garlic cloves, crushed
- 1 fresh red chilli, seeded and chopped
- 1 large tomato, peeled and chopped
- 45ml/3 tbsp chopped fresh coriander (cilantro)
- 1 litre/1¾ pints/4 cups fresh crab or fish stock
- 500g/1¼lb crab meat
- 250ml/8fl oz/1 cup coconut milk
- 30ml/2 tbsp palm oil
- juice of 1 lime
- salt
- hot chilli oil and lime wedges, to serve

1 Heat the olive oil in a pan over a low heat. Stir in the onion and celery, and sauté gently for 5 minutes, until softened and translucent. Stir in the garlic and chilli and cook for a further 2 minutes.

2 Add the tomato and half the coriander and increase the heat. Cook, stirring, for 3 minutes, then add the stock. Bring to the boil, then simmer for 5 minutes.

3 Stir the crab, coconut milk and palm oil into the pan and simmer over a very low heat for a further 5 minutes. The consistency should be thick, but not stew-like, so add some water if needed.

4 Stir in the lime juice and remaining coriander, then season with salt to taste. Serve in heated bowls with the chilli oil and lime wedges on the side.

CHILLI CLAM BROTH

THIS SOUP OF SUCCULENT CLAMS IN A TASTY STOCK COULD NOT BE EASIER TO PREPARE. POPULAR IN COASTAL AREAS OF COLOMBIA, IT MAKES THE PERFECT LUNCH ON A HOT SUMMER'S DAY.

SERVES SIX

INGREDIENTS

- 30ml/2 tbsp olive oil
- 1 onion, finely chopped
- 3 garlic cloves, crushed
- 2 fresh red chillies, seeded and finely chopped
- 250ml/8fl oz/1 cup dry white wine
- 400ml/14fl oz can plum tomatoes, drained
- 1 large potato, about 250g/9oz, peeled and diced
- 400ml/14fl oz/1⅔ cups fish stock
- 1.3kg/3lb fresh clams
- 15ml/1 tbsp chopped fresh coriander (cilantro)
- 15ml/1 tbsp chopped fresh flat leaf parsley
- salt
- lime wedges, to garnish

1 Heat the oil in a pan. Add the onion and sauté for 5 minutes over a low heat. Stir in the garlic and chillies and cook for a further 2 minutes. Pour in the wine and bring to the boil, then simmer for 2 minutes.

2 Add the tomatoes, diced potato and stock. Bring to the boil, cover and lower the heat so that the soup simmers.

3 Season with salt and cook for 15 minutes, until the potatoes are beginning to break up and the tomatoes have made a rich sauce.

4 Meanwhile, wash the clams thoroughly under cold running water. Gently tap any that are open, and discard them if they do not close.

5 Add the clams to the soup, cover the pan and cook for about 3–4 minutes, or until the clams have opened, then stir in the chopped herbs. Season with salt to taste.

6 Check over the clams and throw away any that have failed to open. Ladle the soup into warmed bowls. Offer the lime wedges separately, to be squeezed over the soup just before eating.

CHUNKY PRAWN CHUPE

CHOWDERS, KNOWN AS CHUPES IN SOUTH AMERICA, ARE A MEAL IN THEMSELVES. POTATOES ARE ALWAYS INCLUDED, BUT THE OTHER INGREDIENTS VARY. THIS IS A SEAFOOD VERSION.

SERVES SIX

INGREDIENTS
- 500g/1¼lb raw king prawns (jumbo shrimp)
- 750ml/1¼ pints/3 cups fish stock
- 1 carrot, finely chopped
- 2 celery sticks, thinly sliced
- 45ml/3 tbsp annatto (achiote) oil
- 1 large onion, finely chopped
- 1 red (bell) pepper, seeded and diced
- 2 garlic cloves, crushed
- 2 fresh red chillies, seeded and chopped
- 5ml/1 tsp turmeric
- 1 large tomato, peeled and chopped
- 675g/1½lb potatoes, peeled and cut into 2.5cm/1in cubes
- 115g/4oz/1 cup fresh or frozen peas
- 15ml/1 tbsp chopped fresh mint
- 15ml/1 tbsp chopped fresh coriander (cilantro)
- salt

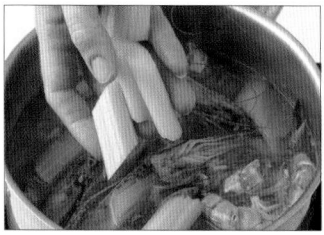

1 Peel the prawns and set them aside. Place the shells in a large pan with the fish stock, carrot and celery. Bring to the boil, then simmer over a low heat for 20 minutes. Strain into a bowl or jug (pitcher) and set the stock aside.

VARIATION
Traditionally this soup would be made using *huacatay*, a pungent Peruvian herb that tastes like a cross between mint and coriander (cilantro).

2 Heat the oil in a large pan over a low heat. Stir in the onion and red pepper and sauté for 5 minutes. Stir in the garlic, chillies and turmeric and cook for a further 2 minutes.

3 Add the chopped tomato and potatoes to the pan, season to taste with salt and cook for about 10 minutes, allowing the tomato to break down slightly and the potatoes to absorb the flavours of the other ingredients.

4 Pour in the strained stock and bring to the boil. Lower the heat and simmer for 15 minutes, or until the potatoes are cooked through.

5 Stir the prawns and peas into the soup and simmer for 4–5 minutes, or until the prawns become opaque. Finally, stir in the mint and coriander, and serve in warmed bowls.

CORN SOUP

CORN SOUP TURNS UP ALL OVER LATIN AMERICA. TOMATOES ARE OFTEN COOKED WITH THE ONION, BUT HERE THEY ARE SPRINKLED OVER THE SOUP, LEAVING THE FLAVOURS FRESH AND DISTINCT.

SERVES FOUR

INGREDIENTS
- 40g/1½oz/3 tbsp butter
- 1 large onion, finely chopped
- 500g/1¼lb fresh or thawed frozen corn kernels
- 1 litre/1¾ pints/4 cups chicken stock
- 250ml/8fl oz/1 cup double (heavy) cream
- salt and ground black pepper
- 1 tomato, peeled, seeded and chopped, to garnish

VARIATION
The corn kernels make this soup very sweet. If it is not to your taste, add 350g/12oz diced potato to the pan at the same time as the corn. Increase the chicken stock accordingly.

1 Melt the butter in a large heavy pan. Stir in the onion and cook over a low heat for 5 minutes or until softened and translucent.

2 Add the corn and the stock, increase the heat and bring to the boil. Lower the heat, cover and simmer for 10 minutes, until the corn is tender.

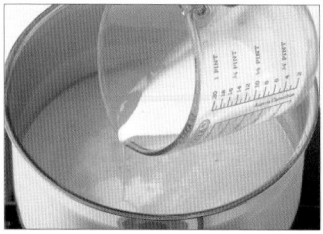

3 Pour the soup into a blender or food processor and process until smooth. Return to the pan and stir in the cream. Bring to the boil, then season with salt and pepper to taste.

4 Ladle the soup into heated bowls, garnish with the chopped tomato and serve immediately.

BEEF AND CASSAVA SOUP

THIS SIMPLE, TASTY SOUP IS ALMOST A STEW. SUCH SOUPS, MADE IN ONE POT, ARE EVERYDAY FARE IN LATIN AMERICA. THE ADDITION OF WINE IS NOT TRADITIONAL, BUT IT ENHANCES THE FLAVOUR.

SERVES FOUR

INGREDIENTS

- 450g/1lb stewing beef, cubed
- 1.2 litres/2 pints/5 cups beef stock
- 300ml/½ pint/1¼ cups white wine
- 15ml/1 tbsp soft brown sugar
- 1 onion, finely chopped
- 1 bay leaf
- 1 bouquet garni
- 1 fresh thyme sprig
- 15ml/1 tbsp tomato purée (paste)
- 1 large carrot, sliced
- 275g/10oz cassava or yam, peeled and cubed
- 50g/2oz fresh spinach, chopped
- a little hot pepper sauce, to taste
- salt and ground black pepper

1 Mix the cubed beef, stock, white wine, sugar, chopped onion, bay leaf, bouquet garni, thyme and tomato purée in a large pan. Bring to the boil, then cover and simmer very gently for about 1¼ hours. If you want very tender meat, allow about 2–2¼ hours.

2 Add the sliced carrot, cubed cassava or yam, spinach and a few drops of hot pepper sauce. Season with salt and ground black pepper to taste and simmer for a further 15 minutes until the meat and vegetables are both tender. Serve in heated bowls.

LAMB AND LENTIL SOUP

LENTILS ARE POPULAR ON CARIBBEAN ISLANDS, SUCH AS TRINIDAD, WHERE THEY WERE INTRODUCED BY SOUTH-EAST ASIAN INDENTURED LABOURERS RECRUITED TO WORK THE SUGAR CANE PLANTATIONS.

SERVES FOUR

INGREDIENTS

- 1.5–1.75 litres/2½–3 pints/ 6¼–7½ cups water or stock
- 900g/2lb neck of lamb, cut into chops
- ½ onion, chopped
- 1 garlic clove, crushed
- 1 bay leaf
- 1 clove
- 2 fresh thyme sprigs
- 225g/8oz potatoes
- 175g/6oz/¾ cup red lentils
- 600ml/1 pint/2½ cups water
- salt and ground black pepper
- chopped fresh parsley

1 Pour 1.5 litres/2½ pints/6¼ cups of the water or stock into a large pan and add the lamb, chopped onion, crushed garlic, bay leaf, clove and thyme sprigs. Bring to the boil, then lower the heat and simmer gently for about 1 hour, until the lamb is tender.

2 Peel the potatoes and cut them into rough 2.5cm/1in cubes. Add them to the soup in the pan and cook for a further 5 minutes.

3 Add the red lentils to the pan, stirring them gently into the stock, then season the soup to taste with a little salt and plenty of ground black pepper. Add approximately 300ml/½ pint/1¼ cups of warm water to completely cover the meat and vegetables.

4 Bring the soup back to the boil, then lower the heat, cover and simmer for 25 minutes or until the lentils are cooked, stirring occasionally. Add a little more water during cooking if the soup becomes too thick. Just before serving, stir in the chopped parsley.

FISH AND SHELLFISH

Fish and shellfish play an important part in Latin-American cuisine and the most popular recipes rely on the freshest fish cooked simply. In parts of Brazil and the Caribbean, where the local cuisine has been shaped by African slave influences, richly flavoured fish and shellfish stews are more popular.

D SEA BASS WITH COCONUT

NT COLOMBIAN DISH IS IDEAL FOR A DINNER PARTY. THE BAY LEAVES GIVE A DEPTH OF FLAVOUR TO THE CHILLI AND COCONUT SAUCE.

SERVES FOUR

INGREDIENTS
- 1 whole large sea bass, about 900g/2lb, cleaned
- 2 fresh red chillies, seeded and finely chopped
- 1 onion, finely sliced
- 2 garlic cloves, crushed
- juice of 1 lime
- 15ml/1 tbsp olive oil
- 2 bay leaves
- 200ml/7fl oz/scant 1 cup coconut milk
- salt

VARIATION
For a complete meal, cook some vegetables in the roasting pan with the sea bass. Sliced carrots, fennel or/and courgettes (zucchini) would all go well with the coconut sauce.

1 Preheat the oven to 180°C/350°F/ Gas 4. Thoroughly rinse the fish inside and out, then pat dry with kitchen paper. Place in a large roasting pan and season all over with salt.

2 Generously sprinkle the chopped chillies, onion, garlic, lime juice and olive oil over the fish. Add the bay leaves to the pan and bake the fish in the oven for about 15 minutes.

3 Pour the coconut milk over the fish and return it to the oven for a further 10 minutes, or until the flesh flakes easily when tested with the tip of a sharp knife.

4 Cut along the back of the fish. This will release the flesh from the bones, making it easy to divide into portions. Serve with the sauce. A rice dish would make a good accompaniment.

PAN-FRIED SEA BREAM WITH LIME AND TOMATO SALSA

THE MOST POPULAR WAY OF COOKING A FRESH PIECE OF FISH IS TO PAN FRY IT OR GRILL IT. IN THIS RECIPE A SIMPLE SALSA IS FLASHED IN THE PAN AT THE END OF COOKING, TO MAKE A LIGHT SAUCE.

SERVES FOUR

INGREDIENTS
- 4 sea bream fillets
- juice of 2 limes
- 30ml/2 tbsp chopped coriander (cilantro)
- 1 fresh red chilli, seeded and finely chopped
- 2 spring onions (scallions), sliced
- 45ml/3 tbsp olive oil, plus extra to serve
- 2 large tomatoes, diced
- salt
- cooked white rice, to serve

1 Place the fish fillets in a shallow china or glass dish large enough to hold them all in a single layer.

2 Mix the lime juice, coriander, chilli and spring onions in a jug (pitcher). Stir in half the oil, then pour this marinade over the fish. Cover and marinate for around 15–20 minutes. Do not be tempted to marinate the fish for longer than this or the acid in the marinade will start to "cook" it.

3 Heat the remaining oil in a large heavy frying pan over a high heat. Lift each piece of fish from the marinade and pat dry with kitchen paper.

4 Season the fish with salt and place in the hot pan, skin side down. Cook for 2 minutes, then turn and cook for a further 2 minutes, until the flesh is opaque all the way through.

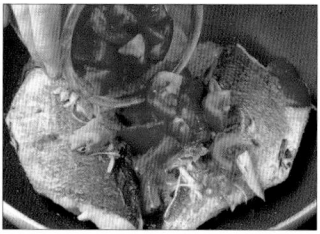

5 Add the marinade and the chopped tomatoes to the pan. Bring the sauce to the boil and cook for about 1 minute, until the tomatoes are lightly cooked but still retain their shape. Drizzle a little olive oil over the fish and serve on individual warm plates, with white rice and the tomato salsa.

UT WITH PEPPERS AND COCONUT MILK

C DISH, KNOWN LOCALLY AS MOQUECA *COMES FROM THE STATE OF BAHIA, ON THE EAST COAST OF BRAZIL. COOKED AND SERVED IN AN EARTHENWARE DISH, IT IS USUALLY ACCOMPANIED BY WHITE RICE AND FLAVOURED CASSAVA FLOUR TO SOAK UP THE DELICIOUS SAUCE.*

SERVES SIX

INGREDIENTS

- 6 halibut, cod, haddock or monkfish fillets, each about 115g/4oz
- juice of 2 limes
- 8 fresh coriander (cilantro) sprigs
- 2 fresh red chillies, seeded and chopped
- 3 tomatoes, sliced into thin rounds
- 1 red (bell) pepper, seeded and sliced into thin rounds
- 1 green (bell) pepper, seeded and sliced into thin rounds
- 1 small onion, sliced into thin rounds
- 200ml/7fl oz/scant 1 cup coconut milk
- 60ml/4 tbsp palm oil
- salt
- cooked white rice, to serve

For the flavoured cassava flour

- 30ml/2 tbsp palm oil
- 1 medium onion, thinly sliced
- 250g/9oz/2¼ cups cassava flour

1 Place the fish fillets in a large, shallow dish and pour over water to cover. Pour in the lime juice and set aside for 30 minutes. Drain the fish thoroughly and pat dry with kitchen paper. Arrange the fish in a single layer in a heavy pan which has a tight-fitting lid.

2 Sprinkle the coriander and chillies over the fish, then top with a layer each of tomatoes, peppers and onion. Pour the coconut milk over, cover and leave to stand for 15 minutes before cooking.

3 Season with salt, then place the pan over a high heat and cook until the coconut milk comes to the boil. Lower the heat and simmer for 5 minutes. Remove the lid, pour in the palm oil, cover again and simmer for 10 minutes.

4 Meanwhile make the flavoured cassava flour. Heat the oil in a large frying pan over a very low heat. Stir in the onion slices and cook for 8–10 minutes until soft and golden. Stir in the cassava flour and cook, stirring constantly, for 1–2 minutes until lightly toasted and evenly coloured by the oil. Season with salt.

5 Serve the *moqueca* with the rice and flavoured cassava flour.

PRAWN AND POTATO OMELETTE

MORE LIKE A SPANISH TORTILLA THAN A FRENCH OMELETTE, THIS DISH MAKES A DELICIOUS LUNCH WHEN SERVED WITH A FRESH LEAFY GREEN SALAD. THE SWEET PRAWNS ARE COOKED GENTLY INSIDE THE OMELETTE, STAYING TENDER AND SUCCULENT.

SERVES SIX

INGREDIENTS

- 200g/7oz potatoes, peeled and diced
- 30ml/2 tbsp olive oil
- 1 onion, finely sliced
- 2.5ml/½ tsp paprika
- 2 large tomatoes, peeled, seeded and chopped
- 200g/7oz peeled raw prawns (shrimp)
- 6 eggs
- 2.5ml/½ tsp baking powder
- salt

1 Cook the potatoes in a pan of salted boiling water for about 10 minutes or until tender.

2 Meanwhile, pour the oil into a 23cm/9in frying pan which can safely be used under the grill (broiler). Place over a medium heat. Add the onion slices and stir well to coat evenly in the oil. Cook for 5 minutes until the onions begin to soften. Sprinkle over the paprika and cook for 1 minute more.

3 Stir in the tomatoes. Drain the cooked potatoes thoroughly and add them to the pan. Stir gently to mix. Increase the heat and cook for 10 minutes, or until the mixture has thickened and the potatoes have absorbed the flavour of the tomatoes. Remove from the heat and stir in the prawns.

4 Preheat the grill. Beat the eggs, stir in the baking powder and salt. Pour into the pan and mix thoroughly. Cover and cook for 8–10 minutes until the omelette has almost set, then finish under the grill.

SALMON IN MANGO AND GINGER SAUCE

MANGO AND SALMON MAY SEEM UNLIKELY PARTNERS, BUT THE FLAVOURS COMPLEMENT EACH OTHER VERY WELL, ESPECIALLY WHEN THE DISTINCT FLAVOUR OF TARRAGON IS ADDED TO THE EQUATION.

SERVES TWO

INGREDIENTS
- 2 salmon steaks, each about 275g/10oz
- a little lemon juice
- 1–2 garlic cloves, crushed
- 5ml/1 tsp dried tarragon, crushed
- 2 shallots, roughly chopped
- 1 tomato, roughly chopped
- 1 large ripe mango, peeled, stoned (pitted) and chopped
- 150ml/¼ pint/⅔ cup fish stock or water
- 15ml/1 tbsp syrup from a jar of preserved ginger
- 25g/1oz/2 tbsp butter
- salt and ground black pepper

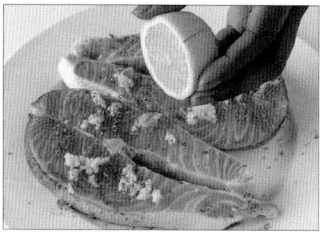

1 Place the salmon steaks in a single layer in a shallow dish and sprinkle with the lemon juice, garlic, tarragon and salt and pepper. Cover and set aside in the refrigerator for at least 1 hour.

2 Meanwhile, place the shallots, tomato and mango in a blender or food processor and blend until smooth. Add the fish stock or water and the ginger syrup, blend again and set aside.

3 Melt the butter in a frying pan and cook the salmon steaks for about 3 minutes on each side.

4 Add the mango purée, cover and simmer for a further 5 minutes, until the salmon is cooked and flakes easily.

5 Transfer the salmon to plates. Heat the sauce, adjust the seasoning and pour over the salmon. Serve hot.

FRIED SNAPPER WITH AVOCADO

THE COMBINATION OF CRISP FRIED FISH AND SILKY SMOOTH AVOCADO WORKS EXTREMELY WELL IN THIS RECIPE. IN THE ISLANDS OF THE CARIBBEAN, WHERE THIS RECIPE ORIGINATED, THE FISH IS OFTEN SERVED WITH FRIED DUMPLINGS OR HARD-DOUGH BREAD.

SERVES FOUR

INGREDIENTS
- 1 lemon
- 4 red snappers, each about 225g/8oz, prepared
- 10ml/2 tsp spice seasoning
- flour, for dusting
- oil, for frying
- 2 avocados and cooked corn, sliced widthways, to serve
- chopped fresh parsley and lime slices, to garnish

1 Squeeze the lemon juice both inside and outside the fish, and sprinkle with the spice seasoning. Place the fish in a shallow dish, cover and set aside in a cool place to marinate for a few hours.

2 Lift the marinated fish out of the dish and dust thoroughly with the flour, shaking off any excess.

3 Heat the oil in a large non-stick frying pan over a medium heat. Add the fish and fry gently for about 10 minutes on each side.

4 Meanwhile, cut the avocados in half, remove the stones (pits) and cut in half again. Peel away the skin and cut the flesh into thin strips.

5 When the fish are cooked through and the skin is crisp and brown, transfer them to warmed serving plates. Add the avocado and corn slices. Garnish with the chopped parsley and lime slices and serve immediately.

COOK'S TIP

Using two frying pans will allow you to cook all four fish simultaneously. Alternatively, cook two and keep them hot in a covered dish in a warm oven while cooking the remaining pair.

TROUT IN WINE SAUCE WITH PLANTAIN

EXOTIC FISH FROM THE WARM CARIBBEAN WATERS, SUCH AS MAHI MAHI OR GROUPER, WOULD ADD A DISTINCTIVE FLAVOUR TO THIS TASTY DISH, WHICH IS EATEN THROUGHOUT THE REGION. IF YOU CANNOT FIND EXOTIC FISH, HOWEVER, TROUT IS IDEAL, OR YOU CAN USE ANY FILLETED WHITE FISH.

SERVES FOUR

INGREDIENTS
- 4 trout fillets
- spice seasoning, for dusting
- 25g/1oz/2 tbsp butter or margarine
- 1–2 garlic cloves
- 150ml/¼ pint/⅔ cup white wine
- 150ml/¼ pint/⅔ cup fish stock
- 10ml/2 tsp clear honey
- 15–30ml/1–2 tbsp chopped fresh parsley
- 1 yellow plantain
- salt and ground black pepper
- oil, for frying
- green salad, to serve

1 Season the trout fillets by coating them in the spice seasoning. Place in a shallow dish, cover with cling film (plastic wrap) and marinate in a cool place for at least 1 hour.

2 Melt the butter or margarine in a large frying pan and heat gently for 1 minute. Add the fish fillets. Sauté for about 5 minutes, until cooked through, turning carefully once. Transfer to a plate and keep hot.

3 Add the garlic, white wine, fish stock and honey to the pan and bring to the boil, stirring. Lower the heat and simmer to reduce slightly. Return the fish to the pan and spoon over the sauce. Sprinkle with the parsley and simmer gently for 2–3 minutes.

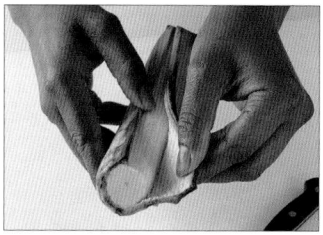

4 Meanwhile, peel the plantain, and cut it into rounds. Heat a little oil in a small frying pan and fry the plantain slices for 2–3 minutes, until golden, turning once. Transfer the fish to warmed serving plates. Stir the sauce, season and pour over the fish. Serve with the fried plantain and a green salad.

COOK'S TIP

Plantains belong to the banana family and can be green, yellow or brown, depending on how ripe they are. Unlike bananas, they must be cooked.

ESCHOVISHED FISH

THIS PICKLED FISH DISH IS OF SPANISH ORIGIN AND IS VERY POPULAR THROUGHOUT THE CARIBBEAN ISLANDS. IT GOES BY VARIOUS NAMES, INCLUDING ESCOVITCH AND CAVEACHED FISH, BUT NO MATTER WHAT THE NAME, IT INEVITABLY TASTES DELICIOUS.

SERVES SIX

INGREDIENTS
- 900g/2lb cod fillet
- ½ lemon
- 15ml/1 tbsp spice seasoning
- flour, for dusting
- oil, for frying
- lemon wedges, to garnish

For the sauce
- 30ml/2 tbsp vegetable oil
- 1 onion, sliced
- ½ red (bell) pepper, sliced
- ½ chayote (christophene), peeled, seeded and cut into small pieces
- 2 garlic cloves, crushed
- 120ml/4fl oz/½ cup malt vinegar
- 75ml/5 tbsp water
- 2.5ml/½ tsp ground allspice
- 1 bay leaf
- 1 small fresh Scotch bonnet or Habañero chilli, chopped
- 15ml/1 tbsp soft brown sugar
- salt and ground black pepper

1 Place the fish in a shallow dish, squeeze over the lemon juice, then sprinkle with the spice seasoning. Pat the seasoning into the fish using your hands, then cover and leave to marinate in a cool place for at least 1 hour.

2 Cut the cod fillet across into 7.5cm/3in pieces. Dust the pieces of fish with a little flour, shaking off any excess.

3 Heat the oil in a heavy frying pan and fry the fish pieces for 2–3 minutes, turning occasionally, until they are golden brown and crisp. Using a fish slice or slotted spoon, lift the cooked fish pieces out of the pan and place in a serving dish. Keep hot.

4 Make the sauce. Heat the oil in a frying pan and fry the onion for 4–5 minutes. Add the pepper, chayote and garlic and stir-fry for 2 minutes.

5 Pour in the vinegar, then add the water, allspice, bay leaf, chilli and sugar. Simmer for 5 minutes, then season. Leave to stand for 10 minutes, then pour the sauce over the fish. Serve hot, garnished with the lemon wedges.

VARIATION

Cod fillets are very expensive so, if they are available, try using whole red snapper or red mullet, which are often used for this dish in the Caribbean.

SEA BASS CEVICHE

THIS TASTY DISH, ALSO KNOWN AS SEVICHE, IS PARTICULARLY POPULAR IN PERU, WHERE IT IS MADE WITH A VARIETY OF FISH AND SHELLFISH. THE RAW FISH SIMPLY "COOKS" IN A FRESH CITRUS MARINADE, AND NEEDS NO HEATING, SO IT IS VITAL THAT THE FISH IS PERFECTLY FRESH.

SERVES FOUR

INGREDIENTS

- 675g/1½lb sea bass fillets
- 300ml/½ pint/1¼ cups lime juice
- 200ml/7 oz orange juice
- 2 fresh red chillies, seeded and finely sliced
- 1 medium red onion, finely sliced
- 30ml/2 tbsp fresh coriander (cilantro) leaves
- 1 large tomato, seeded and chopped
- salt and ground black pepper
- green salad and crusty bread, to serve

1 Cut the sea bass fillets into 2.5cm/1in strips, removing any stray bones with tweezers. Place the fish in a bowl and season with salt and pepper.

2 Pour the lime juice and orange juice over the fish, then gently stir in the chillies and onion slices. The fish must be totally immersed in the marinade, so add a little more juice if necessary.

3 Cover with clear film (plastic wrap) and chill for at least 2 hours, until the fish becomes opaque.

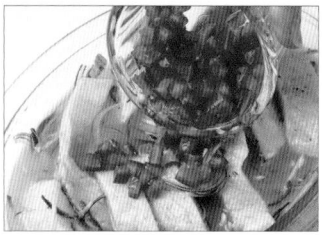

4 Stir the coriander leaves and chopped tomato into the ceviche and serve with a green salad and crusty bread.

COOK'S TIP

The ceviche should be kept covered in the refrigerator right up until it is to be served. It must be eaten on the day it is made.

MACKEREL ESCABECHE

THIS TRADITIONAL WAY OF PRESERVING FISH IN VINEGAR, WAS BROUGHT TO LATIN AMERICA BY THE SPANISH AND PORTUGUESE. OILY FISH, SUCH AS MACKEREL AND SARDINES, LEND THEMSELVES PARTICULARLY WELL TO THIS TREATMENT. IT TAKES AT LEAST A DAY, SO ALLOW PLENTY OF TIME.

SERVES SIX

INGREDIENTS
- 12 small mackerel fillets
- juice of 2 limes
- 90ml/6 tbsp olive oil
- 2 red onions, thinly sliced
- 2 garlic cloves, thinly sliced
- 2 bay leaves
- 6 black peppercorns
- 120ml/4fl oz/½ cup red wine vinegar
- 50g/2oz/½ cup plain (all-purpose) flour
- salt and ground black pepper

1 Place the mackerel fillets side by side in a large, shallow glass or china dish. Pour over the lime juice. Season with salt and pepper and cover. Marinate in the refrigerator for 20–30 minutes, but no longer.

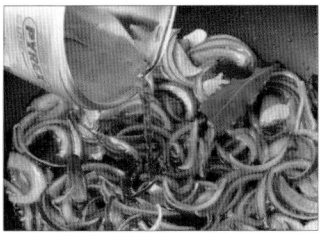

2 Meanwhile, heat half the oil in a frying pan. Add the onions and cook over a low heat for 10 minutes, until softened but not coloured. Stir in the garlic and cook for 2 minutes.

3 Add the bay leaves, peppercorns and vinegar to the pan and simmer over a very low heat for 5 minutes.

COOK'S TIP
If you are planning to keep the fish for more than one day, make sure it is completely immersed in the vinegar, then top with a thin layer of olive oil. Cover tightly. It will keep in the refrigerator for up to 1 month.

4 Pat the mackerel fillets dry and coat them in the flour. Heat the remaining oil in a large frying pan and fry the fish, in batches, for 2 minutes on each side.

5 Return the fish to the dish in which they were originally marinated. Pour the vinegar marinade over the fish. Leave to marinate for 24 hours before serving.

MARINATED RED MULLET

THIS POPULAR LATIN AMERICAN RECIPE IS BASED ON A SPANISH WAY OF COOKING FISH EN ESCABECHE *BY FIRST FRYING IT, THEN MARINATING IT. IF YOU ARE UNABLE TO FIND FRESH MULLET, SNAPPER, SEA BREAM OR TILAPIA ARE ALL GOOD ALTERNATIVES.*

SERVES SIX

INGREDIENTS

- 7.5ml/1½ tsp mild Spanish paprika, preferably Spanish smoked pimentón
- 45ml/3 tbsp plain (all-purpose) flour
- 120ml/4fl oz/½ cup olive oil
- 6 red mullet, each weighing about 300g/11oz, filleted
- 2 aubergines (eggplants), sliced or cut into long wedges
- 2 red or yellow (bell) peppers, seeded and thickly sliced
- 1 large red onion, thinly sliced
- 2 garlic cloves, sliced
- 15ml/1 tbsp sherry vinegar
- juice of 1 lemon
- brown sugar, to taste
- 15ml/1 tbsp chopped fresh oregano
- 18–24 black olives
- 45ml/3 tbsp chopped fresh flat leaf parsley
- salt and ground black pepper

1 Mix 5ml/1 tsp of the paprika with the flour and season well with salt and black pepper. Heat half the oil in a large frying pan. Dip the fish into the flour, turning to coat both sides, and fry for 4–5 minutes, until browned on each side. Place the fish in a glass or china dish suitable for marinating it.

2 Add 30ml/2 tbsp of the remaining oil to the pan and fry the aubergine wedges until softened and browned. Drain thoroughly on a piece of kitchen paper to remove excess oil, then add the aubergine to the fish.

3 Add another 30ml/2 tbsp oil to the pan and cook the peppers and onion gently for 6–8 minutes, until softened but not browned. Add the garlic and remaining paprika, then cook for a further 2 minutes. Stir in the sherry vinegar and lemon juice with 30ml/2 tbsp water and heat until simmering. Season to taste with a pinch of sugar.

4 Stir in the oregano and olives, then spoon over the fish. Set aside to cool, then cover and marinate in the fridge for several hours or overnight.

5 About 30 minutes before serving, bring the fish and vegetables back to room temperature. Stir in the parsley just before serving.

COD CARAMBA

THIS COLOURFUL MEXICAN DISH, WITH ITS CONTRASTING CRUNCHY TOPPING AND TENDER FISH FILLING, CAN BE MADE WITH ANY ECONOMICAL WHITE FISH SUCH AS COLEY OR HADDOCK. SERVE WITH A TASTY GREEN SALAD FOR A HEARTY MIDWEEK SUPPER.

SERVES SIX

INGREDIENTS

- 450g/1lb cod fillets
- 225g/8oz smoked cod fillets
- 300ml/½ pint/1¼ cups fish stock
- 50g/2oz/¼ cup butter
- 1 onion, sliced
- 2 garlic cloves, crushed
- 1 green and 1 red (bell) pepper, seeded and diced
- 2 courgettes (zucchini), diced
- 115g/4oz/⅔ cup drained canned or thawed frozen corn kernels
- 2 tomatoes, peeled and chopped
- juice of 1 lime
- Tabasco sauce
- salt, ground black pepper and cayenne pepper

For the topping

- 75g/3oz tortilla chips
- 50g/2oz/½ cup grated Cheddar cheese
- coriander (cilantro) sprigs, to garnish
- lime wedges, to serve

1 Lay the fish in a shallow pan and pour over the fish stock. Bring to the boil, lower the heat, cover and poach for about 8 minutes, until the flesh flakes easily. Leave to cool slightly, then remove the skin and separate the flesh into large flakes. Keep hot.

2 Melt the butter in a pan, add the onion and garlic and cook gently over a low heat until soft and translucent. Add the peppers, stir and cook for about 2 minutes. Stir in the courgettes and cook for 3 minutes more, until all the vegetables are tender.

3 Stir in the corn and tomatoes, then add lime juice and Tabasco to taste. Season with salt, black pepper and cayenne. Cook for 2 minutes to heat the corn and tomatoes, then stir in the fish and transfer to a dish that can safely be used under the grill (broiler).

4 Preheat the grill. Make the topping by crushing the tortilla chips, then mixing in the grated cheese. Add cayenne pepper to taste and sprinkle over the fish. Place the dish under the grill until the topping is crisp and brown. Garnish with coriander sprigs and lime wedges.

PUMPKIN AND PRAWNS WITH DRIED SHRIMP

THIS CARIBBEAN RECIPE IS AN EXCELLENT WAY OF MAKING A SMALL AMOUNT OF SEAFOOD GO A LONG WAY. THE DRIED SHRIMPS AND COOKED PRAWNS ARE DELICIOUS WITH THE SPICED PUMPKIN.

SERVES FOUR

INGREDIENTS

- 50g/2oz/⅓ cup dried shrimps
- 30ml/2 tbsp vegetable oil
- 25g/1oz/2 tbsp butter or margarine
- 1 red onion, chopped
- 800g/1¾lb pumpkin, peeled and chopped
- 225g/8oz peeled cooked prawns (shrimp)
- 2.5ml/½ tsp ground cinnamon
- 2.5ml/½ tsp five-spice powder
- 2 garlic cloves, chopped
- 2 tomatoes, chopped
- chopped fresh parsley and lime wedges, to garnish

1 Rinse the dried shrimps under cold water and put them in a bowl. Pour in enough hot water to cover, then leave them to soak for about 35 minutes.

2 Meanwhile, heat the oil and butter or margarine in a large frying pan. Add the onion and sauté over a medium heat for 5 minutes, until soft.

3 Add the pumpkin and cook for about 5–6 minutes, until it starts to soften. Tip in the peeled prawns and the dried shrimps with their soaking water. Stir in the cinnamon, five-spice powder and chopped garlic.

4 Add the tomatoes and cook over a gentle heat, stirring occasionally, until the pumpkin is soft.

5 Spoon on to a warmed serving plate and serve hot, garnished with the chopped parsley and lime wedges.

SALT FISH AND ACKEE

THIS IS A CLASSIC JAMAICAN DISH, THAT IS ALSO POPULAR THROUGHOUT THE CARIBBEAN. IT IS OFTEN SERVED WITH BOILED GREEN BANANAS AS WELL AS FRIED DUMPLINGS.

SERVES FOUR

INGREDIENTS

- 450g/1lb salt cod
- 25g/1oz/2 tbsp butter or margarine
- 30ml/2 tbsp vegetable oil
- 1 onion, chopped
- 2 garlic cloves, crushed
- 225g/8oz tomatoes, chopped
- ½ hot chilli, chopped (optional)
- 2.5ml/½ tsp ground black pepper
- 2.5ml/½ tsp dried thyme
- 2.5ml/½ tsp ground allspice
- 30ml/2 tbsp chopped spring onion (scallion)
- 540g/1lb 6oz can ackees, drained
- fried dumplings, to serve

1 Place the salt cod in a bowl and pour in enough cold water to cover. Leave to soak for at least 24 hours, changing the water about five times. Drain and rinse in fresh cold water.

2 Put the salt cod in a large pan of cold water. Bring the water to the boil, then remove the fish and leave it to cool on a plate. Carefully remove and discard the skin and bones, then flake the fish and set it aside.

3 Heat the butter or margarine and oil in a large heavy frying pan over a medium heat. Add the onion and garlic and sauté for 5 minutes. Stir in the tomatoes, with the chilli, if using, and cook gently for a further 5 minutes.

4 Add the salt cod, black pepper, thyme, allspice and spring onion, stir to mix, then stir in the ackees, taking care not to crush them. If you prefer a more moist dish, add a little water or stock. Serve hot with fried dumplings.

CAN FISH CURRY

THIS RECIPE USES SOME OF THE MOST COMMON SPICES IN CARIBBEAN CUISINE, WHERE THE INFLUENCE OF INDIA IS CLEARLY VISIBLE. THE TASTE IS FOR STRONG, PUNGENT FLAVOURS RATHER THAN FIERY HEAT, AND THE RICE IS AN INTEGRAL PART OF THE DISH.

SERVES FOUR

INGREDIENTS

- 2 halibut steaks, total weight about 500–675g/1¼–1½lb
- 30ml/2 tbsp groundnut oil
- 2 cardamom pods
- 1 cinnamon stick
- 6 allspice berries
- 4 cloves
- 1 large onion, chopped
- 3 garlic cloves, crushed
- 10–15ml/2–3 tsp grated fresh root ginger
- 10ml/2 tsp ground cumin
- 5ml/1 tsp ground coriander
- 2.5ml/½ tsp cayenne pepper, or to taste
- 4 tomatoes, peeled, seeded and chopped
- 1 sweet potato, about 225g/8oz, cut into 2cm/¾in cubes
- 475ml/16fl oz/2 cups fish stock or water
- 115g/4oz piece of creamed coconut
- 1 bay leaf
- 225g/8oz/generous 1 cup white long grain rice
- salt

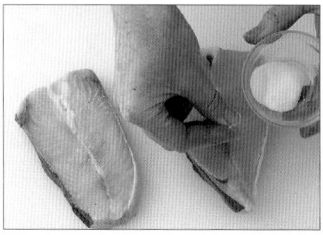

1 Rub the halibut steaks well with salt and set aside.

2 Heat the oil in a flameproof casserole dish and stir-fry the cardamom pods, cinnamon stick, allspice berries and cloves for about 3 minutes to release the delicate aromas.

3 Add the chopped onion, crushed garlic and grated ginger. Continue cooking for about 4–5 minutes over a gentle heat, stirring frequently, until the onion is soft

4 Add the ground cumin, coriander and cayenne pepper and cook briefly, stirring all the time.

5 Stir in the tomatoes, sweet potato, fish stock or water, creamed coconut and bay leaf. Season well with salt. Bring to the boil, then lower the heat, cover and simmer for about 15–18 minutes, until the sweet potato is tender.

6 Cook the rice according to your preferred method. Meanwhile, add the halibut steaks to the pan of curry sauce and spoon the sauce over to cover them completely. Cover the pan with a tight-fitting lid and simmer gently for about 10 minutes until the fish is just tender and flakes easily.

7 Spoon the rice into a warmed serving dish, spoon over the curry sauce and arrange the halibut steaks on top. Garnish with chopped coriander (cilantro), if you like, and serve immediately.

COOK'S TIP

Sweet potato discolours very quickly when cut. If preparing ingredients in advance, put the cubes of potato into a bowl of cold water with 30–45ml/2–3 tbsp lemon juice until ready to use.

KING PRAWNS IN A COCONUT AND NUT CREAM

FOR THIS BRAZILIAN RECIPE, COCONUT MILK IS USED TO MAKE VATAPÁ, *A LUXURIOUS SAUCE THICKENED WITH CASHEWS, PEANUTS AND BREADCRUMBS, THEN USED TO COOK PRAWNS.*

4 Grind the peanuts and cashew nuts in a food processor until they become a fine powder. Stir into the pan and cook for about 1 minute more.

SERVES SIX

INGREDIENTS

- 130g/4½oz/2¼ cups fresh white breadcrumbs
- 105ml/7 tbsp coconut milk
- 30 raw king prawns (jumbo shrimp), about 900g/2lb
- 400ml/14fl oz/1⅔ cups fish stock
- 2 large tomatoes, roughly chopped
- 1 onion, quartered
- 2 fresh red chillies, seeded and roughly chopped
- 130g/4½oz dried shrimps
- 45ml/3 tbsp palm oil
- 2 garlic cloves, crushed
- 25g/1oz fresh root ginger, grated
- 75g/3oz/¾ cup roasted peanuts
- 50g/2oz/½ cup cashew nuts
- 60ml/4 tbsp coconut cream
- juice of 1 lime
- salt and ground black pepper
- chopped fresh coriander (cilantro) and hot chilli oil, to serve

1 Place the breadcrumbs in a bowl and stir in the coconut milk. Leave to soak for at least 30 minutes. Purée, in a blender or food processor, then scrape into a bowl and set aside.

2 Meanwhile, peel the fresh prawns and set them aside in a cool place. Place the shells in a pan and add the fish stock and tomatoes. Bring to the boil, then simmer over a low heat for 30 minutes. Strain into a bowl, pressing the prawn shells against the sides of the sieve with a wooden spoon to extract as much flavour as possible. Reserve the prawn stock but discard the shells.

3 Put the onion, chillies and dried shrimps in a blender or food processor and blend to a purée. Scrape into a large pan and stir in the palm oil. Cook over a very low heat for 5 minutes. Add the garlic and ginger and cook for a further 2 minutes.

5 Stir in the breadcrumb purée and prawn stock and bring to the boil. Reduce the heat and continue to cook, stirring constantly, for 6–8 minutes, until thick and smooth.

6 Add the coconut cream, lime juice and prawns. Stir over the heat for 3 minutes until the prawns are cooked through and the *vatapá* resembles a thin porridge. If necessary, stir in a little water. Season with salt and black pepper.

7 Serve immediately, adding a scattering of chopped coriander and a couple of drops of chilli oil to each portion. Cooked white rice makes a good accompaniment.

VARIATIONS

- Instead of prawns, try using white fish.
- For chicken *vatapá*, replace the prawns with chicken pieces, seasoned and pan-fried in a little olive oil until tender. Use chicken stock rather than fish stock.

STUFFED CRAB

SERVE THIS SIMPLE DISH AS AN APPETIZER FOR A DINNER PARTY. A TRADITIONAL BRAZILIAN RECIPE, IT IS USUALLY SERVED EITHER IN CRAB SHELLS OR SMALL EARTHENWARE DISHES.

SERVES SIX

INGREDIENTS
- 400g/14oz crab meat
- juice of 1 lime
- 50g/2oz/1 cup fresh breadcrumbs
- 105ml/7 tbsp full-fat (whole) milk
- 25g/1oz/2 tbsp butter
- 1 onion, finely chopped
- 2 garlic cloves, crushed
- 2 tomatoes, finely chopped
- 15ml/1 tbsp chopped fresh flat leaf parsley
- 2 egg yolks, plus extra for glazing
- 15ml/1 tbsp dried breadcrumbs
- 15ml/1 tbsp grated Parmesan cheese
- salt
- lemon wedges, to serve

1 Place the crab meat in a large glass bowl and squeeze over the lime juice. Marinate for about 20 minutes. Meanwhile, put the breadcrumbs in a separate bowl with the milk and leave to soak for 10 minutes.

2 Melt the butter in a pan over a low heat. Add the chopped onion and cook gently for 10 minutes until softened. Stir in the crushed garlic and cook for 1 minute more. Drain the crab meat and squeeze out all of the excess liquid from the breadcrumbs.

COOK'S TIP
The crab mixture can be prepared in advance. Spoon it into the individual crab shells or bowls and cover. Keep refrigerated until needed, then add the topping and bake in a preheated oven at 200°C/400°F/Gas 6 for 10–15 minutes.

3 Add the crab meat, tomatoes and breadcrumbs to the pan and stir well to combine. Return to a medium heat and cook, stirring, for 4–5 minutes. Stir in the chopped parsley and season to taste with salt and ground pepper – the mixture should actually taste over-seasoned at this stage.

4 Lower the heat and add the egg yolks, stirring vigorously for 1 minute. Do not allow the mixture to boil.

5 Preheat the grill (broiler). Transfer the mixture to six empty crab shells, or small ovenproof dishes and brush with beaten egg yolk. Combine the dried breadcrumbs and Parmesan and sprinkle a thin coating over the crab meat. Grill (broil) for 3–4 minutes, until golden. Serve with the lemon wedges.

CRAB AND CORN GUMBO

A TYPICALLY CREOLE DISH, THIS IS THICKENED WITH A CLASSIC NUT-BROWN ROUX. IT IS POPULAR ON THE CARIBBEAN ISLANDS OF MARTINIQUE AND ST BARTS.

SERVES FOUR

INGREDIENTS
- 25g/1oz/2 tbsp butter or margarine
- 25g/1oz/¼ cup plain (all-purpose) flour
- 15ml/1 tbsp vegetable oil
- 1 onion, finely chopped
- 115g/4oz okra, trimmed and chopped
- 2 garlic cloves, crushed
- 15ml/1 tbsp finely chopped celery
- 600ml/1 pint/2½ cups fish stock
- 150ml/¼ pint/⅔ cup sherry
- 15ml/1 tbsp tomato ketchup
- 2.5ml/½ tsp dried oregano
- 1.5ml/¼ tsp ground mixed spice (pumpkin pie spice)
- 10ml/2 tsp Worcestershire sauce
- dash of hot pepper sauce
- 2 fresh corn cobs, sliced
- 450g/1lb crab claws
- fresh coriander (cilantro), to garnish

1 Melt the butter or margarine in a large heavy pan over a low heat. Add the flour and stir together to make a roux.

2 Cook for about 10 minutes, stirring constantly to prevent the mixture from burning. The roux will turn golden brown and then darken. As soon as it becomes a rich nut brown, turn the roux on to a plate, scraping it all out of the pan, and set aside.

3 Heat the oil in the same pan over a medium heat, add the chopped onion, the okra, garlic and celery and stir well. Cook for about 2–3 minutes, then add the fish stock, sherry, tomato ketchup, dried oregano, mixed spice, Worcestershire sauce and a dash of hot pepper sauce.

4 Bring to the boil, then lower the heat and simmer gently for about 10 minutes or until all the vegetables are tender. Add the roux, stirring it thoroughly into the sauce, and cook for about 3–4 minutes, until thickened.

5 Add the corn cobs and crab claws and continue to simmer gently over a low heat for about 10 minutes. until both are cooked through.

6 Spoon on to warmed serving plates and garnish with a few sprigs of fresh coriander. Serve immediately.

COOK'S TIP

The roux must not be allowed to burn. Stir it constantly over a low heat. If dark specks appear in the roux, it must be discarded and a fresh roux made.

CREOLE FISH STEW

THIS IS A SIMPLE DISH THAT LOOKS AS GOOD AS IT TASTES. IT IS A GOOD CHOICE FOR A DINNER PARTY, BUT REMEMBER TO ALLOW TIME FOR MARINATING THE FISH.

SERVES SIX

INGREDIENTS
- 2 whole red bream, porgy or large snapper, prepared and cut into 2.5cm/1in pieces
- 30ml/2 tbsp spice seasoning
- 30ml/2 tbsp malt vinegar
- flour, for dusting
- oil, for frying

For the sauce
- 30ml/2 tbsp vegetable oil
- 15ml/1 tbsp butter or margarine
- 1 onion, finely chopped
- 275g/10oz fresh tomatoes, peeled and finely chopped
- 2 garlic cloves, crushed
- 2 fresh thyme sprigs
- 600ml/1 pint/2½ cups fish stock or water
- 2.5ml/½ tsp ground cinnamon
- 1 fresh hot chilli, chopped
- 1 red and 1 green (bell) pepper, seeded and finely chopped
- salt
- fresh oregano sprigs, to garnish

1 Toss the pieces of fish with the spice seasoning and vinegar in a bowl. Cover and set aside to marinate for at least 2 hours at cool room temperature or overnight in the refrigerator.

COOK'S TIP

Take care when preparing the chilli as the capsaicin it contains is a powerful irritant and will burn the skin. Wear gloves if possible and avoid touching your face until you have removed them. Leave the chilli seeds in, or remove them for a slightly milder result.

2 When ready to cook, place a little flour in a large shallow bowl and use to coat the fish pieces, shaking off any excess flour.

3 Heat a little oil in a large frying pan. Add the fish pieces and fry for about 5 minutes, turning the pieces carefully, until golden brown, then set aside. Do not worry if the fish is not quite cooked through; it will finish cooking in the sauce.

4 To make the sauce, heat the oil and butter or margarine in a frying pan and stir-fry the onion for 5 minutes. Add the tomatoes, garlic and thyme and simmer for a further 5 minutes. Stir in the stock or water, cinnamon and chilli.

5 Add the fish pieces and the chopped peppers. Simmer until the fish is cooked and the stock has reduced to a thick sauce. Season with salt. Serve hot, garnished with the oregano.

CUBAN SEAFOOD RICE

THIS IS THE PERFECT DISH FOR A LARGE GATHERING. THE MORE PEOPLE YOU MAKE IT FOR, THE MORE TYPES OF SEAFOOD YOU CAN ADD, AND THE TASTIER IT WILL BECOME.

SERVES EIGHT

INGREDIENTS

- 450g/1lb raw prawns (shrimp)
- 1 litre/1¾ pints/4 cups fish stock
- 450g/1lb squid
- 16 clams
- 16 mussels
- 60ml/4 tbsp olive oil
- 1 onion, finely chopped
- 1 fresh red chilli, seeded and finely chopped
- 2 garlic cloves, crushed
- 350g/12oz/1⅔ cups long grain rice
- 45ml/3 tbsp chopped fresh coriander (cilantro)
- juice of 2 limes
- salt and ground black pepper

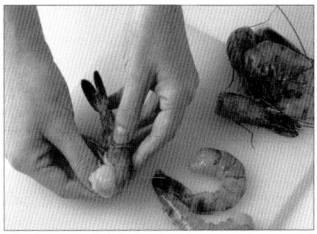

1 Peel the prawns and set them aside. Place the shells in a pan and add the fish stock. Bring to the boil, then simmer for 15 minutes. Strain into a bowl, discarding the shells.

2 Clean the squid under cold running water. Pull the tentacles away from the body. The squid's entrails will come out easily. Remove the clear piece of cartilage from inside the body cavity and discard it. Wash the body thoroughly.

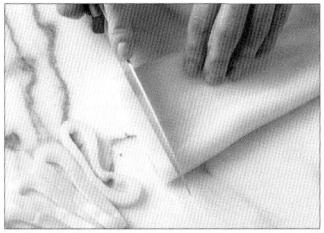

3 Pull away the purplish-grey membrane that covers the body. Now cut between the tentacles and head, discarding the head and entrails. Leave the tentacles whole but discard the hard beak in the middle. Cut the body into thin rounds.

4 Scrub the clams and mussels under cold running water. Pull away the 'beard' from the mussels and discard any open shells that fail to close when tapped. Place the shellfish in a bowl, cover with a wet piece of kitchen paper and put in the refrigerator until needed.

COOK'S TIP

Live shellfish are best kept in a cool moist environment. Place them in a bowl covered with wet kitchen paper and store them in the refrigerator.

5 Pour half the olive oil into a pan with a tight fitting lid. Place over a high heat. When the oil is very hot, add the squid and season well. Stir-fry for 2–3 minutes, until the squid curls and begins to brown. Remove the pieces from the pan with a slotted spoon and set aside.

6 Add the prawns to the pan and cook for 2 minutes. The moment they turn pink, remove them from the heat.

7 Pour the remaining oil into the pan. Stir in the onion and sauté over a low heat for 5 minutes. Add the chilli and garlic and cook for 2 minutes. Tip in the rice, and cook, stirring, for 1 minute, until lightly toasted but not coloured.

8 Add the prawn stock and bring to the boil. Cover, lower the heat and simmer, for 15–18 minutes.

9 Add the clams and mussels and cover the pan. Cook for 3–4 minutes, until their shells open. Remove from the heat and discard any that have remained closed. Stir the cooked squid, prawns, coriander and lime juice into the rice. Season and serve immediately.

CHILEAN SQUID CASSEROLE

THIS HEARTY STEW IS IDEAL ON A COLD EVENING. THE POTATOES DISINTEGRATE TO THICKEN AND ENRICH THE SAUCE, MAKING A WARMING, COMFORTING MAIN COURSE.

SERVES SIX

INGREDIENTS

- 800g/1¾lb squid
- 45ml/3 tbsp olive oil
- 5 garlic cloves, crushed
- 4 fresh jalapeño chillies, seeded and finely chopped
- 2 celery sticks, diced
- 500g/1¼lb small new potatoes or baby salad potatoes, scrubbed, scraped or peeled and quartered
- 400ml/14fl oz/1⅔ cups dry white wine
- 400ml/14fl oz/1⅔ cups fish stock
- 4 tomatoes, diced
- 30ml/2 tbsp chopped fresh flat leaf parsley
- salt
- white rice or *arepas* (corn breads), to serve

1 Clean the squid under cold water. Pull the tentacles away from the body. The squid's entrails will come out easily. Remove the cartilage from inside the body cavity and discard it. Wash the body thoroughly.

2 Pull away the membrane that covers the body. Cut between the tentacles and head, discarding the head and entrails. Leave the tentacles whole but discard the hard beak in the middle. Cut the body into thin rounds.

COOK'S TIP

Adding the tomatoes and parsley at the end gives a real freshness to the sauce. If you'd prefer an even heartier dish, add these ingredients to the pan with the potatoes. Replace the white wine with a Chilean cabernet sauvignon.

3 Heat the oil, add the garlic, chillies and celery and cook for 5 minutes. Stir in the potatoes, then add the wine and stock. Bring to the boil, then simmer, covered, for 25 minutes.

4 Remove from the heat and stir in the squid, tomatoes and parsley. Cover the pan and leave to stand until the squid is cooked. Serve immediately.

CHILEAN SEAFOOD PLATTER

FRESHNESS IS IMPORTANT FOR THIS RAW SEAFOOD APPETIZER, SO CHILEAN COOKS USE THE PRIME CATCH OF THE DAY, INCLUDING EXOTIC SHELLFISH. YOU CAN USE WHATEVER IS AVAILABLE LOCALLY.

SERVES SIX

INGREDIENTS
- 450g/1lb raw king prawns (jumbo shrimp)
- 12 clams
- 12 mussels
- 6 scallops
- 6 oysters
- 12 razor clams
- lime wedges, to serve

For the salsa
- 60ml/4 tbsp chopped fresh coriander (cilantro)
- 15ml/1 tbsp chopped fresh flat leaf parsley
- 2 shallots, finely chopped
- 1 fresh green chilli, seeded and finely chopped
- juice of 2 limes
- 30ml/2 tbsp olive oil
- salt

1 Combine the salsa ingredients in a bowl and season to taste. Make the salsa a few hours in advance, if possible, so that the delicate flavours have time to develop.

2 Bring a pan of salted water to the boil. Plunge the prawns into the water and remove from the pan as soon as they turn pink. Refresh the prawns in a bowl of cold water, drain and set aside.

COOK'S TIP
If you prefer to cook the shellfish, it could be steamed quickly and then refreshed in cold water before being served. Do not overcook the shellfish, or it will become tough.

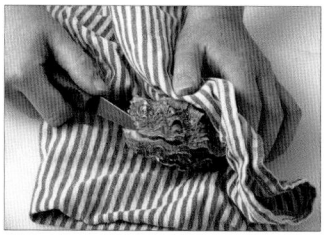

3 Use an oyster knife to open the raw shellfish. Push the point of the knife into the hinge, then twist to loosen. Push the knife along the edge of the whole shell so it can be opened.

4 Use the knife to loosen the fish from their shells and carefully remove the black "string" that runs along the edge of the scallop.

5 Arrange the seafood, in the shells, on a platter and serve with the fresh coriander and chilli salsa, and lime wedges, if you like. Eat immediately.

MEAT

The gaucho nations of Argentina, Paraguay and Uruguay are real meat-eaters, and large cuts of beef, lamb and pork are cooked whole at their famous barbecues. Richly flavoured stews and pot roasts are also popular, made with herbs, spices and fruits, or as a combination of mixed meats, as in the Brazilian national dish Feijoada.

THE GAUCHO BARBECUE

THERE IS NO BETTER WAY OF ENJOYING THE PRESTIGIOUS PAMPAS BEEF THAN WITH A TRADITIONAL BARBECUE. THE MEAT IS COOKED SIMPLY, WITH NO NEED FOR RUBS OR MARINADES, THEN ENJOYED WITH A DELICIOUS SELECTION OF SALADS AND SALSAS.

SERVES SIX

INGREDIENTS
- 50g/2oz/¼ cup coarse sea salt
- 200ml/7fl oz/ scant 1 cup warm water
- 6 pork sausages
- 1kg/2¼lb beef short ribs
- 1kg/2¼lb rump (round) steak, in one piece
- salads, salsas and breads, to serve

COOK'S TIP
Regularly basting the meat in salted water keeps it moist and succulent.

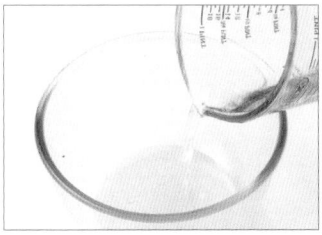

1 Dissolve the sea salt in the warm water in a bowl. Leave to cool.

2 Prepare the barbecue. If you are using a charcoal grill, light the coals about 40 minutes before you want to start cooking. Wait until the coals are no longer red but are covered in white ash. Occasionally add coals to the barbecue to maintain this temperature.

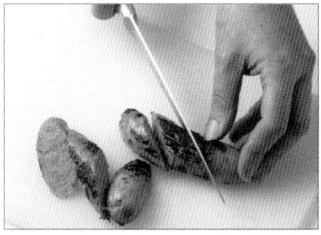

3 Start by cooking the sausages, which should take 15–20 minutes depending on the size. Once cooked on all sides, slice the sausages thickly and arrange on a plate. Let guests help themselves while you cook the remaining meats.

4 The short ribs should be placed bony side down on the grill. Cook for 15 minutes, turn, brush the cooked side of each rib with brine and grill for a further 25–30 minutes. Slice and transfer to a plate for guests to help themselves.

5 Place the whole rump steak on the grill and cook for 5 minutes, then turn over and baste the browned side with brine. Continue turning and basting in this way for 20–25 minutes in total, until the meat is cooked to your liking. Allow the meat to rest for 5 minutes, then slice thinly and serve with salads, salsa and bread.

VARIATION
A selection of meat cuts can be used, from sirloin to flank steak or chuck steak. Sweetbreads, skewered chicken hearts and kidneys are popular additions to the Gaucho barbecue, as well as chicken, lamb and pork. The star of the show, however, will always be the beef.

BEEF STUFFED WITH EGGS AND SPINACH

THIS TRADITIONAL ARGENTINIAN DISH MAKES A GREAT LUNCH WHEN SERVED COLD WITH A SALAD, BUT CAN ALSO BE SERVED HOT FOR DINNER WITH SOME BOILED POTATOES. ITS NAME, MATAMBRE *("KILL HUNGER") IS SOMEWHAT UNFAIR; FOR ALTHOUGH FILLING, IT IS NOT A HEAVY DISH.*

SERVES SIX

INGREDIENTS
- 60ml/4 tbsp olive oil
- 1 small carrot, finely chopped
- 1 celery stick, finely chopped
- 1 onion, finely chopped
- 2 eggs
- 675g/1½lb flank steak
- 250g/9oz spinach, trimmed
- 2.5ml/½ tsp cayenne pepper
- 1.5 litres/2½ pints/6¼ cups beef stock
- salt and ground black pepper
- boiled potatoes or salad, to serve

1 Heat half the olive oil in a frying pan over a medium heat. Add the carrot, celery and onion and sauté for 5 minutes, until soft and beginning to colour.

2 Meanwhile hard boil the eggs. Place them in a pan with cold water to cover. Bring to the boil, then lower the heat to a simmer. Cook for 10 minutes then lift out and cool in a bowl of cold water. Shell the eggs, then slice them thinly.

3 Season the steak generously with salt and ground black pepper. Spread the cooked onion mixture over the beef, leaving a 1cm/½in border round the edge. Arrange the spinach over the onion, then top with the egg. Season with extra salt and cayenne pepper.

COOK'S TIP
Flank steak is ideal for slow cooking, becoming so tender you can almost cut it with a fork. If you cannot get flank, skirt steak is very similar.

4 Roll the meat up tightly, being careful not to lose any of the stuffing. Tie with string four or five times along the length of the roll.

5 Heat the remaining oil in a pan. Add the beef roll to the pan and cook on all sides until golden brown. Pour in the stock, then bring to the boil. Lower the heat, cover and simmer gently for 1½–2 hours, until very tender.

6 Remove the beef from the stock and slice it as thinly as possible. Serve hot with boiled potatoes or as part of a buffet or picnic.

CARBONADA CRIOLLA

MEAT AND FRUIT ARE OFTEN COMBINED IN ARGENTINIAN COOKING, AND THIS COLOURFUL STEW IS A PRIME EXAMPLE. THE TENDER BEEF COOKED IN RED WINE BALANCES THE SWEETNESS OF THE PEACHES, POTATOES AND PUMPKIN. MAKE SURE THE PUMPKIN FITS IN YOUR OVEN.

SERVES EIGHT

INGREDIENTS

- 1 large pumpkin, about 5kg/11lb
- 60ml/4 tbsp olive oil
- 1kg/2¼lb braising steak, cut into 2.5cm/1in cubes
- 1 large onion, finely chopped
- 3 fresh red chillies, seeded and chopped
- 2 garlic cloves, crushed
- 1 large tomato, roughly chopped
- 2 fresh bay leaves
- 600ml/1 pint/2½ cups beef stock
- 350ml/12fl oz/1½ cups red wine
- 500g/1¼lb potatoes, peeled and cut into 2cm/¾in cubes
- 500g/1¼lb sweet potatoes, peeled and cut into 2cm/¾in cubes
- 1 corn cob, cut widthways into 6 slices
- 3 peaches, peeled, stoned (pitted) and cut into thick wedges
- salt and ground black pepper

1 Wash the outside of the pumpkin. Using a sharp knife, carefully cut a slice off the top 6cm/2½in from the stem, to make a lid. Using a spoon, scoop out the seeds and stringy fibres and discard. Scoop out some of the flesh, leaving a shell about 2cm/¾in thick inside of the pumpkin. Cut the flesh you have removed into 1cm/½in pieces.

COOK'S TIP

Calabaza is a large West Indian pumpkin with a greenish orange skin that is often used for *carbonada criolla*. Look for it in Caribbean markets.

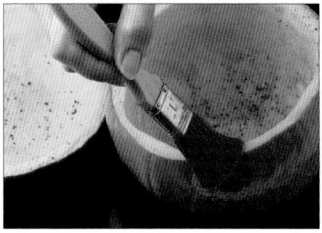

2 Brush the inside of the pumpkin and the flesh side of the lid with a little olive oil. Season with salt and ground black pepper. Place both pumpkin and lid on a baking sheet, flesh-side up. Set aside.

3 Preheat the oven to 200°C/400°F/Gas 6. Heat half the remaining oil in a large heavy pan over a high heat. Add the beef, season and sauté for 8–10 minutes, until golden brown, then remove with a slotted spoon – you may need to do this in batches. Avoid adding too much beef to the pan or it will steam rather than brown.

4 Lower the heat and add the remaining oil to the pan. Stir in the onion and chillies, and sauté for 5 minutes. Scrape the base of the pan with a wooden spoon, to loosen any sediment. Add the garlic and tomato and cook for 2 minutes more.

5 Return the meat to the pan and add the bay leaves, stock and red wine. Bring to the boil, then lower the heat to a gentle simmer. Cook for 1 hour or until the meat is tender.

6 Place the baking sheet containing the pumpkin and its lid in the oven and bake for 30 minutes.

7 Add the potatoes, sweet potatoes, pieces of pumpkin and corn to the stew. Pour in more liquid if needed and bring to the boil. Reduce the heat to a simmer, cover and cook for 15 minutes.

8 Finally add the peach wedges and season with salt and black pepper to taste. Spoon the stew into the partially cooked pumpkin, cover with the pumpkin lid and bake for 15 minutes or until the pumpkin is tender.

9 Carefully lift the filled pumpkin on to a large, strong platter and take it to the table. Ladle the stew on to plates, then cut the empty pumpkin into six to eight wedges, depending on the number of people to be served.

PEPPERED STEAK IN SHERRY CREAM SAUCE

THE VAST SUBCONTINENT OF SOUTH AMERICA IS SUBJECT TO MANY CULINARY INFLUENCES, ALL OF WHICH HARMONIZE WITH THE NATIVE RECIPES OF EACH COUNTRY. VERSIONS OF THIS DISH ARE TO BE FOUND ALL OVER THE WORLD, BUT THE ADDITION OF PLANTAIN IS A CARIBBEAN ADAPTATION.

2 Season the meat with pepper and spice seasoning, place in a shallow dish and cover. Leave to marinate in a cool place for 30 minutes.

3 Melt the butter in a large frying pan and sauté the strips of steak for about 4–5 minutes, until browned on all sides. Using a slotted spoon, transfer to a warm plate and set aside.

4 Add the shallots and garlic, fry gently for 2–3 minutes, then stir in the sherry and water. Simmer for 5 minutes.

SERVES FOUR

INGREDIENTS

675g/1½lb frying steak
5ml/1 tsp spice seasoning
25g/1oz/2 tbsp butter
6–8 shallots, sliced
2 garlic cloves, crushed
120ml/4fl oz/½ cup sherry
45ml/3 tbsp water
75ml/5 tbsp single (light) cream
salt and ground black pepper
chopped fresh chives, to garnish
cooked plantain, to serve

1 Cut the frying steak into thin strips, of even length and thickness, discarding any fat or gristle.

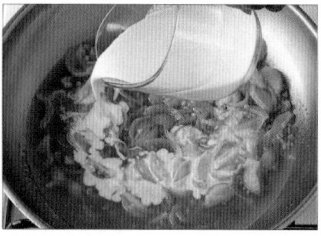

5 Stir in the cream and season. Return the meat to the pan and heat through. Serve with plantain and chopped chives.

OXTAIL AND BUTTER BEANS

This is a traditional Caribbean stew – old-fashioned, economical and full of goodness. It requires patience because of the long cooking time. There is not much meat on the oxtail, so it is necessary to buy a large amount.

SERVES FOUR

INGREDIENTS

- 1.6kg/3½lb oxtail, chopped into pieces
- 1 onion, finely chopped
- 3 bay leaves
- 4 fresh thyme sprigs
- 3 whole cloves
- 1.75 litres/3 pints/7½ cups water
- 175g/6oz/scant 1 cup dried butter (lima) beans, soaked overnight
- 2 garlic cloves, crushed
- 15ml/1 tbsp tomato purée (paste)
- 400g/14oz can chopped tomatoes
- 5ml/1 tsp ground allspice
- 1 fresh hot chilli
- salt and ground black pepper

1 Put the pieces of oxtail in a large heavy pan, add the chopped onion, bay leaves, thyme and cloves and cover with water. Bring to the boil.

2 Reduce the heat, cover the pan and simmer gently for at least 2½ hours or until the meat is very tender. If the meat looks like it might dry out, add a little extra water, being careful not to add too much at one time.

3 Meanwhile, drain the butter beans and tip them into a large pan. Pour in water to cover. Bring to the boil, lower the heat and simmer for about 1–1¼ hours or until just tender. Drain and set aside until ready to use.

COOK'S TIP

Unless you are confident using a meat cleaver to chop the oxtail into short lengths, ask your butcher to do it for you.

VARIATION

Haricot (navy) beans can be used in the same way as butter beans in the recipe.

4 When the oxtail is cooked, add the garlic, tomato purée, tomatoes, allspice, and chilli, and season. Add the beans, simmer for 20 minutes, then serve.

BLACK BEAN CHILLI CON CARNE

FRESH GREEN AND DRIED RED CHILLIES ADD PLENTY OF FIRE TO THIS CLASSIC TEX-MEX DISH OF TENDER BEEF COOKED IN A RICH AND SPICY TOMATO SAUCE.

SERVES SIX

INGREDIENTS
- 225g/8oz/1¼ cups dried black beans
- 500g/1¼lb braising steak
- 30ml/2 tbsp vegetable oil
- 2 onions, chopped
- 1 garlic clove, crushed
- 1 fresh green chilli, seeded and finely chopped
- 15ml/1 tbsp paprika
- 10ml/2 tsp ground cumin
- 10ml/2 tsp ground coriander
- 400g/14oz can chopped tomatoes
- 300ml/½ pint/1¼ cups beef stock
- 1 dried red chilli, crumbled
- 5ml/1 tsp hot pepper sauce
- 1 fresh red (bell) pepper, seeded and chopped
- salt
- fresh coriander (cilantro), to garnish
- boiled rice, to serve

1 Put the beans in a large pan. Cover with cold water, bring to the boil and boil vigorously for about 10 minutes. Drain, tip into a bowl, cover with cold water and leave to soak overnight.

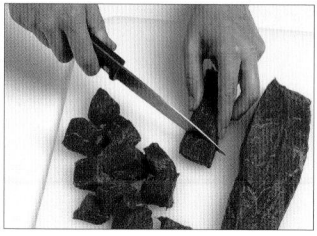

2 Preheat the oven to 150°C/300°F/ Gas 2. Cut the steak into small dice. Heat the oil in a large, flameproof casserole. Add the onion, garlic and green chilli and cook gently for 5 minutes until soft. Transfer the mixture to a plate.

3 Increase the heat to high, add the meat to the casserole and brown on all sides, then stir in the paprika, ground cumin and ground coriander.

4 Add the tomatoes, beef stock, dried chilli and hot pepper sauce. Drain the beans and add them to the casserole, with enough water to cover. Bring to simmering point, cover and cook in the oven for about 2 hours. Stir occasionally and add extra water, if necessary, to prevent the casserole from drying.

5 Season the casserole with salt and add the chopped red pepper. Replace the lid, return the casserole to the oven and cook for about 30 minutes more, or until the meat and beans are tender. Sprinkle over the fresh coriander and serve with boiled rice.

VARIATION

Use minced (ground) beef in place of the braising steak.

COOK'S TIP

Red kidney beans are traditionally used in chilli con carne, but in this recipe black beans are used instead. They are the same shape and size as red kidney beans but have a shiny black skin.

MEXICAN SPICY BEEF TORTILLA

THIS DISH IS NOT UNLIKE A LASAGNE, EXCEPT THAT THE SPICY MEAT IS MIXED WITH RICE AND IS LAYERED BETWEEN MEXICAN TORTILLAS, WITH A HOT SALSA SAUCE FOR AN EXTRA KICK.

SERVES FOUR

INGREDIENTS
- 1 onion, chopped
- 2 garlic cloves, crushed
- 1 fresh red chilli, seeded and thinly sliced
- 350g/12oz rump (round) steak, cut into small cubes
- 15ml/1 tbsp oil
- 225g/8oz/2 cups cooked long grain rice
- beef stock, to moisten
- 3 large wheat tortillas

For the salsa picante
- 2 x 400g/14oz cans chopped tomatoes
- 2 garlic cloves, halved
- 1 onion, quartered
- 1–2 fresh red chillies, seeded and roughly chopped
- 5ml/1 tsp ground cumin
- 2.5–5ml/½–1 tsp cayenne pepper
- 5ml/1 tsp fresh oregano or 2.5ml/½ tsp dried oregano
- tomato juice or water, if required

For the cheese sauce
- 50g/2oz/4 tbsp butter
- 50g/2oz/½ cup plain (all-purpose) flour
- 600ml/1 pint/2½ cups milk
- 115g/4oz/1 cup grated Cheddar cheese
- salt and ground black pepper

1 Preheat the oven to 180°C/350°F/Gas 4. Make the salsa picante. Place the tomatoes, garlic, onion and chillies in a blender or food processor and process until smooth. Pour into a small pan, add the spices and oregano and season with salt.

2 Gradually bring the mixture to the boil, stirring occasionally. Boil for 1–2 minutes, then lower the heat, cover with a lid and simmer gently for about 15 minutes. The sauce should be thick, but of a pouring consistency. If it is too thick, dilute it with a little fresh tomato juice or water.

3 Make the cheese sauce. Melt the butter in a pan and stir in the flour. Cook for 1 minute. Add the milk, stirring all the time until the sauce boils and thickens. Stir in all but 30ml/2 tbsp of cheese and season to taste. Cover the pan with a lid and set aside.

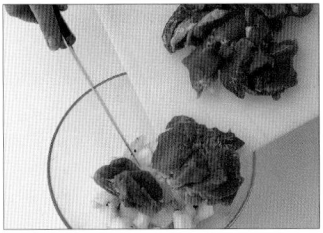

4 Mix the onion, garlic and chilli in a bowl. Add the steak cubes and mix well.

5 Heat the oil in a frying pan and stir-fry the meat mixture for about 10 minutes, until the meat cubes have browned and the onion is soft. Stir in the rice and enough beef stock to moisten. Season to taste with salt and freshly ground black pepper.

6 Pour about a quarter of the cheese sauce into the bottom of a round ovenproof dish. Add a tortilla and then spread over half the salsa followed by half the meat mixture.

7 Repeat these layers, then add half the remaining cheese sauce and the final tortilla. Pour over the remaining cheese sauce and sprinkle the reserved grated cheese on top. Bake in the preheated oven for about 15–20 minutes, or until golden on top.

FEIJOADA

This mixed meat and black bean stew is indisputably the national dish of Brazil and is traditionally served for Saturday lunch. It's impossible to make a good FEIJOADA *for fewer than ten people, since there are so many different types of meat involved. The meats can vary, but the beans have to be very small and black.*

SERVES TWELVE

INGREDIENTS

- 1kg/2¼lb/5½ cups black turtle beans
- 1 smoked pig's tongue, optional
- 500g/1¼lb *carne seca* or beef jerky
- 250g/9oz salted pork ribs
- 350g/12oz smoked streaky (fatty) bacon, in one piece
- 500g/1¼lb smoked pork ribs
- 300g/11oz pork sausages
- 300g/11oz smoked chorizo
- 2 fresh bay leaves
- 60ml/4 tbsp vegetable oil
- 5 garlic cloves, crushed
- salt
- fresh orange slices, peeled, to serve
- cooked white rice
- toasted cassava flour
- stir-fried kale
- chilli oil

1 Wash the beans in running water, then place in a bowl with cold water to cover. Soak overnight. Rinse the tongue, *carne seca* or beef jerky, and salted pork ribs in cold running water and place in a separate bowl. Pour over water to cover and soak for 8 hours, or overnight, changing the soaking water three or four times.

2 Drain the beans and place them in a very large heavy pan. Pour in enough water to cover, and bring to the boil over a high heat. Skim the surface, then lower the heat. Cover the pan and simmer for 1 hour.

3 Meanwhile, drain the soaked meats, rinse them again under cold running water and transfer to a second large heavy pan. Add the streaky bacon and smoked pork ribs, then cover with water. Bring to the boil over a high heat, skim the surface, then cover the pan. Lower the heat and simmer for 1 hour.

4 Transfer the cooked meats, with their cooking liquid, to the pan with the beans. Add the pork sausages, chorizo and bay leaves. If necessary, add more water to cover. Bring to the boil, skim the surface, cover, and continue simmering for about 30 minutes.

5 Heat the oil in a large frying pan over a low heat. Add the crushed garlic cloves and cook, stirring, for about 2 minutes, being careful not to let it burn.

6 Ladle some beans from the large pan into the frying pan and fry, mashing the beans with a wooden spoon. Return the mashed beans to the meat mixture and lower the heat for 5 minutes. Taste the stew and add some salt if needed.

7 Lift the meats from the pan and cut them into even-size pieces. Arrange on a platter, keeping each type of meat separate. Spoon a ladleful of beans over the meats. Pour the remaining beans into a large serving bowl.

8 Take the beans and meats to the table with a platter of peeled, sliced oranges, cooked white rice, toasted cassava flour, stir-fried kale and chilli oil.

COOK'S TIPS

- *Carne seca*, a Brazilian beef jerky, can be bought in Brazilian or Portuguese food stores. You can make a *feijoada* without it, but it won't be as rich.
- Toasted cassava flour is sold in Latin American or Portuguese food stores. Here it is served from the packet, but it can be flavoured with palm oil or eggs.

SPICY MEATBALLS WITH TOMATO SAUCE

WHEREVER YOU GO IN LATIN AMERICA, YOU'LL FIND A DIFFERENT INTERPRETATION OF THIS HEARTY FAMILY DISH. SPANISH IN ORIGIN, THE MEATBALLS ARE OFTEN MADE WITH PORK OR VEAL, OR A MIXTURE OF MEATS, AND KNOWN AS ALBONDIGAS.

SERVES FOUR

INGREDIENTS

- 500g/1¼lb minced (ground) beef
- 3 garlic cloves, crushed
- 1 small onion, finely chopped
- 50g/2oz/1 cup fresh breadcrumbs
- 2.5ml/½ tsp ground cumin
- 1 egg, beaten
- 50g/2oz/½ cup plain (all-purpose) flour
- 60ml/4 tbsp olive oil
- salt
- cooked white rice, to serve

For the sauce

- 30ml/2 tbsp olive oil
- 1 small onion, thinly sliced
- 2 red (bell) peppers, seeded and diced
- 2 fresh red chillies, seeded and chopped
- 2 garlic cloves, crushed
- 150ml/¼ pint/⅔ cup canned chopped tomatoes
- 400ml/14fl oz/1⅔ cups light beef stock
- ground black pepper

COOK'S TIP

An electric frying pan is ideal for cooking the meatballs, as its large surface area will allow you to fry them in one or two batches, and there is plenty of room for reheating them in the sauce.

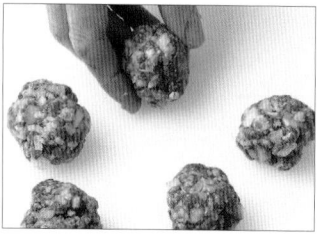

1 Place all the meatball ingredients, except the flour and oil, in a large bowl. Using your hands, mix until thoroughly combined. Season with salt and shape the mixture into even-size balls. Wet your hands to prevent the mixture from sticking. Dust lightly with flour.

2 Heat the oil in a large frying pan and cook the meatballs, in batches, for 6–8 minutes or until golden. When all the meatballs have been browned, wipe the pan clean with kitchen paper.

3 Pour the olive oil into the pan and cook the onion and peppers over a low heat for 10 minutes, until soft. Add the chillies and garlic, and cook for a further 2 minutes. Pour in the tomatoes and stock, and bring to the boil. Lower the heat, cover the pan and simmer for 15 minutes. Season to taste.

4 Add the meatballs to the pan and spoon the sauce over them. Bring back to the boil, then cover and simmer for 10 minutes. Serve with rice.

SCRAMBLED EGGS WITH CHORIZO

THIS POPULAR MEXICAN DISH IS OFTEN EATEN FOR BREAKFAST. DRIED, SPANISH-STYLE CHORIZO GIVES THE EGGS A RICH GOLDEN COLOUR AND DELICIOUS SMOKY FLAVOUR. BUY THE SAUSAGE IN ONE PIECE AND SLICE IT JUST BEFORE COOKING.

SERVES FOUR

INGREDIENTS
- 15ml/1 tbsp olive oil
- 150g/5oz dried chorizo, cut into 1cm/½in slices
- 2.5ml/½ tsp paprika
- 8 eggs, lightly beaten
- salt
- country bread and green salad, to serve

VARIATION
For extra fire and spice, add a dash of a hot pepper sauce, such as Tabasco, to the beaten egg mixture.

1 Heat the oil in a large frying pan over a medium heat and pan-fry the chorizo slices for 1–2 minutes, until golden brown.

COOK'S TIP
The chorizo will brown very quickly, so do not leave it to cook unattended, or it may burn.

2 Add the paprika, stir for 30 seconds, then pour in the beaten eggs. Season lightly with salt. As the eggs start to set, break them up with a fork.

3 Remove the pan from the heat when the mixture is still quite moist; it will continue cooking off the heat. Serve with the bread and a green salad.

Hearty Beef Stew

Brown ale enriches this Caribbean beef stew and gives it a real kick. Vary the amount to suit your taste, but don't overdo it or you will overwhelm the taste of the paprika.

SERVES FOUR

INGREDIENTS

- 50g/2oz/⅓ cup black-eyed beans (peas)
- 25g/1oz/2 tbsp butter or margarine
- 1 onion, chopped
- 675g/1½lb stewing beef, cubed
- 5ml/1 tsp paprika
- 2 garlic cloves, crushed
- 10ml/2 tsp ground cinnamon
- 10ml/2 tsp sugar
- 600ml/1 pint/2½ cups beef stock
- 150ml/¼ pint/⅔ cup brown ale
- 45ml/3 tbsp evaporated (unsweetened condensed) milk
- salt and ground black pepper
- steamed baby patty-pan squash

1 Put the black-eyed beans in a bowl and pour over water to cover. Leave to soak overnight, then drain, tip into a large pan, cover with water and bring to the boil. Boil rapidly for 3–4 minutes, then reduce the heat.

2 Simmer the beans for 30 minutes or until tender, but still quite firm. Drain the beans, reserving the cooking liquid.

3 Melt the butter or margarine in a large pan and sauté the onion for a few minutes. Add the beef, paprika, garlic, cinnamon and sugar and fry for about 5 minutes, stirring frequently.

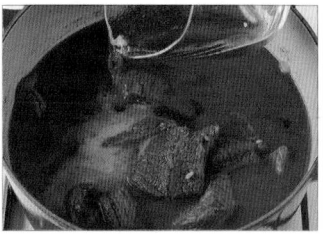

4 Pour in the beef stock and brown ale, cover and cook gently for 1½ hours, until the beef is almost cooked.

5 Add the evaporated milk and beans. Season with salt and pepper and continue cooking until the beans and beef are tender. Serve with steamed baby patty-pan squash.

CARIBBEAN LAMB CURRY

THIS JAMAICAN DISH IS POPULARLY KNOWN AS CURRIED GOAT OR CURRY GOAT, ALTHOUGH KID, LAMB OR MUTTON ARE EQUALLY LIKELY TO BE USED TO MAKE IT.

SERVES SIX

INGREDIENTS

- 900g/2lb boned leg of mutton or lamb
- 50g/2oz/4 tbsp curry powder
- 3 garlic cloves, crushed
- 1 large onion, chopped
- leaves from 4 fresh thyme sprigs, or 5ml/1 tsp dried thyme
- 3 bay leaves
- 5ml/1 tsp ground allspice
- 30ml/2 tbsp vegetable oil
- 50g/2oz/¼ cup butter or margarine
- 900ml/1½ pints/3¾ cups lamb stock or water
- 1 fresh hot chilli, chopped
- fresh coriander (cilantro) sprigs, to garnish
- cooked rice, to serve

1 Cut the meat into 5cm/2in cubes, discarding excess fat and any gristle. Place it in a large bowl.

2 Add the curry powder, garlic, onion, thyme, bay leaves, allspice and oil. Mix well, then cover the bowl and place in the refrigerator. Marinate for at least 3 hours or overnight.

3 Melt the butter or margarine in a large heavy pan. Add the seasoned mutton or lamb and fry over a medium heat for about 10 minutes, turning the meat frequently.

4 Stir in the stock or water and chilli, and bring to the boil. Lower the heat, cover and simmer for 1½ hours or until the meat is tender. Garnish with coriander and serve with rice.

"SEASONED-UP" LAMB IN SPINACH SAUCE

IN THE CARIBBEAN, ESPECIALLY IN THE ENGLISH-SPEAKING ISLANDS, YOU WILL OFTEN HEAR DISHES DESCRIBED AS "SEASONED UP". THIS IMPLIES THE USE OF A SPICY RUB OR MARINADE, A TECHNIQUE THAT WORKS WELL WITH CHEAPER CUTS OF MEAT.

SERVES FOUR

INGREDIENTS
- 675g/1½lb boneless lamb, cubed
- 2.5ml/½ tsp ground ginger
- 2.5ml/½ tsp dried thyme
- 30ml/2 tbsp olive oil
- 1 onion, chopped
- 2 garlic cloves, crushed
- 15ml/1 tbsp tomato purée (paste)
- ½ fresh hot chilli, chopped (optional)
- 600ml/1 pint/2½ cups lamb stock or water
- 115g/4oz fresh spinach, finely chopped
- salt and ground black pepper

1 Put the lamb cubes in a dish. Sprinkle over the ginger and thyme, season and mix well to coat. Cover and marinate for at least 2 hours or overnight in the refrigerator.

2 Heat the olive oil in a heavy pan, add the onion and garlic and fry gently for 5 minutes or until the onion is soft.

3 Add the lamb with the tomato purée and chilli, if using. Fry over a medium heat for about 5 minutes, stirring frequently, then add the lamb stock or water. Cover and simmer for about 30 minutes, until the lamb is tender.

4 Stir in the spinach and simmer for around 8 minutes. Serve hot.

LAMB PELAU

INDIAN IMMIGRANTS INTRODUCED THE PILAU TO THE CARIBBEAN. THE NAME HAS CHANGED SLIGHTLY, BUT RICE DISHES LIKE THIS ONE REMAIN TRUE TO THEIR ORIGINS.

SERVES FOUR

INGREDIENTS
- 450g/1lb stewing lamb
- 15ml/1 tbsp curry powder
- 1 onion, finely chopped
- 2 garlic cloves, crushed
- 2.5ml/½ tsp dried thyme
- 2.5ml/½ tsp dried oregano
- 1 fresh or dried chilli
- 25g/1oz/2 tbsp butter or margarine, plus extra for serving
- 600ml/1 pint/2½ cups beef or chicken stock or coconut milk
- 5ml/1 tsp ground black pepper
- 2 tomatoes, chopped
- 10ml/2 tsp sugar
- 30ml/2 tbsp chopped spring onion (scallion)
- 450g/1lb/2½ cups basmati rice
- spring onion (scallion) strips, to garnish

1 Cut the lamb into cubes and place in a dish. Add the curry powder, onion, garlic, herbs and chilli and stir well. Cover with clear film (plastic wrap) and leave to marinate for 1 hour.

2 Melt the butter or margarine in a pan and fry the lamb for 5–10 minutes. Pour in the stock or coconut milk, bring to the boil, then lower the heat and simmer for 35 minutes or until tender.

3 Add the black pepper, tomatoes, sugar, chopped spring onion and rice. Stir well and reduce the heat. Make sure that the rice is covered by 2.5cm/1in of liquid; add a little water if necessary. Cover the pan; simmer the pelau for 25 minutes or until the rice has absorbed the liquid and is cooked. Spoon into a serving bowl and stir in a little extra butter or margarine. Garnish with spring onion strips and serve.

SPICED ROAST LEG OF LAMB

PEPPERS AND BEANS ARE DELICIOUS COOKED WITH THIS SPICED LAMB – THE BEANS SOAK UP THE MEAT JUICES AND COMBINE WITH SWEET RED PEPPERS TO MAKE A SUCCULENT ONE-POT MEAL.

SERVES SIX

INGREDIENTS

- 1 leg of lamb, about 1.8kg/4lb
- 4 garlic cloves, crushed
- 5ml/1 tsp ground cumin
- 10ml/2 tsp ground annatto (achiote) seeds
- 10ml/2 tbsp sweet paprika
- 5ml/1 tsp dried oregano
- 45ml/3 tbsp olive oil
- 3 red (bell) peppers, cored, seeded and thickly sliced
- 2 x 400g/14oz can black-eyed beans (peas), drained
- 105ml/7 tbsp dry white wine
- salt and ground black pepper
- cooked white rice or polenta, to serve

COOK'S TIP

Look for ground annatto in South American or Caribbean markets, or replace with saffron or turmeric.

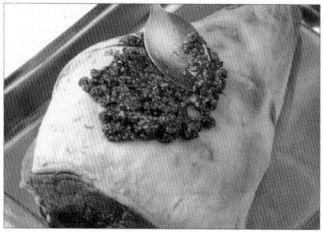

1 Weigh the lamb and calculate the cooking time. For medium-cooked lamb, allow 20 minutes per 450g/1lb, plus 20 minutes. Allow either 5 minutes more or less per 450/1lb for rare and well-done meat.

2 Mix the garlic, cumin, annatto, paprika and oregano in a bowl. Stir in half the olive oil. Using a spoon, rub the paste all over the lamb. Cover and marinate in a cool place for 2–3 hours.

3 Preheat the oven to 180°C/350°F/Gas 4. Place the lamb in a roasting pan with the peppers and beans. Pour in the wine and drizzle with the remaining oil. Season, then roast for the calculated time. Check occasionally, adding water if the vegetables begin to dry out.

4 When the lamb is cooked, remove from the oven and cover the meat loosely with foil. Leave to rest for 15 minutes, then serve with rice or polenta.

RABBIT IN COCONUT MILK

THIS UNUSUAL DISH COMES FROM COLOMBIA. THE RABBIT IS STEWED IN A LIGHTLY SPICED TOMATO SAUCE, AND WHEN IT IS ALMOST READY, COCONUT MILK IS STIRRED IN TO ENRICH THE SAUCE.

SERVES FOUR

INGREDIENTS

- 1 rabbit, cut into 8 pieces (ask your butcher to do this for you)
- 3 garlic cloves, crushed
- 1.5ml/¼ tsp paprika
- 1.5ml/¼ tsp ground cumin
- 45ml/3 tbsp olive oil
- 1 large onion, thinly sliced
- 1 bay leaf
- 400g/14oz can plum tomatoes, drained and roughly chopped
- 150ml/¼ pint/⅔ cup chicken stock
- 250ml/8fl oz/1 cup coconut milk
- salt and ground black pepper
- white rice or boiled potatoes, to serve

1 Wash the rabbit under cold water, then pat the pieces dry with kitchen paper. Combine the garlic, paprika and cumin in a bowl and rub the mixture all over the rabbit. Cover with clear film (plastic wrap) and leave to marinate for 1 hour, or overnight in the refrigerator.

2 Heat the oil in a pan, add the onion slices and cook for 5 minutes, until tender. Remove the onion with a slotted spoon and set aside.

3 Add the rabbit to the oil remaining in the pan, season and cook until golden. Do this over a very low heat to avoid burning the spices.

4 Return the onion slices to the pan and add the bay leaf. Stir in the tomatoes and stock and bring to the boil. Lower the heat, cover and simmer for 45 minutes.

VARIATION

This dish is often made with chicken rather than rabbit. The ingredients remain the same, but the cooking time should be reduced by 15 minutes.

5 Stir in the coconut milk. Continue to simmer, uncovered, for a further 15 minutes, until the rabbit is tender and the sauce has thickened. Serve immediately with white rice or boiled potatoes.

PORK ROASTED WITH HERBS, SPICES AND RUM

IN THE CARIBBEAN, THIS SPICY ROAST PORK IS A FAVOURITE DISH THAT IS USUALLY COOKED ON A BARBECUE AND SERVED ON SPECIAL OCCASIONS AS PART OF A BUFFET.

SERVES EIGHT

INGREDIENTS
- 2 garlic cloves, crushed
- 45ml/3 tbsp soy sauce
- 15ml/1 tbsp malt vinegar
- 15ml/1 tbsp finely chopped celery
- 30ml/2 tbsp chopped spring onion (scallion)
- 7.5ml/1½ tsp dried thyme
- 5ml/1 tsp dried sage
- 2.5ml/½ tsp ground mixed spice (pumpkin pie spice)
- 10ml/2 tsp curry powder
- 120ml/4fl oz/½ cup rum
- 15ml/1 tbsp demerara (raw) sugar
- 1.6kg/3½lb boned loin of pork
- salt and ground black pepper
- spring onion (scallion) curls, to garnish
- creamed sweet potato, to serve

For the sauce
- 25g/1oz/2 tbsp butter or margarine, diced
- 15ml/1 tbsp tomato purée (paste)
- 300ml/½ pint/1¼ cups chicken or pork stock
- 15ml/1 tbsp chopped fresh parsley
- 15ml/1 tbsp demerara (raw) sugar
- hot pepper sauce, to taste

1 In a bowl, mix the garlic, soy sauce, vinegar, celery, spring onion, thyme, sage, spice, curry powder, rum, and sugar. Add a little salt and pepper.

2 Open out the pork and slash the meat, without cutting through it completely. Place it in a shallow dish. Spread most of the spice mixture all over the pork, pressing it well into the slashes. Rub the outside of the joint with the remaining mixture, cover the dish with clear film (plastic wrap) and chill in the refrigerator overnight.

COOK'S TIP

In the Caribbean, pork is baked until it is very well done, so reduce the cooking time if you prefer meat slightly more moist. To get the full flavour from the marinade, start preparation the day before.

3 Preheat the oven to 190°C/375°F/Gas 5. Roll the meat up, then tie it tightly in several places with strong cotton string to hold the meat together.

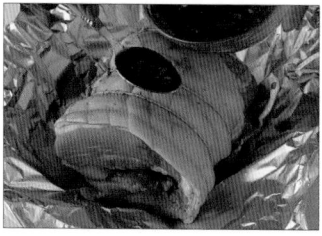

4 Spread a large piece of foil across a roasting pan and place the marinated pork loin in the centre. Baste the pork with a few spoonfuls of the marinade and wrap the foil around the meat.

5 Roast the pork in the oven for 1¾ hours, then slide the foil out from under the meat and discard it. Baste the pork with any remaining marinade and cook for a further 1 hour. Check occasionally that the meat is not drying out and baste with the pan juices.

6 Meanwhile, make the sauce. Transfer the pork to a warmed serving dish, cover with foil and leave to stand in a warm place for 15 minutes. Pour the pan juices into a pan. Add the butter or margarine, tomato purée, stock, parsley and sugar, with hot pepper sauce and salt to taste. Simmer until reduced.

7 Serve the pork sliced, with the creamed sweet potato. Garnish with the spring onion curls and serve the sauce separately.

PORK WITH PINEAPPLE

THIS UNUSUAL DISH FROM MEXICO COMBINES THE SWEET, JUICY TASTE OF FRESH PINEAPPLE WITH FIERY HOT CHILLIES, AND THE REFRESHING TANG OF COOL MINT.

SERVES SIX

INGREDIENTS
- 30ml/2 tbsp corn oil
- 900g/2lb boneless pork shoulder or loin, cut into 5cm/2in cubes
- 1 onion, finely chopped
- 1 large red (bell) pepper, seeded and finely chopped
- 1 or more jalapeño chillies, seeded and finely chopped
- 450g/1lb fresh pineapple chunks
- 8 fresh mint leaves, chopped
- 250ml/8fl oz/1 cup chicken stock
- salt and ground black pepper
- fresh mint sprigs, to garnish
- boiled rice, to serve

1 Heat the oil in a large frying pan and sauté the pork in batches until the cubes are lightly coloured. Transfer the pork to a flameproof casserole, leaving the oil behind in the pan.

2 Add the chopped onion, red pepper and the chillies to the oil remaining in the pan. Sauté until the onion is tender, then add to the casserole with the pineapple. Stir to mix.

3 Add the mint, then cover the casserole with a tight-fitting lid and simmer gently for about 2 hours, or until the pork is tender.

4 Season to taste, garnish the casserole with fresh sprigs of mint and serve with plain boiled rice. Serve immediately, while still hot.

COOK'S TIP

If fresh pineapple is not available, use pineapple chunks from a can. Make sure it is canned in its own juice, however, and not in syrup or other fruit juice.

PORK IN MILK

ITALIAN IMMIGRANTS FIRST TOOK THIS TUSCAN RECIPE TO ARGENTINA. IN PERU, RAISINS AND SEVERAL SWEET SPICES ARE ADDED, BUT FOR THIS VERSION ONLY CLOVES ARE USED, GIVING A SUBTLE FLAVOUR.

SERVES SIX

INGREDIENTS
- 1kg/2¼lb pork loin, on the bone
- 25g/1oz/2 tbsp butter
- 15ml/1 tbsp olive oil
- 1 litre/1¾ pints/4 cups full-fat (whole) milk
- 3 whole cloves
- 4 garlic cloves, peeled but left whole
- 1 bay leaf
- juice of 2 lemons
- salt and ground black pepper
- boiled potatoes, to serve

COOK'S TIP
The milk will curdle because of the addition of lemon juice. Don't be tempted to strain it, or you'll lose half the flavour. When you blend it, it will become perfectly smooth again.

1 Preheat the oven to 180°C/350°F/Gas 4. Season the pork and select a roasting pan that will hold it snugly. Heat the butter and oil in the roasting pan over a medium heat. When the butter has melted, add the pork and baste it all over. Cook for 10–15 minutes, turning, until golden brown all over.

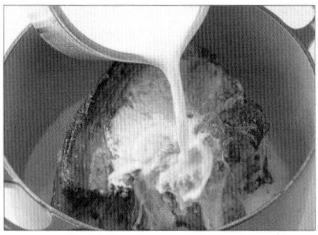

2 Pour in the milk and add the cloves, garlic, bay leaf and lemon juice. Cook in the oven for 1¾–2 hours.

3 Remove the roasting pan from the oven and transfer the pork loin to a serving platter to rest for 5 minutes. Skim the fat from the cooking liquid and, using a teaspoon, remove the cloves and bay leaf. Place the pan on the hob and boil over a high heat until the sauce is reduced by half.

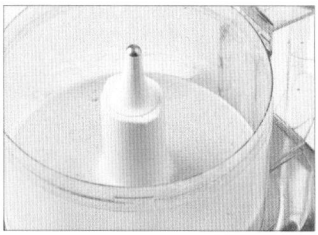

4 Process the sauce in a food processor until smooth. Carve the pork and serve it with the sauce and boiled potatoes.

BAKED HAM WITH ORANGE AND LIME

THE DELICIOUS CITRUS GLAZE ON THIS HAM CONTRASTS BEAUTIFULLY WITH THE SWEETNESS OF THE MEAT FOR THIS PERFECT SUNDAY LUNCH DISH. PLAIN RICE AND BLACK BEANS, THOSE FAVOURITE LATIN AMERICAN SIDE DISHES, ARE THE OBVIOUS ACCOMPANIMENT.

SERVES EIGHT

INGREDIENTS
- 1 green gammon (unsmoked ham), about 2kg/4½lb
- grated rind of 1 orange
- grated rind of 1 lime
- 1 bay leaf
- 3 fresh parsley stalks
- 6 black peppercorns
- 5 garlic cloves, crushed
- 15ml/1 tbsp dried oregano
- 2 fresh red chillies, seeded and finely chopped
- juice of 1 orange
- juice of 2 limes
- 30ml/2 tbsp soft brown sugar
- ground black pepper

1 Put the gammon in a large pan and pour in cold water to cover. Add the orange and lime rind, the bay leaf, parsley and peppercorns. Bring to the boil over a high heat, cover and lower the heat so that the water is bubbling at a gentle simmer. Cook the gammon for about 2 hours.

2 Preheat the oven to 220°C/425°F/Gas 7. When the gammon is cooked, remove the pan from the heat. Leave until the gammon is cool enough to handle, then transfer it to a chopping board. Carefully pull away the skin, leaving the fat on the meat.

3 Mix the crushed garlic, oregano, chopped chillies, orange and lime juice and sugar in a bowl and stir well to combine. Add a generous amount of ground black pepper. Rub the mixture all over the gammon, coating it evenly. Transfer to a roasting pan and bake for 20–25 minutes or until golden.

4 Slice the ham and serve. Alternatively, enjoy as part of a buffet or picnic.

POULTRY

Chicken is the meat most frequently eaten in the Caribbean and Latin America. The Caribbean Sunday roast is extremely popular, but for delicious weekday meals try thyme and lime chicken or chicken with okra. Colombian chicken hot-pot and carapulcra, *a chicken and pork dish from Peru, are both national dishes. Turkey and duck are also popular throughout the region.*

CUBAN CHICKEN PIE

THIS IS A GREAT FAMILY MEAL, PERFECT FOR A SUNDAY LUNCH. THE FILLING, WHICH INCLUDES CAPERS, OLIVES AND RAISINS, PROVIDES A FLAVOURSOME CONTRAST TO THE CRISP CORN TOPPING.

SERVES SIX

INGREDIENTS
- 1 chicken, about 1.6kg/3½lb
- 6 peppercorns
- 1 bay leaf
- 3 fresh parsley sprigs
- 30ml/2 tbsp olive oil
- 1 large onion, finely chopped
- 2 hard-boiled eggs, chopped
- 2 tomatoes, roughly chopped
- 50g/2oz/½ cup pitted green olives, roughly chopped
- 15ml/1 tbsp drained bottled capers
- 65g/2½oz/scant ½ cup raisins
- salt and ground black pepper

For the topping
- 500g/1¼lb/3⅓ cups drained canned or thawed frozen corn kernels
- 90g/3½oz butter
- 10ml/2 tsp caster (superfine) sugar
- 3 eggs, lightly beaten
- salt

1 Put the chicken in a large, heavy pan and add enough water to cover. Add the peppercorns, bay leaf and parsley and bring to the boil over a high heat. Lower the heat, cover and simmer gently for 1 hour or until cooked through.

2 Allow the chicken to cool in the cooking liquid. When cold enough to handle, lift the chicken out of the pan and, using two forks, shred the flesh roughly. Discard the skin and bones.

3 Make the topping. Tip the corn kernels into a blender or food processor and purée until smooth. Melt the butter in a pan over a low heat. Stir in the puréed corn and sugar. Season generously with salt and cook, stirring, for 10 minutes, until the mixture thickens and comes away from the sides of the pan.

4 Remove from the heat and leave to cool for 10 minutes, then slowly stir in the beaten eggs, a little at a time. Set the topping mixture aside.

5 Preheat the oven to 180°C/350°F/Gas 4. Heat the oil in a large frying pan and stir in the chopped onion. Cook gently for 5 minutes, until soft and translucent, and season with salt and black pepper to taste.

6 Stir in the chopped hard-boiled eggs, chopped tomatoes, olives, capers and raisins. Fold in the shredded chicken, making sure that it is well distributed throughout the mixture.

7 Spoon the pie filling into a 25 x 20cm/10 x 8in baking dish. Using a spoon, spread the corn topping evenly over the top of the chicken filling and bake for 45 minutes, until golden brown. Leave to stand for about 10 minutes before serving on warm plates.

VARIATION

Shortcrust pastry can be used instead of the corn topping.

CHICKEN WITH OKRA

SERVE THIS CLASSIC BRAZILIAN DISH FOR A FAMILY SUPPER. IT IS TOTALLY FUSS-FREE, TAKING VERY LITTLE TIME AND EFFORT TO PREPARE.

SERVES FOUR

INGREDIENTS

- 15ml/1 tbsp olive oil
- 4 chicken thighs
- 1 large onion, finely chopped
- 2 garlic cloves, finely crushed
- 2 fresh red chillies, seeded and finely chopped
- 120ml/4fl oz/½ cup water
- 350g/12oz okra
- 2 large tomatoes, finely chopped
- salt
- boiled white rice or polenta, to serve
- hot chilli oil (optional)

COOK'S TIP

As okra cooks, the pods release a sticky juice, which coats and flavours the chicken. If you don't like this sticky texture, however, cook the pods whole, simply trimming off the tops but not cutting into the pods themselves.

1 Heat the oil in a wide pan over a low heat. Season the chicken thighs with salt and add them to the pan, skin side down. Cook until golden brown, turn them over and add the chopped onion.

2 Sauté for 5 minutes, until the onion has softened; then add the garlic and chopped chillies. Cook for a further 2 minutes. Add half the water to the pan and bring to the boil. Lower the heat, cover and cook for 30 minutes.

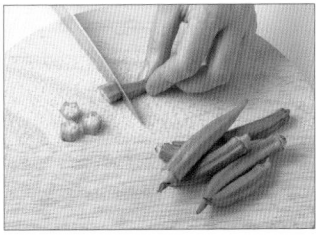

3 Trim the okra and slice into thin rounds. Add to the pan with the tomatoes. Season with salt and pour in the remaining water. Cover and simmer gently for about 10–15 minutes, or until the chicken pieces are tender and fully cooked. The chicken is ready when the flesh can be pulled off the bone easily.

4 Serve immediately with boiled white rice or polenta, and offer some hot chilli oil on the side.

COLOMBIAN CHICKEN HOT-POT

COLOMBIANS ARE JUSTIFIABLY PROUD OF THIS NATIONAL DISH. TRADITIONALLY, THREE NATIVE VARIETIES OF POTATOES ARE USED, EACH WITH A DIFFERENT TEXTURE, TO CREATE A TASTY THICK BROTH. THE ADDITION OF CORIANDER AND CORN PROVIDES A COMPLEMENTARY SWEETNESS.

SERVES EIGHT

INGREDIENTS

- 1.6kg/3½lb chicken
- 3 spring onions (scallions)
- 2 bay leaves
- 6 fresh coriander (cilantro) sprigs
- 6 whole black peppercorns
- 675g/1½lb floury potatoes, peeled and cut into 1cm/½in chunks
- 675g/1½lb waxy potatoes, peeled and cut into 1cm/½in chunks
- 675g/1½lb baby new potatoes or salad potatoes
- 2 corn cobs, each cut into 4 pieces
- salt
- capers and sour cream, to serve

For the avocado salsa

- 1 hard-boiled egg
- 1 large ripe avocado
- 1 spring onion (scallion), finely chopped
- 15ml/1 tbsp chopped fresh coriander (cilantro)
- 1 fresh green chilli, seeded and finely chopped
- salt

1 Put the chicken in a large pan or flameproof casserole and cover with water. Add the spring onions (scallions), bay leaves, coriander sprigs and peppercorns. Season, bring to the boil and skim the surface of the liquid.

2 Reduce the heat to a gentle simmer, cover and cook for 1 hour or until the chicken is tender and fully cooked. Remove from the heat and allow the chicken to cool in the cooking liquid.

3 Drain the chicken, reserving the cooking liquid to use as stock. Place the chicken on a board and cut it into 8 pieces. It should be so tender that the legs are easy to pull off.

4 Separate the thighs from the drumsticks. Use a knife to cut between the two breasts, then gently ease the meat off the bone. Cut the breasts in half, set the chicken pieces aside on a plate and discard the rest of the carcass.

5 Skim the fat from the top of the cooking liquid, then strain it into a clean pan. Bring to the boil. Add the floury and waxy potatoes and simmer for 15 minutes. Stir in the new potatoes or salad potatoes and corn and simmer for a further 20 minutes.

6 By this time, the floury potatoes will have broken up and they will have helped to thicken the liquid. The waxy potatoes should be soft and partly broken. The new or salad potatoes should be tender but still whole. Return the chicken pieces to the pan and reheat gently but thoroughly.

7 Meanwhile, make the fresh avocado salsa. Peel and roughly chop the hard-boiled egg. Using a fork, mash it in a small bowl.

8 Just before serving, cut the avocado in half lengthways and, using a teaspoon, scoop the flesh into a separate bowl. Mash well with a fork, then stir in the chopped hard-boiled egg until thoroughly combined. Add the spring onion, fresh coriander and chilli, mix well, then season to taste with salt.

9 Serve the chicken mixture in a heated casserole or earthenware dish, with bowls of hot tomato salsa, capers and sour cream on the side, if you like.

COOK'S TIP

The quality and flavour of the chicken stock in this dish will depend entirely on what kind of chicken you use. It is worth spending a bit more and buying the best bird you can find, preferably free range, corn-fed or organic. You will really taste the difference.

BARBECUED JERK CHICKEN

JERK SEASONING IS A BLEND OF HERBS AND SPICES THAT IS RUBBED INTO MEAT BEFORE IT IS ROASTED OVER CHARCOAL SPRINKLED WITH PIMIENTO BERRIES. IN JAMAICA, JERK SEASONING WAS ORIGINALLY USED ONLY FOR PORK, BUT JERKED CHICKEN TASTES JUST AS GOOD.

SERVES FOUR

INGREDIENTS
- 8 chicken pieces
- oil, for brushing
- salad leaves, to serve

For the jerk seasoning
- 5ml/1 tsp ground allspice
- 5ml/1 tsp ground cinnamon
- 5ml/1 tsp dried thyme
- 1.5ml/¼ tsp freshly grated nutmeg
- 10ml/2 tsp demerara (raw) sugar
- 2 garlic cloves, crushed
- 15ml/1 tbsp finely chopped onion
- 15ml/1 tbsp chopped spring onion (scallion)
- 15ml/1 tbsp vinegar
- 30ml/2 tbsp oil
- 15ml/1 tbsp lime juice
- 1 fresh hot chilli pepper, chopped
- salt and ground black pepper

1 Make the jerk seasoning. Combine the ground allspice, cinnamon, thyme, grated nutmeg, sugar, garlic, both types of onion, vinegar, oil, lime juice and chilli pepper in a small bowl. Use a fork to mash them together until a thick paste is formed. Season to taste with a little salt and plenty of ground black pepper.

2 Make several lengthways slits in the flesh on the chicken pieces. Place the chicken pieces in a dish and spoon the jerk seasoning over them. Use your hands to rub the seasoning into the chicken, especially into the slits.

3 Cover with clear film (plastic wrap) and marinate for at least 4–6 hours or overnight in the refrigerator.

4 Preheat the grill (broiler) or prepare the barbecue. Shake off any excess seasoning from the chicken and brush the pieces with oil. Either place on a baking sheet and grill (broil) for 45 minutes, or cook on the barbecue for about 30 minutes. Whichever method you choose, it is important to turn the chicken pieces frequently. Serve hot with salad leaves.

COOK'S TIP

The flavour is best if you marinate the chicken overnight. If cooking on the barbecue, sprinkle the charcoal with aromatic herbs, such as rosemary or bay leaves, for even more flavour.

THYME AND LIME CHICKEN

LIMES GROWN IN LATIN AMERICA TEND TO BE PALER THAN THE ONES IN OUR SUPERMARKETS, BUT THEY ARE JUICY AND FULL OF FLAVOUR. THIS CARIBBEAN RECIPE, WHICH COMBINES THEM WITH FRAGRANT THYME, IS A GREAT VEHICLE FOR THEM.

SERVES FOUR

INGREDIENTS
- 8 chicken thighs
- 30ml/2 tbsp chopped spring onion (scallion)
- 10ml/2 tsp chopped fresh thyme or 5ml/1 tsp dried thyme
- 2 garlic cloves, crushed
- juice of 2 limes or 1 lemon
- 75g/3oz/6 tbsp butter, melted
- salt and ground black pepper
- cooked rice, to serve

To garnish
- lime slices
- fresh coriander (cilantro) sprigs

1 Put the chicken thighs skin-side down in a baking dish or roasting pan. Using a sharp knife, make a lengthways slit along the thigh bone of each. Mix the spring onion with a little salt and pepper and press the mixture into the slits.

2 Mix the thyme, garlic and lime or lemon juice in a small bowl. Add 50g/2oz/4 tbsp of the butter and mix well, then spoon a little of the mixture over each chicken thigh, spreading evenly.

3 Spoon the remaining butter evenly over the top of the chicken pieces. Cover the dish tightly with clear film (plastic wrap) and leave to marinate for at least 3–4 hours in the refrigerator. For the best flavour, prepare the chicken the day before and leave to marinate overnight.

4 Preheat the oven to 190°C/375°F/Gas 5. Remove the film and cover the chicken with foil. Bake for about 1 hour, then remove the foil and cook for a further 5–10 minutes, until the chicken turns golden brown. Garnish with lime slices and fresh coriander and serve with rice.

CHICKEN, PORK AND POTATOES IN PEANUT SAUCE

THIS TRADITIONAL PERUVIAN DISH, KNOWN AS CARAPULCRA, *IS MADE WITH* PAPASECA *(DRIED POTATOES), WHICH BREAK UP WHEN COOKED TO THICKEN THE SAUCE. THE SAME EFFECT IS ACHIEVED HERE BY USING FLOURY POTATOES, THE KIND THAT DISINTEGRATE WHEN COOKED FOR A LONG TIME.*

SERVES SIX

INGREDIENTS
- 75g/3oz/¾ cup unsalted peanuts
- 60ml/4 tbsp olive oil
- 3 chicken breast portions, halved
- 500g/1¼lb boneless pork loin, cut into 2cm/¾in pieces
- 1 large onion, chopped
- 30–45ml/2–3 tbsp water
- 3 garlic cloves, crushed
- 5ml/1 tsp paprika
- 5ml/1 tsp ground cumin
- 500g/1¼lb floury potatoes, peeled and thickly sliced
- 550ml/18fl oz/scant 2½ cups vegetable stock
- salt and ground black pepper
- cooked rice, to serve

To garnish
- 2 hard-boiled eggs, sliced
- 50g/2oz/½ cup pitted black olives
- chopped fresh flat leaf parsley

1 Place the peanuts in a large dry frying pan over a low heat. Toast for about 2–3 minutes, until golden all over. Watch them closely, shaking the pan frequently, as they have a tendency to burn. Leave to cool, then process in a food processor until finely ground.

2 Heat half the olive oil in a heavy pan. Add the chicken pieces, season with salt and ground black pepper and cook for 10 minutes, until golden brown all over. Transfer the pieces of chicken to a plate, using a slotted spoon.

3 Heat the remaining oil in the pan. When it is very hot, add the pork. Season and sauté for 3–4 minutes, until golden brown. Transfer to the plate containing the chicken pieces.

4 Lower the heat and stir the onion into the oil in the pan. Cook for 5 minutes, adding the water if it begins to stick. Stir in the garlic, paprika and cumin and cook for 1 minute more.

5 Add the potatoes, stir and cover the pan. Cook for 3 minutes. Add the peanuts and stock. Bring to the boil, and simmer gently for 20–30 minutes.

6 Return the chicken and pork to the pan and bring to the boil. Lower the heat, replace the lid and simmer for 6–8 minutes, until the meat is fully cooked. Avoid overcooking the meat or it will become tough and stringy.

7 Garnish the stew with the egg slices, black olives and chopped parsley. Serve with the rice.

COOK'S TIP

If you cannot locate unsalted peanuts, buy a pack of salted ready-roasted peanuts, wash them under cold running water, then pat dry and grind.

SPICY FRIED CHICKEN

THIS TRADITIONAL CARIBBEAN CRISPY CHICKEN DISH IS SUPERB EATEN HOT OR COLD. SERVED WITH A SALAD OR VEGETABLES, IT MAKES A DELICIOUS LUNCH AND IS ALSO IDEAL FOR PICNICS OR SNACKS.

SERVES FOUR

INGREDIENTS
- 4 chicken drumsticks
- 4 chicken thighs
- 10ml/2 tsp curry powder
- 2.5ml/½ tsp garlic granules or 1 garlic clove, crushed
- 2.5ml/½ tsp ground black pepper
- 2.5ml/½ tsp paprika
- about 300ml/½ pint/1¼ cups milk
- oil, for deep frying
- 50g/2oz/½ cup plain (all-purpose) flour
- salt
- dressed salad leaves, to serve

1 Sprinkle the chicken pieces with curry powder, garlic, pepper, paprika and a little salt. Rub into the chicken, then cover and marinate for at least 2 hours, or overnight in the refrigerator.

2 Preheat the oven to 180°C/350°F/ Gas 4. Cover the chicken with milk and leave to stand for a further 15 minutes.

3 Heat the oil in a large pan or deep-fryer and tip the flour on to a plate. Dip the chicken pieces in flour and add to the oil, taking care not to overcrowd the pan. Fry until golden, but not fully cooked.

4 Remove the chicken pieces with a slotted spoon and place on a baking sheet. Continue until all the chicken pieces have been fried.

5 Place the baking sheet in the oven and bake the chicken for around 30 minutes. Serve hot or cold with dressed salad leaves.

SUNDAY ROAST CHICKEN

MUCH OF THE PREPARATION FOR THIS DISH IS DONE THE NIGHT BEFORE, MAKING IT IDEAL FOR A FAMILY LUNCH. THE CHICKEN IS SUCCULENT AND FULL OF FLAVOUR, WITH A RICH GRAVY.

SERVES SIX

INGREDIENTS
- 1.6kg/3½lb chicken
- 5ml/1 tsp paprika
- 5ml/1 tsp dried thyme
- 2.5ml/½ tsp dried tarragon
- 5ml/1 tsp garlic granules or 1 garlic clove, crushed
- 15ml/1 tbsp lemon juice
- 30ml/2 tbsp clear honey
- 45ml/3 tbsp dark rum
- melted butter, for basting
- 300ml/½ pint/1¼ cups chicken stock
- lime quarters, to garnish

1 Place the chicken in a roasting pan and sprinkle with paprika, thyme, tarragon, garlic and salt and pepper. Rub the mixture all over the chicken, including underneath the skin. Cover with clear film (plastic wrap) and leave to marinate for at least 2 hours or overnight in the refrigerator.

2 Preheat the oven to 190°C/375°F/ Gas 5. Mix the lemon, honey and rum in a bowl. Stir well, then pour over and under the chicken skin, rubbing it in well to ensure the flavours are absorbed.

3 Spoon melted butter all over the chicken, then transfer to the oven and roast for 1½–2 hours, until fully cooked.

VARIATION

Extra herbs and rum can be used to make a richer, tastier gravy, if you like.

4 Transfer the chicken to a serving dish while you make the gravy. Pour the pan juices into a small pan. Add the chicken stock. Simmer for 10 minutes or until the gravy has reduced and thickened slightly. Adjust the seasoning and pour into a serving jug. Garnish the chicken with the lime quarters and serve.

PEANUT CHICKEN

THE RICH SAUCE FOR THIS POPULAR CARIBBEAN DISH IS BEST MADE WITH SMOOTH PEANUT BUTTER, ALTHOUGH IT CAN ALSO BE MADE WITH GROUND PEANUTS.

SERVES FOUR

INGREDIENTS
- 900g/2lb boneless chicken breast portions, skinned and cut into cubes
- 2 garlic cloves, crushed
- 2.5ml/½ tsp dried thyme
- 2.5ml/½ tsp ground black pepper
- 15ml/1 tbsp curry powder
- 15ml/1 tbsp lemon juice
- 25g/1oz/2 tbsp butter or margarine
- 1 onion, chopped
- 45ml/3 tbsp chopped tomatoes
- 1 fresh hot chilli, seeded and chopped
- 30ml/2 tbsp smooth peanut butter
- 450ml/¾ pint/scant 2 cups warm water
- salt
- fresh coriander (cilantro) sprigs, to garnish
- fried plantain, to serve
- okra, to serve

1 Put the chicken in a large bowl and stir in the garlic, thyme, black pepper, curry powder, lemon juice and a little salt. Cover and marinate in a cool place for 3–4 hours.

2 Melt the butter or margarine in a large pan. Add the onion, sauté gently for 5 minutes, then add the seasoned chicken. Fry over a medium heat for 10 minutes, turning frequently, and then stir in the tomatoes and chilli.

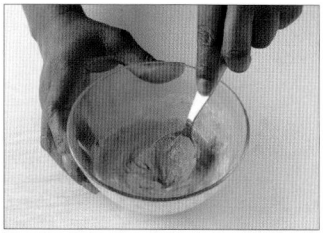

3 In a small bowl, blend the peanut butter to a smooth paste with a little of the warm water and stir this paste into the chicken mixture.

4 Gradually stir in the remaining water, then simmer gently for about 30 minutes or until the chicken is fully cooked. Add a little more water if the sauce begins to dry out. Garnish with sprigs of fresh coriander and serve hot with slices of fried plantain and okra.

BREAST OF TURKEY WITH MANGO AND WINE

FRESH TROPICAL MANGO AND WARM CINNAMON COMBINE TO GIVE A REAL TASTE OF THE CARIBBEAN.

SERVES FOUR

INGREDIENTS
- 4 turkey breast fillets
- 1 small ripe mango
- 1 garlic clove, crushed
- 1.5ml/¼ tsp ground cinnamon
- 15ml/1 tbsp finely chopped fresh parsley
- 15ml/1 tbsp crushed cream crackers (oyster crackers)
- 40g/1½oz/3 tbsp butter or margarine
- 1 garlic clove, crushed
- 6 shallots, sliced
- 150ml/¼ pint/⅔ cup white wine
- salt and ground black pepper
- diced fresh mango and chopped fresh parsley, to garnish

1 Cut a slit horizontally into each turkey fillet to make a pocket. Using a sharp knife, peel the mango and cut the flesh off the stone (pit). Finely chop enough of the flesh to make 30ml/2 tbsp and roughly dice the remainder.

2 Mix the garlic, cinnamon, parsley, cracker crumbs and finely chopped mango in a bowl. Add 15ml/1 tbsp of the butter or margarine with salt and pepper to taste and mash together.

3 Spoon a little of the mango mixture into each of the pockets in the turkey breast fillets and close, securing with a wooden cocktail stick (toothpick) if necessary. Season with a little extra ground black pepper.

4 Melt the remaining butter in a frying pan and sauté the crushed garlic and sliced shallots for about 5 minutes. Add the turkey fillets and cook for 15 minutes, turning once. Add the wine, cover and simmer for 5–10 minutes, until the turkey is cooked. Add the mango, heat, and serve garnished with parsley.

PERUVIAN DUCK WITH RICE

DUCK IS VERY POPULAR IN PERU. IN THIS RECIPE, THE RICE IS COOKED IN THE SAME LIQUID AS THE DUCK, SO IT ABSORBS THE AROMATIC FLAVOURS OF THE HERBS AND SPICES.

SERVES SIX

INGREDIENTS
- 2 fresh red chillies, seeded
- 4 garlic cloves, roughly chopped
- 5 fresh coriander (cilantro) stalks
- 5ml/1 tsp ground cumin
- 3 duck legs
- salt and ground black pepper
- 1 large onion, finely chopped
- 650ml/1 pint/2½ cups chicken stock
- 250ml/8fl oz/1 cup red wine
- 350g/12oz/1¾ cups long grain rice
- 115g/4oz/1 cup frozen peas, thawed
- 15ml/1 tbsp chopped fresh coriander (cilantro), to garnish

VARIATION

If you find duck too fatty for your tastes, try making this dish with chicken legs or rabbit. It will be just as delicious.

1 Put the fresh chillies, garlic cloves, coriander (cilantro) stalks and ground cumin in a blender or food processor and process to a thick paste.

2 Cut the duck legs in half to separate the thigh from the drumstick. Place in a large heavy pan with a tight-fitting lid. Place over a low heat. Season the duck with salt and ground black pepper. Cook until golden brown on all sides, set the duck aside and pour away most of the fat, leaving about 30ml/2 tbsp.

3 Add the onion to the pan and cook gently for 5 minutes. Stir in the chilli and coriander paste and cook for a further 2 minutes. Return the duck to the pan, pour in the stock and wine and bring to the boil. Cover, reduce the heat and simmer for 45 minutes.

4 Stir the rice into the pan, replace the lid and cook for 18–20 minutes. Stir in the peas and remove from the heat. Leave to stand for 5 minutes and serve with a scattering of chopped coriander.

DRUNKEN DUCK

THIS IS A LOVELY DISH FOR A DINNER PARTY. THE DUCK AND SWEET POTATOES COOK IN THE RED WINE AND WARM SPICES, CREATING A RICH, ALMOST CHOCOLATE-LIKE SAUCE.

SERVES FOUR

INGREDIENTS
- 1 duck, about 2.25kg/5lb
- 1 large onion, thinly sliced
- 2.5ml/½ tsp crushed dried chillies
- 2 garlic cloves, crushed
- 1.5ml/¼ tsp ground cloves
- 1.5ml/¼ tsp ground allspice
- 2.5ml/½ tsp ground cinnamon
- 800g/1¾lb sweet potatoes, peeled and cut into thick wedges
- 250ml/8fl oz/1 cup red wine
- 250ml/8fl oz/1 cup chicken stock
- salt and ground black pepper
- polenta or cooked rice, to serve

1 Preheat the oven to 200°C/400°F/Gas 6. Season the inside and outside of the duck. Place the duck in a large flameproof casserole over a low heat and cook, turning occasionally, until the skin has released some of its fat and turned a rich golden brown. Transfer the duck to a plate.

2 Pour away most of the duck fat from the pan, leaving about 30ml/2 tbsp. Return the casserole to the heat, add the onion and crushed chillies and stir well to coat in the fat, incorporating any sediment on the bottom of the pan.

3 Cook for 5 minutes until the onion is soft and translucent. Stir in the garlic and spices and cook for 1 minute more.

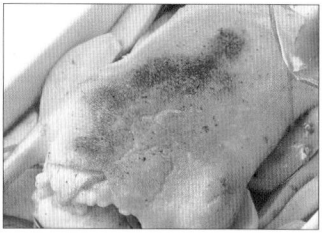

4 Return the duck to the casserole, arrange the sweet potatoes around it and pour in the wine and stock. Bring to the boil and cover. Move the dish to the oven and cook for 1¼–1½ hours.

5 Skim the fat from the top of the sauce and serve with soft polenta or plain rice.

Vegetarian Dishes and Salads

Although vegetarianism is not widespread in the Caribbean and Latin America, root vegetables, corn and what might be considered exotic fruit and vegetables, such as heart of palm and okra are used extensively. The salads in this chapter can either be enjoyed as a light lunch, as an appetizer or as side dishes.

CORN SOUFFLÉ

LATIN AMERICAN SOUFFLÉS ARE QUITE DIFFERENT FROM THEIR FRENCH COUNTERPARTS. FOR EXAMPLE, THIS ONE WILL RISE ONLY SLIGHTLY, YET THE TEXTURE WILL STILL BE LIGHT AND AIRY.

SERVES SIX

INGREDIENTS
- 75g/3oz/6 tbsp butter
- 300g/11oz sweet potato, peeled and cubed
- 300g/11oz pumpkin, peeled and cubed
- 300g/11oz/scant 2 cups frozen corn kernels, thawed
- 3 spring onions (scallions), roughly chopped
- 150g/5oz Cheddar cheese, grated
- 5 eggs
- salt and ground black pepper

1 Preheat the oven to 180°C/350°F/Gas 4. Using 15g/½oz/1 tbsp of the butter, grease a 28 x 18cm/11 x 7in baking dish. Cook the sweet potato and pumpkin in a pan of lightly salted boiling water for 10 minutes, until tender. Drain and set aside.

2 Put 250g/9oz/1½ cups of corn kernals into a food processor. Add the chopped spring onions and process until smooth. Melt the remaining butter in a pan and stir in the corn and onion mixture. Cook, stirring, over a low heat, for about 1–2 minutes.

3 Add the cheese, stirring until it has melted. Season generously with salt and pepper. Remove from the heat.

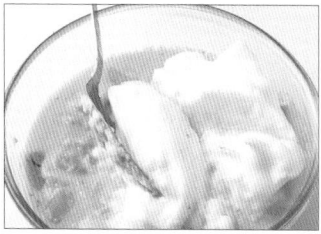

4 Separate three of the eggs and add the remaining whole eggs to the bowl containing the yolks. Mix lightly, then stir the yolk mixture into the pan. Add the sweet potato, pumpkin and remaining corn. Whisk the egg whites until stiff, then fold them into the soufflé mixture.

5 Transfer the mixture to the prepared dish and place the dish in a roasting pan. Pour in hot water to come halfway up the side of the dish and bake for 35–40 minutes, until golden. If the soufflé still wobbles when shaken gently, cook for a further 5–10 minutes. Leave to cool, then serve.

COOK'S TIP

For the best results, whisk the egg whites with a pinch of salt in a clean glass or metal bowl. When they are very stiff and no longer slide around the bowl when it is moved, they are ready for use.

LAYERED POTATO BAKE WITH CHEESE

INSPIRED BY THE PERUVIAN SIDE DISH, OCOPA AREQUIPENA, *THIS FAMILY-SIZED POTATO CAKE IN A SPICY CHEESE AND WALNUT SAUCE IS SUBSTANTIAL ENOUGH FOR A MAIN COURSE.*

SERVES SIX

INGREDIENTS

- 105ml/7 tbsp olive oil
- 1 large onion, chopped
- 2 garlic cloves, crushed
- 5ml/1 tsp crushed dried chillies
- 130g/4½oz/generous 1 cup walnut halves
- 130g/4½oz/generous ½ cup fresh cheese, such as ricotta
- 105ml/7 tbsp warm water
- 3 eggs
- 450g/1lb large potatoes, peeled
- butter, for greasing
- 65g/2½oz/scant ¾ cup pitted black olives
- 4 pimientos, cut into strips
- salt

1 Heat 30ml/2 tbsp of the oil in a small pan over a low heat. Add the chopped onion and sauté gently for 5 minutes, until softened. Stir in the garlic and crushed dried chillies and cook for a further 2 minutes.

2 Put the walnuts in a blender or food processor. Blend until smooth, then add the cooked onion mixture, with the cheese and remaining olive oil. Season generously with salt and pour in the warm water. Blend to make a smooth paste. Set aside.

3 Put the eggs in a small pan of cold water. Bring to the boil, then lower the heat to a simmer. Cook for 10 minutes then cool in a bowl of cold water.

4 Add the potatoes to a pan of salted water and cover. Bring to the boil, then simmer for 10 minutes. Drain and refresh under cold water. Drain again and cut into 1cm/½in slices. Shell the eggs and cut them into slices.

5 Preheat the oven to 180°C/350°F/ Gas 4. Grease a 28 x 18cm/11 x 7in baking dish with butter. Arrange a layer of potatoes in the dish and generously spread with the prepared paste. Top with egg slices and a sprinkling of olives and pimiento strips. Continue layering until all the ingredients have been used, finishing with olives and pimientos.

6 Bake for 30 minutes, until the potatoes are very tender. Leave to cool for 5 minutes before serving.

HEART OF PALM PIE

THE DELICATE CREAMY FILLING IN THIS PIE CONTRASTS BEAUTIFULLY WITH THE CRUMBLY PASTRY. THIS RECIPE CAN ALSO BE USED TO MAKE SMALL BRAZILIAN EMPADINHAS *– BABY SAVOURY PIES – NOT TO BE CONFUSED WITH* EMPANADAS, *THE LITTLE TURNOVERS.*

SERVES EIGHT

INGREDIENTS
- 500g/1¼lb/5 cups plain (all-purpose) flour
- 5ml/1 tsp salt
- 175g/6oz/¾ cup butter
- 75g/3oz/6 tbsp lard or white cooking fat
- 1 egg yolk
- 45ml/3 tbsp cold water

For the filling
- 25g/1oz/2 tbsp butter
- 1 large onion, finely chopped
- 4 garlic cloves, crushed
- 15ml/1 tbsp plain (all-purpose) flour
- 200ml/7fl oz/scant 1 cup full-fat (whole) milk
- 2 hard-boiled eggs, roughly chopped
- 1 large tomato, peeled, seeded and cubed
- 1 fresh red chilli, seeded and finely chopped
- 2 x 400g/14oz cans heart of palm, drained and cut into 2cm/¾in slices
- 15ml/1 tbsp chopped fresh flat leaf parsley
- salt and ground black pepper

To glaze
- 1 egg yolk
- 15ml/1 tbsp water

1 Place the flour, salt, butter and lard or cooking fat in a food processor and process until the mixture resembles fine breadcrumbs. With the motor still running, add the egg yolk and the cold water. As soon as the mixture comes together, transfer to a floured surface. Knead it lightly until smooth. Divide the pastry into two rounds, one slightly larger than the other, wrap both in cling film (plastic wrap) and place in the refrigerator while you make the filling.

2 Melt the butter in a frying pan over a low heat. Stir in the chopped onion and cook for 5 minutes until soft. Add the garlic and cook for a further 2 minutes.

3 Stir the flour into the pan and cook, stirring, for 1 minute. Remove from the heat and slowly pour in the milk, a little at a time, stirring to prevent any lumps from forming.

4 Return to the heat and cook, stirring constantly, for 2 minutes to make a thin white sauce. Remove from the heat and stir in the chopped hard-boiled eggs, cubed tomato, chilli, palm hearts and parsley. Season with salt and pepper.

5 Preheat the oven to 190°C/375°F/ Gas 5. Place a large baking sheet on the central shelf so that it heats up.

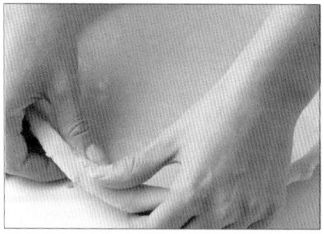

6 On a floured surface, roll out the larger piece of pastry and line the base and sides of a 23cm/9in round loose-based quiche pan. The pastry will be very crumbly, so it may tear in a few places. Should this happen, use your fingers to push the pastry together again. There should be no gaps.

7 Add the filling, then roll out the remaining pastry and use to top the pie. Do not worry about any small gaps in the pastry, as they add to the rustic character of the dish.

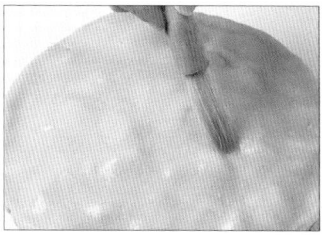

8 Make the glaze by mixing the egg yolk with the water. Using a pastry brush glaze the pastry, then place the quiche pan on the heated baking sheet and bake the pie for 45 minutes, until the pastry is golden.

9 Leave the pie to cool for 5 minutes on a wire rack before removing it from the pan and putting it on to a large plate. Serve warm or at room temperature.

COOK'S TIP

Cooking the pie on a heated baking sheet ensures that the pastry cooks thoroughly, avoiding a soggy base.

MACARONI CHEESE PIE

MACARONI CHEESE IS A FAVOURITE DISH ON THE ISLAND OF BARBADOS, WHERE IT IS OFTEN SERVED AS AN ACCOMPANIMENT, INSTEAD OF A STARCHY VEGETABLE SUCH AS POTATO. THIS TREATMENT MAKES AN EXCELLENT VEGETARIAN MAIN COURSE.

SERVES FOUR

INGREDIENTS

- 225g/8oz/2 cups macaroni
- 40g/1½oz/3 tbsp butter or margarine
- 20g/¾oz/3 tbsp plain (all-purpose) flour
- 450ml/¾ pint/scant 2 cups milk
- 5ml/1 tsp mild mustard
- 2.5ml/½ tsp ground cinnamon
- 175g/6oz mature (sharp) Cheddar cheese, grated
- 1 egg, beaten
- 15ml/1 tbsp butter or margarine
- 25g/1oz/2 tbsp chopped spring onion (scallion)
- 40g/1½oz/3 tbsp canned chopped tomatoes
- 115g/4oz/⅔ cup corn kernels
- salt and ground black pepper
- chopped fresh parsley, to garnish

1 Heat the oven to 180°C/350°F/Gas 4. Cook the macaroni in a pan of salted boiling water for 10 minutes. Drain, rinse under cold water and drain again.

2 Melt 25g/1oz/2 tbsp of the butter in a pan and add the flour. Cook for 1 minute, then add the milk, whisking constantly. Heat until the mixture boils, then simmer gently for 5–10 minutes.

3 Stir in the mustard and cinnamon, with two-thirds of the cheese. Season to taste. Cook gently, stirring frequently, until the cheese has melted, then remove from the heat and whisk in the egg. Cover closely and set aside.

4 Heat the remaining butter or margarine in a small frying pan and cook the spring onion, chopped tomatoes and corn over a gentle heat for 5–10 minutes.

5 Tip half the cooked macaroni into a greased ovenproof dish. Pour over half the cheese sauce and mix well, then spoon the tomato and corn mixture evenly over the mixture.

6 Tip the remaining macaroni into the pan containing the cheese sauce, stir well and then spread carefully over the tomato and corn mixture.

7 Top with the remaining grated cheese. Bake for about 45 minutes, or until the top is golden and bubbly. If possible, leave to stand for 30 minutes before serving, garnished with parsley.

RED BEAN CHILLI

SATISFYING, SPICY AND SIMPLE TO PREPARE, THIS VEGETARIAN CARIBBEAN VERSION OF THE CLASSIC MEXICAN CHILLI IS COMFORT FOOD AT ITS BEST. EXPERIMENT WITH DIFFERENT TYPES OF CHILLI PEPPERS, INCLUDING DRIED VARIETIES LIKE THE MEXICAN CHIPOTLES.

SERVES FOUR

INGREDIENTS
- 30ml/2 tbsp vegetable oil
- 1 onion, chopped
- 400g/14oz can chopped tomatoes
- 2 garlic cloves, crushed
- 300ml/½ pint/1¼ cups white wine
- about 300ml/½ pint/1¼ cups vegetable stock
- 115g/4oz/1 cup red lentils
- 2 fresh thyme sprigs or 5ml/1 tsp dried thyme
- 10ml/2 tsp ground cumin
- 45ml/3 tbsp dark soy sauce
- ½ fresh hot chilli, seeded and finely chopped
- 5ml/1 tsp ground mixed spice (pumpkin pie spice)
- 15ml/1 tbsp oyster sauce (optional)
- 225g/8oz can red kidney beans, drained
- 10ml/2 tsp sugar
- salt
- boiled white rice with corn, to serve

1 Heat the oil in a pan and fry the onion for 2–3 minutes, until slightly softened.

2 Add the tomatoes and garlic, cook for about 10 minutes, then stir in the white wine and vegetable stock.

VARIATION
This vegetarian chilli can be adapted to accommodate meat-eaters by substituting either minced (ground) beef or lamb for the lentils.

3 Stir in the lentils, thyme, cumin, soy sauce, chilli, spice and oyster sauce, if using.

COOK'S TIP
Fiery chillies can irritate the skin, so always wash your hands thoroughly after handling them and avoid touching your eyes.

4 Cover and simmer for 40 minutes or until the lentils are cooked, stirring occasionally and adding more water if the lentils begin to dry out.

5 Stir in the kidney beans and sugar and cook for 10 minutes more. Season to taste and serve with boiled white rice and corn.

PEPPERS STUFFED WITH BEANS

STUFFED PEPPERS ARE A POPULAR MEXICAN DISH. A SPECIAL VERSION – CHILES EN NOGADA – IS SERVED ON 28 AUGUST TO MARK INDEPENDENCE DAY. THE GREEN PEPPERS ARE SERVED WITH A FRESH WALNUT SAUCE AND POMEGRANATE SEEDS TO REPRESENT THE COLOURS OF THE MEXICAN FLAG.

SERVES SIX

INGREDIENTS

- 6 large green (bell) peppers
- 2 eggs, separated
- 2.5ml/½ tsp salt
- corn oil, for frying
- plain (all-purpose) flour, for dusting
- 120ml/4fl oz/½ cup whipping cream
- 115g/4oz/1 cup grated Cheddar cheese
- fresh coriander (cilantro) sprigs, to garnish

For the beans

- 350g/12oz/1¼ cups dried red kidney, pinto or black haricot (navy) beans
- 2 onions, finely chopped
- 2 garlic cloves, finely chopped
- 1 bay leaf
- 1 or more serrano chillies
- 120–150ml/8–10 tbsp corn oil
- 2 tomatoes, peeled, seeded and chopped
- salt

1 Put the beans into a pan and add cold water to cover. Add half the chopped onion, half the garlic, the bay leaf and the chillies. Bring to the boil and boil vigorously for about 10 minutes. Transfer the beans and liquid into a large flameproof casserole or pan, then cover and cook over a low heat for 30 minutes.

2 Add 15ml/1 tbsp of the corn oil to the beans and cook for a further 30 minutes or until the beans are tender. Add salt to taste and cook for 30 minutes more.

3 Remove the beans from the heat. Heat the remaining oil in a small frying pan and sauté the remaining onion and garlic until soft. Add the tomatoes and cook for a few minutes more. Add the tomato and onion mixture to the beans and set aside.

4 Roast the peppers over a gas flame or under a medium grill (broiler), turning occasionally, until the skins have blackened and blistered. Transfer the peppers to a plastic bag, secure the top and leave for 15 minutes.

5 Meanwhile, heat 30ml/2 tbsp of the oil in a large frying pan. Add about 45ml/3 tbsp of the beans. Mash them with a wooden spoon or potato masher, gradually adding more beans and oil until they have formed a heavy paste.

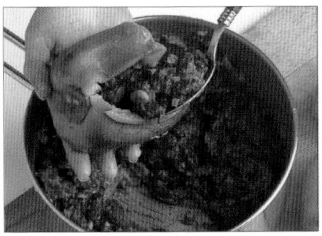

6 Preheat the oven to 180°C/350°F/Gas 4. Remove the peppers from the bag. Hold each pepper in turn under cold running water and rub off the skins. Slit the peppers down one side and remove the seeds and ribs. Stuff with the beans.

7 Beat the egg whites in a bowl until they stand in firm peaks. In another bowl, beat the yolks together with the salt. Fold gently into the whites.

8 Pour the corn oil into a large frying pan to a depth of about 2.5cm/1in and heat. Spread out the flour in a shallow bowl or dish.

9 Dip the filled peppers in the flour and then in the egg mix. Fry in batches until golden brown all over. Arrange the peppers in an ovenproof dish. Pour over the cream and sprinkle with the cheese. Bake for 30 minutes or until the topping is golden brown and the peppers are hot. Serve garnished with fresh coriander.

GREEN BEAN AND SWEET RED PEPPER SALAD

THIS FRESH MEXICAN SALAD LOOKS AND TASTES DELICIOUS, AND MAKES THE PERFECT SIDE DISH FOR A SUMMER PICNIC OR BARBECUE. TRY USING A COMBINATION OF GREEN, BLACK AND STUFFED OLIVES AS THE GARNISH, TO ADD COLOUR AND VARIETY.

SERVES FOUR

INGREDIENTS
- 350g/12oz/2½ cups cooked green beans, quartered
- 2 red (bell) peppers, seeded and chopped
- 2 spring onions (scallions), white and green parts, chopped
- 1 or more drained pickled serrano chillies, well rinsed, seeded and chopped
- 1 iceberg lettuce, coarsely shredded, or mixed salad leaves
- olives, to garnish

For the dressing
- 45ml/3 tbsp red wine vinegar
- 135ml/9 tbsp olive oil
- salt and ground black pepper

1 Combine the cooked green beans, chopped peppers, chopped spring onions and chillies in a salad bowl.

2 Make the salad dressing. Pour the red wine vinegar into a bowl or jug (pitcher). Add salt and ground black pepper to taste, then gradually whisk in the olive oil until well combined.

3 Pour the salad dressing over the prepared vegetables and toss lightly together to mix and coat thoroughly.

4 Line a large platter with the shredded lettuce leaves and arrange the salad-dressed vegetables on top. Garnish with the olives and serve.

SPICY VEGETABLE CHOW MEIN

CHOW MEIN IS POPULAR IN GUYANA, WHERE IT IS USUALLY MADE WITH SHREDDED CHICKEN OR PRAWNS. THIS VEGETARIAN VERSION CAN BE ADAPTED TO SUIT ALL TASTES.

SERVES THREE

INGREDIENTS
- 225g/8oz egg noodles
- 30–45ml/2–3 tbsp vegetable oil
- 2 garlic cloves, crushed
- 1 onion, chopped
- 1 small red (bell) pepper, chopped
- 1 small green (bell) pepper, chopped
- 115g/4oz fine green beans, blanched
- 2 celery sticks, finely chopped
- 2.5ml/½ tsp five-spice powder
- 1 vegetable stock cube, crumbled
- 2.5ml/½ tsp ground black pepper
- 15ml/1 tbsp soy sauce (optional)
- salt

COOK'S TIP
Shredded omelette or sliced hard-boiled eggs are popular garnishes for chow mein.

1 Cook the noodles in a large pan of salted boiling water for 10 minutes or according to the instructions on the packet, then drain and cool.

2 Heat the oil in a wok or large frying pan and stir-fry the garlic, onion, red and green peppers, beans and celery, tossing them together to mix.

3 Add the five-spice powder, vegetable stock cube and ground black pepper, stir well and cook for 5 minutes until the vegetables are just tender but still slightly crunchy.

4 Stir in the noodles and soy sauce, if using. Taste the chow mein and season with salt if required. Serve.

AUBERGINES STUFFED WITH SWEET POTATO

SLICES OF AUBERGINE ROLLED AROUND A SWEET POTATO AND CHEESE FILLING MAKE AN UNUSUAL CARIBBEAN SUPPER DISH, OR TRY THEM AS AN APPETIZER FOR A VEGETARIAN MEAL.

SERVES FOUR

INGREDIENTS
- 225g/8oz sweet potatoes, peeled and quartered
- 2.5ml/½ tsp chopped fresh thyme
- 75g/3oz Cheddar cheese, diced
- 25g/1oz/2 tbsp chopped spring onion (scallion)
- 15ml/1 tbsp each chopped red and green (bell) pepper
- 1 garlic clove, crushed
- 2 large aubergines (eggplant)
- 30ml/2 tbsp plain (all-purpose) flour
- 15ml/1 tbsp spice seasoning
- olive oil, for frying
- butter, for greasing
- 2 tomatoes, sliced
- salt and ground black pepper
- chopped fresh parsley, to garnish

1 Preheat the oven to 180°C/350°F/Gas 4. Cook the sweet potatoes in a pan of boiling water for 15–20 minutes, until tender, then drain and mash.

2 Add the thyme, cheese, spring onion, peppers and garlic. Mix well and season.

3 Cut each aubergine lengthways into four slices. Mix the flour and spice seasoning on a plate and dust over each aubergine slice.

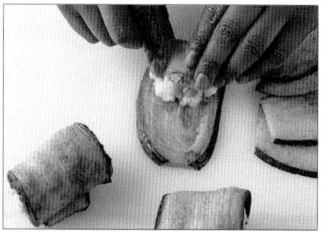

4 Heat a little oil in a large frying pan and fry each aubergine slice until browned, but not fully cooked. Drain and cool. Spoon a little of the potato mixture into the middle of each aubergine slice and roll up.

5 Butter two large pieces of foil and place four rolls on each. Top with slices of tomato. Wrap up the parcels and bake for 20 minutes. Serve hot, garnished with the parsley.

SPINACH PLANTAIN ROUNDS

THIS DELECTABLE WAY OF SERVING PLANTAINS IS POPULAR THROUGHOUT THE CARIBBEAN ISLANDS. THE PLANTAINS MUST BE FAIRLY RIPE, BUT STILL FIRM. THE ROUNDS CAN BE SERVED EITHER HOT OR COLD, WITH A SALAD, OR AS A VEGETABLE ACCOMPANIMENT.

SERVES FOUR

INGREDIENTS
- 2 large ripe plantains
- oil, for frying
- 15g/½oz/2 tbsp butter or margarine
- 25g/1oz/2 tbsp finely chopped onion
- 2 garlic cloves, crushed
- 450g/1lb fresh spinach, chopped
- pinch of freshly grated nutmeg
- 1 egg, beaten
- wholemeal (whole-wheat) flour, for dusting
- salt and ground black pepper

1 Using a small sharp knife, carefully cut each plantain lengthways into four pieces.

2 Heat a little oil in a large frying pan and fry the pieces of plantain on both sides until golden brown but not fully cooked. Lift out and drain on kitchen paper. Reserve the oil in the pan.

3 Melt the butter or margarine in a separate pan and sauté the onion and garlic for 2–3 minutes, until the onion is soft. Add the spinach and nutmeg, with salt and pepper to taste. Cover and cook for about 5 minutes, until the spinach has wilted. Cool, then tip into a sieve (strainer) and press out any excess moisture.

4 Curl the plantain pieces into rings and secure each ring with half a wooden cocktail stick (toothpick). Pack each ring with a little of the spinach mixture.

5 Place the egg and flour in two separate shallow dishes. Add a little more oil to the frying pan, if necessary, and heat until medium hot. Dip the plantain rings in the egg and then in the flour and fry on both sides for 1–2 minutes until golden brown. Drain on kitchen paper and serve.

PEPPERY BEAN SALAD

THIS PRETTY CARIBBEAN SALAD USES CANNED BEANS FOR SPEED AND CONVENIENCE. THE CONTRAST BETWEEN THE CRISP RADISHES AND PEPPERS AND THE SOFTER TEXTURE OF THE BEANS IS ONE REASON WHY IT WORKS SO WELL. THE TASTY DRESSING PLAYS A PART, TOO.

SERVES SIX

INGREDIENTS
- 425g/15oz can kidney beans, drained
- 425g/15oz can black-eyed beans (peas), drained
- 425g/15oz can chickpeas, drained
- ¼ red (bell) pepper
- ¼ green (bell) pepper
- 6 radishes
- 15ml/1 tbsp chopped spring onion (scallion)
- sliced spring onion, to garnish

For the dressing
- 5ml/1 tsp ground cumin
- 15ml/1 tbsp tomato ketchup
- 30ml/2 tbsp olive oil
- 15ml/1 tbsp white wine vinegar
- 1 garlic clove, crushed
- 2.5ml/½ tsp hot pepper sauce
- salt

1 Drain the canned beans and chickpeas into a colander and rinse them thoroughly under cold running water. Shake off the excess water and tip them into a large salad bowl.

2 Core, seed and roughly chop the peppers. Trim the radishes and slice them thinly. Add to the beans with the chopped pepper and spring onion.

3 In a small bowl, mix the ground cumin, ketchup, olive oil, white wine vinegar and garlic. Add the hot pepper sauce and a little salt to taste and stir again until thoroughly mixed.

4 Pour the dressing over the salad and mix thoroughly with a fork. Cover with clear film (plastic wrap) and chill for at least 1 hour before serving, garnished with sliced spring onion.

COOK'S TIP

For maximum flavour, it is best to allow the ingredients to marinate for at least 3–4 hours.

AVOCADO AND GRAPEFRUIT SALAD

THIS IS A LIGHT, REFRESHING LUNCH-TIME SALAD. THE BUTTERY TEXTURE OF THE AVOCADOS, COMBINES WITH THE TANGINESS OF THE GRAPEFRUIT TO MAKE THE PERFECT SUMMER DISH. SERVE IT AS A LIGHT MAIN COURSE OR AS AN ACCOMPANIMENT TO BARBECUED MEATS.

SERVES FOUR

INGREDIENTS
- 90ml/6 tbsp olive oil
- 30ml/2 tbsp white wine vinegar
- 1 pink grapefruit
- 2 large ripe avocados
- 1 cos or romaine lettuce, separated into leaves
- salt and ground black pepper

1 Using a balloon whisk or a fork, whisk the olive oil and white wine vinegar together in a large bowl, season to taste with salt and ground black pepper and vigorously whisk again.

VARIATIONS

Try other fruit combinations. Mango and strawberries go well together, as do papaya and limes.

2 Slice the top and bottom off the grapefruit. Peel the fruit by running a small knife all around it, between the peel and flesh. Make sure all the bitter pith is removed. Hold the grapefruit over the bowl containing the dressing and cut carefully between the membranes, so that all the segments fall into the bowl. Squeeze the remaining pulp over the bowl to extract all the juice.

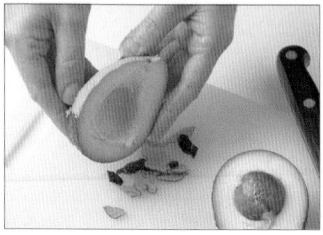

3 Run a knife around the length of the avocados. Twist the sides in opposite directions to separate the halves. Use a large spoon to remove the stone (pit), then peel the halves. Slice the flesh and cover these with the dressing, to stop them from discolouring.

4 Tear the lettuce into pieces and add to the bowl. Toss to coat. Adjust the seasoning to taste and serve.

QUINOA SALAD WITH CITRUS DRESSING

QUINOA IS A TYPE OF GRAIN GROWN IN THE ANDES. A STAPLE FOOD OF THE REGION, IT HAS BEEN CULTIVATED SINCE THE TIME OF THE INCAS AND AZTECS. QUINOA IS PACKED WITH PROTEIN AND IS ALSO GLUTEN FREE, SO IT IS IDEAL FOR VEGETARIANS AND THOSE WHO ARE GLUTEN INTOLERANT.

SERVES SIX

INGREDIENTS
- 175g/6oz/1 cup quinoa
- 90ml/6 tbsp olive oil
- juice of 2 limes
- juice of 1 large orange
- 2 fresh green chillies, seeded and finely chopped
- 2 garlic cloves, crushed
- ½ cucumber, peeled
- 1 large tomato, seeded and cubed
- 4 spring onions (scallions), sliced
- 30ml/2 tbsp chopped fresh mint
- 15ml/1 tbsp chopped fresh flat leaf parsley
- salt

COOK'S TIP
Quinoa can also be eaten plain as an accompaniment to meat or fish dishes.

1 Put the quinoa in a sieve (strainer), rinse thoroughly under cold water, then tip into a large pan. Pour in cold water to cover and bring to the boil. Lower the heat and simmer for 10–12 minutes, until tender. Drain and leave to cool.

2 Make a dressing by whisking the oil with the citrus juices. Stir in the chillies and garlic and season with salt.

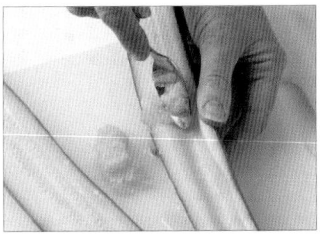

3 Cut the cucumber in half lengthways and, using a teaspoon, scoop out and discard the seeds. Cut into 5mm/¼in slices and add to the cooled quinoa with the tomato, spring onions and herbs. Toss well to combine.

4 Pour the dressing over the salad and toss again until well mixed. Check the seasoning and serve.

OKRA AND TOMATO SALAD

FOR THIS SALAD THE OKRA IS COOKED AS LITTLE AS POSSIBLE, KEEPING IT CRUNCHY. SERVE AS A SIDE SALAD, OR STIR IN SOME BABY SPINACH FOR A MEMORABLE MAIN COURSE.

SERVES FOUR

INGREDIENTS
- 60ml/4 tbsp olive oil
- 15ml/1 tbsp red wine vinegar
- 1 red onion, very thinly sliced
- 3 tomatoes, peeled and seeded
- 400g/14oz okra
- salt and ground black pepper

1 In a large bowl, whisk together the olive oil and red wine vinegar. Season with salt and ground black pepper. Toss the slices of red onion into the dressing and leave to marinate while you prepare and cook the okra.

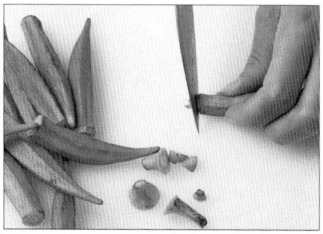

2 Trim the tough stalks from the okra, but avoid cutting into the pods, otherwise you will release a sticky liquid. Cook the okra in a pan of lightly salted boiling water for 4–5 minutes, until just tender. Drain and dry on kitchen paper. Leave the small okra whole, but cut any larger ones diagonally in half.

3 Stir the cooked okra into the dressing, mix thoroughly and leave to marinate for about 20–25 minutes.

4 Cut the tomatoes into thin wedges and add them to the bowl. Gently toss them together with the okra. Season to taste with salt and ground black pepper and serve immediately.

TOMATO, HEART OF PALM AND ONION SALAD

THIS SIMPLE SALAD CAN BE ASSEMBLED IN MINUTES. IT IS AN EXCELLENT DISH FOR INTRODUCING ANYONE TO THE DELICATE FLAVOUR OF PALM HEARTS.

SERVES FOUR

INGREDIENTS
- 4 beefsteak tomatoes
- 1 small onion, thinly sliced
- 400g/14oz can hearts of palm

For the dressing
- juice of 1 lime
- 10ml/2 tsp Dijon mustard
- 60ml/4 tbsp olive oil
- salt and ground black pepper

COOK'S TIP
If the tomatoes are not perfectly ripe, sprinkle the slices with a large pinch of caster (superfine) sugar, to help bring out their sweetness.

1 Cut the tomatoes into 1cm/½in slices and arrange on a large serving platter. Sprinkle the thin onion slices over the tomatoes and season to taste with salt and ground black pepper.

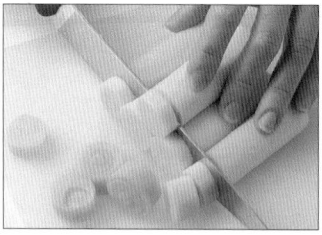

2 Drain the canned hearts of palm thoroughly, cut them into 1cm/½in slices and sprinkle the slices over the tomatoes and onions.

3 Make the dressing by whisking the lime juice, mustard and oil in a bowl. Season with salt and ground pepper. Drizzle over the salad and serve.

VARIATION
If you cannot get hearts of palm, this salad will be just as delicious using artichoke hearts instead.

SPICY POTATO SALAD

ADDING JUST A LITTLE CHILLI GIVES THIS CARIBBEAN SALAD A DELECTABLE SPICY FLAVOUR, WHICH IS BALANCED BY THE CREAMY DRESSING. IT MAKES A GOOD ACCOMPANIMENT TO GRILLED MEAT OR FISH.

SERVES SIX

INGREDIENTS
- 900g/2lb new potatoes, peeled
- 2 red (bell) peppers
- 2 celery sticks
- 1 shallot
- 2–3 spring onions (scallions)
- 1 fresh green chilli
- 1 garlic clove, crushed
- 10ml/2 tsp finely chopped fresh chives, plus extra to garnish
- 10ml/2 tsp finely chopped fresh basil
- 15ml/1 tbsp finely chopped fresh parsley
- 15ml/1 tbsp single (light) cream
- 15ml/1 tbsp mayonnaise
- 30ml/2 tbsp salad cream or extra mayonnaise
- 5ml/1 tsp mild mustard
- 2.5ml/½ tsp sugar

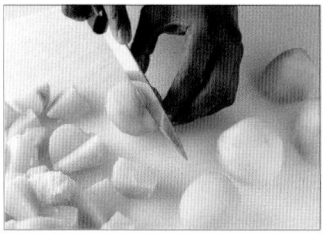

1 Cook the potatoes in a large pan of salted boiling water until tender but still firm. Drain and cool, then cut into 2.5cm/1in cubes and place in a large salad bowl.

COOK'S TIP
It is best to use waxy new potatoes for this dish, as older, floury ones may crumble or break up when boiled.

2 Cut the red peppers in half, cut away and discard the core and seeds, then cut into small pieces. Finely chop the celery, shallot and spring onions. Slice the chilli very thinly, discarding the seeds. Add the vegetables to the potatoes, with the garlic and chopped chives, basil and parsley.

3 Mix the cream, mayonnaise, salad cream or extra mayonnaise, mustard and sugar together in a small bowl. Stir until the mixture is well combined.

4 Pour the dressing over the potato and vegetable salad and stir gently to coat all the ingredients evenly. Garnish the salad with the extra chives just before it is served.

MANGO, TOMATO AND RED ONION SALAD

THIS SALAD MAKES A DELICIOUS APPETIZER AND IS OFTEN EATEN ON THE ISLANDS OF THE CARIBBEAN. UNDER-RIPE MANGO CONTRIBUTES A SUBTLE SWEETNESS THAT GOES WELL WITH THE TOMATO.

SERVES FOUR

INGREDIENTS
- 1 firm under-ripe mango
- 2 large tomatoes or 1 beefsteak tomato, sliced
- ½ cucumber, peeled and thinly sliced
- ½ red onion, sliced into rings
- 1 garlic clove, crushed
- 30ml/2 tbsp sunflower or vegetable oil
- 15ml/1 tbsp lemon juice
- 2.5ml/½ tsp hot pepper sauce
- salt and ground black pepper
- sugar, to taste
- chopped chives, to garnish

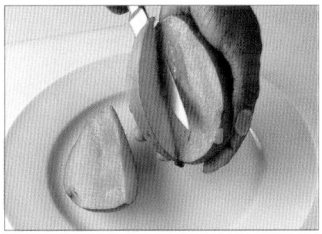

1 Using a sharp knife, cut a thick slice or "cheek" from either side of the mango stone. Peel away the skin and slice the flesh into thin strips. Peel the remaining mango, remove the rest of the flesh and slice it thinly.

2 Arrange a layer of tomato slices on a large serving plate or platter. Top with the cucumber slices, followed by the mango, and finish off with the thin slices of red onion.

3 Make the salad dressing. Crush the garlic clove into a small glass bowl. Add the oil, lemon juice, hot pepper sauce, salt, ground black pepper and sugar, if you like. Using a balloon whisk or a fork, whisk these ingredients together until thoroughly mixed.

4 Drizzle the dressing evenly over the salad and garnish with chopped chives. Serve immediately.

COOK'S TIP
Choose the freshest, ripest tomatoes available for the best flavour.

PERUVIAN SALAD

THIS IS A SPECTACULAR-LOOKING SALAD THAT COULD BE SERVED AS A SIDE DISH OR A LIGHT LUNCH. IN PERU, WHITE RICE WOULD BE USED, BUT BROWN RICE ADDS AN INTERESTING TEXTURE AND FLAVOUR.

SERVES FOUR

INGREDIENTS

- 225g/8oz/2 cups cooked long grain brown or white rice
- 15ml/1 tbsp chopped fresh parsley
- 1 red (bell) pepper
- 1 small onion, sliced into rings
- olive oil, for sprinkling
- 115g/4oz green beans, halved
- 50g/2oz/½ cup baby corn
- 4 quail's eggs, hard-boiled and halved
- 25–50g/1–2oz Spanish ham, cut into thin slices (optional)
- 1 small avocado
- lemon juice, for sprinkling
- 75g/3oz mixed salad leaves
- 15ml/1 tbsp capers
- about 10 stuffed olives, halved

For the dressing

- 1 garlic clove, crushed
- 60ml/4 tbsp olive oil
- 45ml/3 tbsp sunflower oil
- 30ml/2 tbsp lemon juice
- 45ml/3 tbsp natural (plain) yogurt
- 2.5ml/½ tsp mustard
- 2.5ml/½ tsp granulated sugar
- salt and ground black pepper

1 Make the dressing by placing all the ingredients in a bowl and whisking with a fork or whisk until smooth. Alternatively, place the ingredients in an empty jam jar, screw the lid on tightly and shake well.

2 Put the cooked rice into a large, glass salad bowl and spoon in half the dressing. Add the chopped parsley, stir well and set aside.

3 Cut the pepper in half, remove the seeds and pith, then place the halves, cut side down, in a small roasting pan. Add the onion rings. Sprinkle the onion with a little olive oil, place the pan under a hot grill (broiler) and cook for 5–6 minutes until the pepper blackens and blisters and the onion turns golden. You may need to stir the onion once or twice so that it cooks evenly.

4 Stir the onion in with the rice. Put the pepper in a plastic bag and knot the bag. When the steam has loosened the skin on the pepper halves and they are cool enough to handle, peel them and cut the flesh into thin strips.

5 Cook the green beans in boiling water for 2 minutes, then add the corn and cook for 1–2 minutes more, until tender. Drain both vegetables, refresh them under cold water, then drain again. Place in a large mixing bowl and add the red pepper strips, quail's eggs and ham, if using.

6 Peel the avocado, remove the stone (pit), and cut the flesh into slices or chunks. Sprinkle with the lemon juice. Put the salad leaves in a separate mixing bowl, add the avocado and mix lightly. Arrange the salad leaves and avocado on top of the rice.

7 Stir about 45ml/3 tbsp of the dressing into the green bean and pepper mixture. Pile this on top of the salad.

8 Sprinkle the capers and stuffed olives on top and serve the salad with the remaining dressing.

PUMPKIN SALAD

RED WINE VINEGAR BRINGS OUT THE SWEETNESS OF THE PUMPKIN. NO SALAD LEAVES ARE USED, JUST PLENTY OF FRESH PARSLEY. EATEN THROUGHOUT LATIN AMERICA, IT IS GREAT FOR A COLD BUFFET.

SERVES FOUR

INGREDIENTS

- 1 large red onion, peeled and very thinly sliced
- 200ml/7fl oz/scant 1 cup olive oil
- 60ml/4 tbsp red wine vinegar
- 675g/1½lb pumpkin, peeled and cut into 4cm/1½in pieces
- 40g/1½oz/¾ cup fresh flat leaf parsley leaves, chopped
- salt and ground black pepper

VARIATIONS

Try replacing the pumpkin with sweet potatoes. Wild rocket (arugula) or fresh coriander (cilantro) can be used instead of the parsley, if you prefer.

1 Mix the onion, olive oil and vinegar in a large bowl. Stir well to combine.

2 Put the pumpkin in a large pan of cold salted water. Bring to the boil, then lower the heat and simmer gently for 15–20 minutes. Drain.

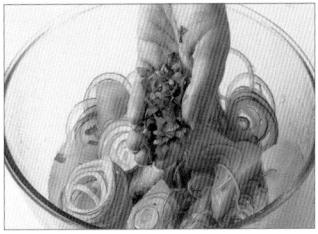

3 Immediately add the drained pumpkin to the bowl containing the dressing and toss lightly with your hands. Leave to cool. Stir in the chopped parsley, cover with clear film (plastic wrap) and chill. Allow the salad to come back to room temperature before serving.

Side Dishes and Salsas

Traditionally, Caribbean and Latin American meals consist of a meat, fish or poultry dish accompanied by rice, beans or potatoes and a combination of side dishes, such as rice and peas, or stir-fried kale. Salsa, whether hot and spicy or cool and refreshing, is served as a dish or stirred into dishes.

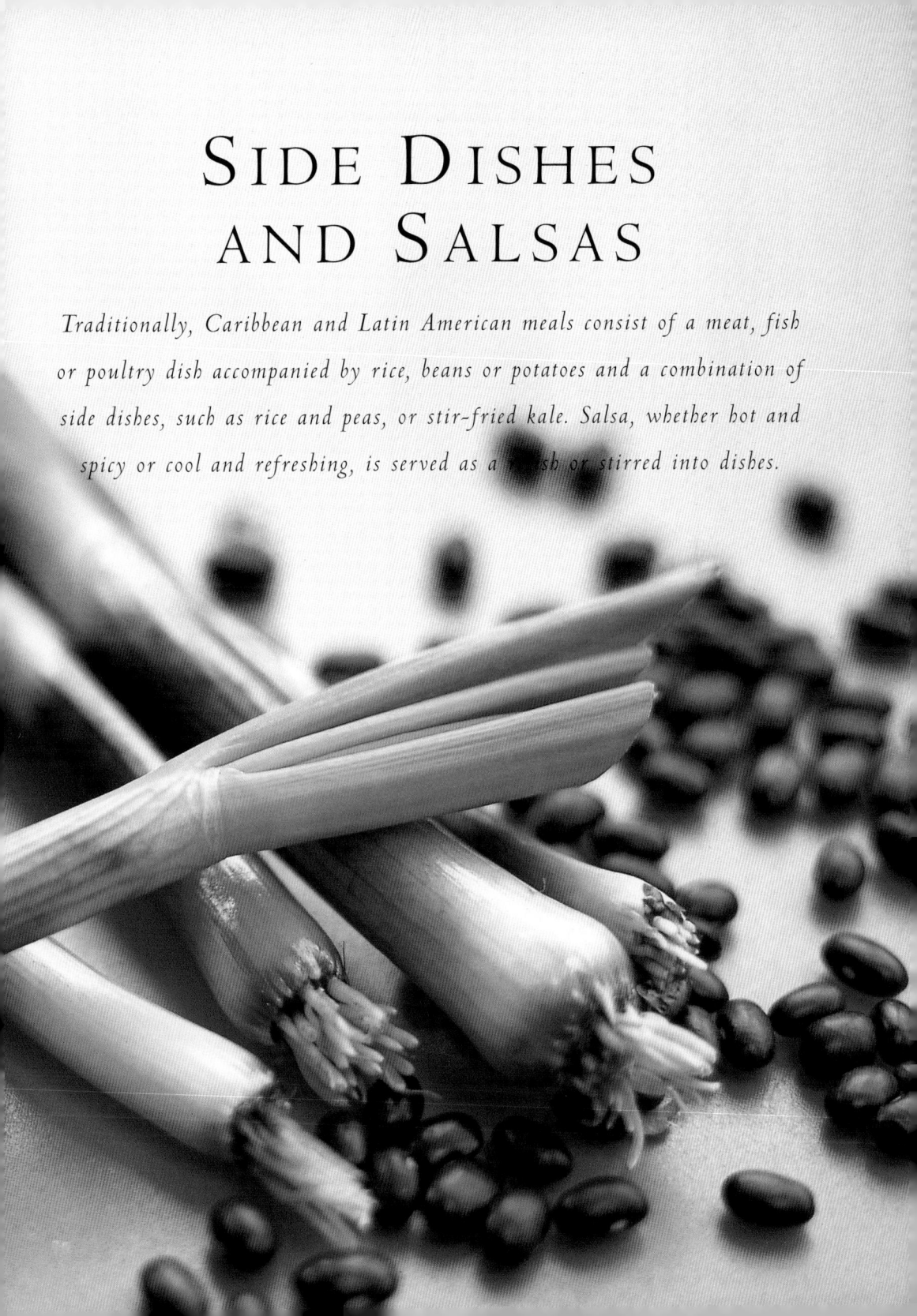

PLAIN RICE

RICE IS A STAPLE FOOD IN MANY PARTS OF LATIN AMERICA – IT IS EATEN AT MOST MEALS WITH ANYTHING AND EVERYTHING, AND IS OFTEN ACCOMPANIED BY BLACK BEANS.

SERVES FOUR

INGREDIENTS
- 200g/7oz/1 cup long grain rice
- 30ml/2 tbsp vegetable oil
- 2 garlic cloves, crushed
- 450ml/¾ pint/scant 2 cups water
- salt

COOK'S TIP
If the rice is still tough after steaming, add a little water, cover and return to the heat for a few minutes. If, instead, the rice is still sticky, return to the heat and cook over a very low heat with the lid off, until the excess moisture has evaporated.

1 Rinse the rice in a large bowl of cold water, then drain thoroughly in a fine sieve (strainer). Pour the oil into a heavy pan that has a tight-fitting lid. Heat gently, then add the garlic and cook, stirring, for 1 minute. Add the rice and stir for 2 minutes, until the grains are lightly toasted.

2 Pour in the water and season with salt. Bring to the boil, cover and lower the heat again to a very gentle simmer. Cook for 18 minutes, without lifting the lid. Remove from the heat and leave the rice to rest, covered, for 5 minutes. Transfer to a serving bowl and fluff up with a fork before taking to the table.

BLACK BEANS

YOU'LL FIND BEANS ON MOST LATIN TABLES, WHATEVER THE DAY OF THE WEEK OR OCCASION. THE RECIPE WILL VARY SLIGHTLY, DEPENDING ON THE COUNTRY, THE AVAILABILITY OF ADDITIONAL INGREDIENTS AND PERSONAL CHOICE. CHILLIES AND OTHER SPICES ARE OFTEN INCLUDED.

SERVES SIX

INGREDIENTS
- 450g/1lb/2½ cups black turtle beans, soaked overnight in water to cover
- 115g/4oz smoked streaky (fatty) bacon, in one piece
- 1 bay leaf
- 30ml/2 tbsp vegetable oil
- 2 garlic cloves, crushed
- salt

COOK'S TIP
Do not season the beans until they are cooked, or they will become tough. As the sauce thickens, the beans have a tendency to stick, so stir frequently after returning the refried beans to the pan.

1 Drain the beans and put them in a large heavy pan. Cover generously with cold water. Add the bacon and bay leaf and bring to the boil. Skim the surface of the liquid, then lower the heat to a simmer. Cook for at least 1 hour or until the beans are tender, topping up the water if necessary.

2 Heat the oil in a pan over medium heat. Cook the garlic for 2 minutes. Add two ladles of cooked beans and fry for 2–3 minutes, breaking up the beans.

3 Tip the refried beans back into the saucepan and season. Simmer over a very low heat for 10 minutes, then serve.

COCONUT RICE

DELICIOUSLY MOIST AND FULL OF FLAVOUR, COCONUT RICE IS AN EXCELLENT ACCOMPANIMENT FOR ALL SORTS OF MAIN DISHES – THIS COLOMBIAN VERSION IS PARTICULARLY GOOD WITH FISH.

SERVES FOUR

INGREDIENTS
- 3 x 400ml/14fl oz cans coconut milk
- 5ml/1 tsp light brown sugar
- 200g/7oz/1 cup long grain rice
- salt
- 15g/½oz/1 tbsp butter

1 Pour the coconut milk into a large pan that has a tight-fitting lid. Stir in the sugar. Bring to the boil and simmer until the liquid is reduced by half.

2 Add the rice to the pan, season with salt and bring to the boil. Lower the heat to a simmer and cook, stirring often, for 5 minutes.

3 Stir the butter into the rice and cover the pan tightly. Simmer gently for a further 15 minutes, then remove from the heat. Leave covered for 5 minutes before transferring to a serving bowl.

COOK'S TIP
Canned coconut milk is available sweetened as well as plain – be sure to buy the unsweetened, plain type for savoury cooking.

VARIATION
This tasty side dish is equally good when made with other varieties of rice. Depending on preference, try using short-grain, medium-grain or basmati.

TOASTED CASSAVA FLOUR WITH EGG AND BACON

BRAZILIAN COOKS MAKE GREAT USE OF FAROFA, *FLAVOURED TOASTED CASSAVA FLOUR, SPRINKLING IT OVER MEAT OR FISH DISHES TO MOP UP THE JUICES. TRY THIS VERSION WITH RICE AND BEANS.*

SERVES SIX

INGREDIENTS
- 15g/½oz/1 tbsp butter
- 90g/3½oz streaky (fatty) bacon, in one piece
- 2 eggs, lightly beaten
- 15ml/1 tbsp water
- 225g/8oz/2 cups toasted cassava flour
- 15ml/1 tbsp chopped fresh parsley
- salt

COOK'S TIP
Cassava flour resembles dried breadcrumbs. Look for it in Latin American or Portuguese stores, where it will be labelled *farinha de mandioca*. It is sometimes called cassava meal.

1 Melt the butter in a pan over a low heat. Dice the bacon and add to the pan. Sauté for 5 minutes, until golden.

2 Mix the eggs with the water in a cup or small bowl. Tip the mixture into the pan and stir until it starts to set. The eggs should have the consistency of soft scrambled eggs – do not overcook them.

3 Add the cassava flour and stir vigorously over the heat for 1 minute, until thoroughly combined. Remove from the heat and stir in the chopped parsley. Season to taste with salt and transfer to a bowl to serve.

RICE AND PEAS

IT MAY SEEM ODD THAT A DISH WITH KIDNEY BEANS AS A PRIMARY INGREDIENT IS CALLED RICE AND PEAS, BUT IN JAMAICA, WHERE IT ORIGINATED, FRESH PIGEON PEAS WERE ORIGINALLY USED. SINCE THE PEAS ARE SEASONAL, THE DISH IS MORE OFTEN MADE WITH DRIED KIDNEY BEANS.

SERVES SIX

INGREDIENTS

- 200g/7oz/1 cup red kidney beans
- 2 fresh thyme sprigs
- 50g/2oz piece of creamed coconut or 120ml/4fl oz/½ cup coconut cream
- 2 bay leaves
- 1 onion, finely chopped
- 2 garlic cloves, crushed
- 2.5ml/½ tsp ground allspice
- 1 red or green (bell) pepper, seeded and chopped
- 600ml/1 pint/2½ cups water
- 450g/1lb/2½ cups long grain rice
- salt and ground black pepper

1 Put the red kidney beans in a large bowl. Pour in enough cold water to cover the beans generously. Cover the bowl and leave the beans to soak overnight.

2 Drain the beans and tip them into a large pan with a tight-fitting lid. Pour in enough water to cover the beans. Bring to the boil and boil for 10 minutes, then lower the heat and simmer for 1½ hours or until the beans are tender.

3 Add the thyme, creamed coconut or coconut cream, bay leaves, onion, garlic, allspice and pepper. Season and stir in the measured water.

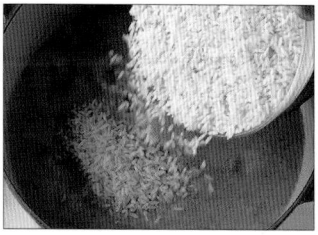

4 Bring to the boil and add the rice. Stir well, reduce the heat and cover the pan. Simmer for 25–30 minutes, until all the liquid has been absorbed. Serve as an accompaniment to fish, meat or vegetarian dishes.

COU-COU

THIS TASTY OKRA AND MASHED CORN MEAL PUDDING IS A BAJAN NATIONAL DISH. TRADITIONALLY, IT IS SERVED WITH FRESH FLYING FISH COOKED IN A CARIBBEAN GRAVY, BUT IT CAN ALSO BE SERVED WITH ANY OTHER FISH, MEAT OR VEGETABLE STEW.

SERVES FOUR

INGREDIENTS

- 115g/4oz okra, trimmed and roughly chopped
- 225g/8oz/1½ cups coarse corn meal
- 600ml/1 pint/2½ cups water or coconut milk
- 25g/1oz/2 tbsp butter
- salt and ground black pepper

COOK'S TIP

Adding unsweetened coconut milk instead of water will give your cou-cou a special, rich flavour.

1 Bring a pan of water seasoned with a little salt and pepper to the boil. Add the chopped okra and cook for about 10 minutes. Remove the okra with a slotted spoon and set it aside.

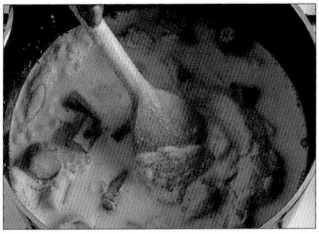

2 Pour away half the liquid from the pan, then return the pan to the heat. Return the okra to the pan, then gradually beat in the corn meal.

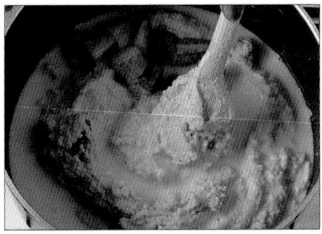

3 Cook on a very low heat, beating the mixture vigorously. Gradually add the measured water or coconut milk, beating after each addition to prevent the mixture from sticking to the pan and burning.

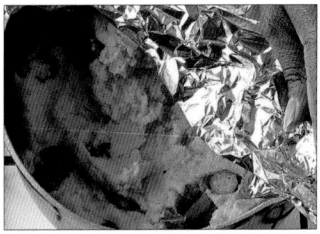

4 Cover and cook for about 20 minutes, beating occasionally. The cou-cou is cooked when the corn meal granules are soft. Cover with foil and then a lid to keep the mixture moist and hot until required. Spread with butter before serving.

BUTTERED SPINACH AND RICE

THE LAYER OF FRESH COOKED SPINACH IN THIS POPULAR CARIBBEAN DISH IS SAID TO HAVE BEEN THE RESULT OF A HAPPY ACCIDENT. IT WAS INTENDED FOR A SEPARATE DISH, BUT THE COOK FORGOT TO ADD IT SO SIMPLY USED IT TO TOP THE RICE INSTEAD.

SERVES FOUR

INGREDIENTS
- 40g/1½oz/3 tbsp butter or margarine
- 1 onion, finely chopped
- 2 fresh tomatoes, chopped
- 450g/1lb/2½ cups basmati rice, rinsed
- 2 garlic cloves, crushed
- 600ml/1 pint/2½ cups stock or water
- 350g/12oz fresh spinach, shredded
- salt and ground black pepper
- 2 tomatoes, sliced, to garnish

COOK'S TIP
If you are unable to get fresh spinach, use frozen leaf spinach instead. Thaw and drain approximately 225g/8oz frozen spinach and cook on top of the rice for about 5 minutes. If you prefer, finely shredded spring greens (collards) make a delicious alternative to spinach.

1 Melt 25g/1oz/2 tbsp of butter or margarine in a large pan with a tight-fitting lid. Gently fry the onion for 3–4 minutes, until soft and translucent. Stir in the fresh chopped tomatoes.

2 Add the basmati rice and crushed garlic, gently cook for 5 minutes, then gradually add the stock or water, stirring constantly. Season to taste with plenty of salt and ground black pepper.

3 Cover and simmer gently for 10–15 minutes, until the rice is almost cooked, then reduce the heat to low.

4 Spread the spinach in a thick layer over the rice. Cover the pan and cook over a low heat for 5–8 minutes, until the spinach has wilted. Spoon into a serving dish, dot the remaining butter over the top and garnish with the sliced tomatoes. Serve immediately.

CREAMED SWEET POTATOES

SIMILAR TO TRADITIONAL MASHED POTATOES, THIS CARIBBEAN SPECIALITY USES WHITE SWEET POTATOES INSTEAD OF THE ORANGE VARIETY. THE GRATED NUTMEG ADDS AN EXTRA, IRRESISTIBLE SWEETNESS.

SERVES FOUR

INGREDIENTS
- 900g/2lb sweet potatoes
- 50g/2oz/¼ cup butter
- 45ml/3 tbsp single (light) cream
- freshly grated nutmeg
- 15ml/1 tbsp chopped fresh chives
- salt and ground black pepper

COOK'S TIP
If you cannot get white sweet potatoes, white yams make a good substitute, especially poona (Ghanaian) yam.

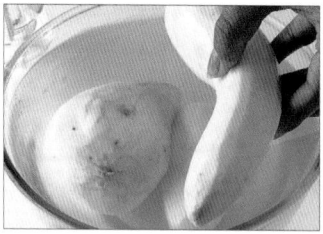

1 Peel the sweet potatoes under cold running water and place in a bowl of salted water to prevent them from discolouring. Cut them into large chunks and place in a pan of cold water. Cook, covered, for 20–30 minutes until tender.

2 Drain the potatoes and return them to the dry pan. Add the butter, cream, nutmeg, chives and seasoning. Mash with a potato masher and then fluff up with a fork. Serve warm as an accompaniment to a curry or stew.

COLOMBIAN CHEESY POTATOES

TENDER NEW POTATOES TOPPED WITH A CREAMY CHEESE AND TOMATO SAUCE MAKE A DELICIOUS SIDE DISH, WHICH IS GREAT SERVED WITH MEAT, POULTRY OR FISH DISHES.

SERVES SIX

INGREDIENTS
- 1kg/2¼lb new or salad potatoes
- 25g/1oz/2 tbsp butter
- 4 spring onions (scallions), thinly sliced
- 2 large tomatoes, peeled, seeded and chopped
- 200ml/7fl oz/scant 1 cup double (heavy) cream
- 90g/3½oz/1 cup grated mozzarella
- salt and ground black pepper

1 Place the potatoes in a large pan of salted cold water. Cover and bring to the boil. Lower the heat and simmer for 18-20 minutes, until tender.

2 Meanwhile, melt the butter in a frying pan over a low heat, add the spring onions and cook gently, stirring occasionally, for 5 minutes, until softened. Stir in the tomatoes and cook for a further 2–3 minutes, stirring occasionally, until the tomatoes break up.

3 Drain the potatoes and put them in a warmed serving bowl. Add the cream to the onion and tomato mixture, bring to the boil, then add the cheese, stirring until it melts. Season with salt and pepper to taste. Pour the hot sauce over the potatoes and serve immediately.

CARIBBEAN POTATO SALAD

COLOURFUL VEGETABLES IN A CREAMY SMOOTH DRESSING MAKE THIS PIQUANT CARIBBEAN SALAD IDEAL TO SERVE ON ITS OWN OR WITH GRILLED OR COLD MEATS.

SERVES SIX

INGREDIENTS

- 900g/2lb small waxy or salad potatoes
- 2 red (bell) peppers, seeded and diced
- 2 celery sticks, finely chopped
- 1 shallot, finely chopped
- 2 or 3 spring onions (scallions), finely chopped
- 1 mild fresh green chilli, seeded and finely chopped
- 1 garlic clove, crushed
- 10ml/2 tsp finely snipped chives
- 10ml/2 tsp finely chopped basil
- 15ml/1 tbsp finely chopped parsley
- 15ml/1 tbsp single (light) cream
- 30ml/2 tbsp salad cream
- 15ml/1 tbsp mayonnaise
- 5ml/1 tsp Dijon mustard
- 7.5ml/½ tbsp sugar
- snipped chives, to garnish
- chopped red chilli, to garnish

1 Cook the potatoes in a large saucepan of boiling water until tender but still firm. Drain and leave to one side. When cool enough to handle, cut the cooked potatoes into 2.5cm/1in cubes and place in a large salad bowl.

2 Add all the vegetables to the potatoes in the salad bowl, together with the chopped chilli, crushed garlic and all the chopped herbs.

3 Mix together the cream, salad cream, mayonnaise, mustard and sugar in a small bowl. Stir well until the mixture is thoroughly combined and forms a smooth dressing.

4 Pour the dressing over the potato mixture and stir gently to coat evenly. Serve immediately, garnished with the snipped chives and chopped red chilli.

VARIATIONS

Try adding other vegetables to this potato salad, such as tomatoes for flavour or lightly cooked green beans for a tasty crunch. Many traditional potato salads also include a coarsely chopped hard-boiled egg. This would work just as well in this Caribbean version, if you like.

OKRA FRIED RICE

OKRA WAS INTRODUCED TO MAINLAND SOUTH AMERICA AND THE ISLANDS OF THE CARIBBEAN BY THE AFRICAN SLAVES WHO WERE BROUGHT OVER TO WORK THE SUGAR PLANTATIONS. IT BECAME AN IMPORTANT AND MUCH-VALUED INGREDIENT.

SERVES FOUR

INGREDIENTS
- 15ml/1 tbsp butter or margarine
- 30ml/2 tbsp vegetable oil
- 1 garlic clove, crushed
- ½ red onion, finely chopped
- 115g/4oz okra, trimmed
- 30ml/2 tbsp diced green and red (bell) peppers
- 2.5ml/½ tsp dried thyme
- 2 fresh green chillies, finely chopped
- 2.5ml/½ tsp five-spice powder
- 1 vegetable stock (bouillon) cube
- 30ml/2 tbsp soy sauce
- 15ml/1 tbsp chopped fresh coriander (cilantro)
- 225g/8oz/2 cups cooked long grain white rice
- salt and ground black pepper
- fresh coriander, to garnish

1 Melt the butter or margarine in the oil in a frying pan or wok. Add the garlic and onion, and cook over a medium heat for 5 minutes, until the onion is soft but not browned.

2 Trim the okra, cutting off the stalks and points, then thinly slice the pods. Add to the pan or wok and cook gently for 6–7 minutes.

3 Add the green and red peppers, thyme, chillies and five-spice powder. Cook for 3 minutes, then crumble in the stock cube.

4 Add the soy sauce, chopped coriander and rice, and heat through, stirring well. Season with salt and pepper. Spoon into a dish and serve hot, garnished with the coriander sprigs.

AUBERGINES WITH GARLIC AND SPRING ONIONS

THIS IS A SUPERB WAY OF SERVING AUBERGINES. IT CAN BE MADE EVEN MORE DELICIOUS BY ADDING LITTLE STRIPS OF SMOKED SALMON AT THE LAST MINUTE AND LETTING THEM JUST WARM THROUGH.

SERVES FOUR

INGREDIENTS
- 45ml/3 tbsp vegetable oil
- 2 garlic cloves, crushed
- 3 tomatoes, peeled and chopped
- 900g/2lb aubergines (eggplants), cut into chunks
- 150ml/¼ pint/⅔ cup vegetable stock or water
- 30ml/2 tbsp soy sauce
- 60ml/4 tbsp chopped spring onion (scallion)
- ½ red (bell) pepper, seeded and chopped
- 1 fresh hot chilli, seeded and chopped
- 30ml/2 tbsp chopped fresh coriander (cilantro)
- salt and ground black pepper

1 Heat the oil in a wok or frying pan and fry the garlic and tomatoes for 3–4 minutes. Add the aubergines and toss with the garlic and tomatoes.

2 Pour in the stock or water and cover the pan. Simmer gently until the aubergines are very soft. Stir in the soy sauce and half of the spring onions.

3 Add the red pepper and chilli to the aubergine. Season with salt and pepper to taste. Mix well.

4 Stir in the coriander and sprinkle with the remaining spring onion. Spoon the aubergine mixture into a dish and serve at once. Alternatively, allow to cool until warm before serving.

CASSAVA WITH A CITRUS SALSA

THIS DISH CONSISTS OF DICED CASSAVA IN A CLASSIC CUBAN SAUCE CALLED MOJO. *WHEN THE COOKED CASSAVA IS COATED IN THE SHARP DRESSING, IT BECOMES IMBUED WITH THE DELICIOUS FLAVOURS OF FRESH ORANGE, LIME AND GARLIC.*

SERVES FOUR

INGREDIENTS
- 800g/1¾lb cassava, peeled and cut into chunks
- 2 garlic cloves, crushed
- juice of 1 small orange
- juice of 1 lime
- 45ml/3 tbsp olive oil
- 15ml/1 tbsp chopped fresh flat leaf parsley
- salt

VARIATION

Mojo is also delicious with cooked pumpkin and sweet potatoes.

1 Cook the cassava in a large pan of salted boiling water for 20–25 minutes, until beginning to break up. Drain in a colander and then transfer to a large serving plate.

2 Mix the garlic, orange juice and lime juice in a bowl. Whisk in the oil, season with salt and stir in the parsley. Drizzle the dressing over the cooked cassava and serve.

STIR-FRIED SPRING GREENS

SPRING GREENS ARE VERY POPULAR IN BRAZIL. THEY ARE EATEN WITH MEAT AND ARE THE TRADITIONAL ACCOMPANIMENT TO FEIJOADA. *GARLIC ENHANCES THEIR SLIGHTLY BITTER FLAVOUR, AND THEY TASTE EVEN BETTER WHEN COOKED WITH BACON AND CHILLIES.*

SERVES SIX

INGREDIENTS

- 450g/1lb spring (collard) greens
- 15ml/1 tbsp vegetable oil
- 150g/5oz smoked streaky (fatty) bacon, in one piece
- 2 garlic cloves, crushed
- 1.5ml/¼ tsp crushed dried chillies
- salt

VARIATIONS

- If you cannot find spring greens, use curly kale or Savoy cabbage instead. These may not be as vibrant in colour, but the taste will be very similar.
- Cubed pancetta can be used instead of the bacon.

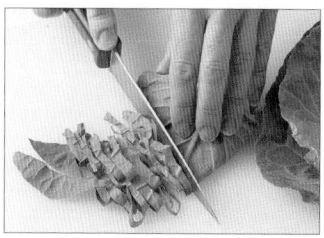

1 Cut off the hard stalks from the spring greens. Lay the leaves flat on top of each other and roll into a tight cigar-shape. Slice very thinly, using a sharp knife.

2 Heat the oil in a large frying pan over a low heat. Cut the bacon into small cubes and sauté in the oil for 5 minutes, or until golden brown. Lift the cubes out of the pan with a slotted spoon and drain on kitchen paper.

3 Increase the heat, add the crushed garlic and dried chillies to the oil remaining in the pan, and stir-fry for about 30 seconds.

4 Add the shredded spring greens and toss over the heat until just tender. Season to taste with salt, stir in the cooked bacon cubes and serve immediately.

CORN STICKS

THIS TRADITIONAL CARIBBEAN RECIPE PRODUCES PERFECT CORN BREAD IN A LOAF TIN. ALTERNATIVELY, IF YOU CAN FIND THE MOULDS, IT CAN BE USED TO MAKE ATTRACTIVE CORN STICKS.

MAKES FORTY

INGREDIENTS
- 225g/8oz/2 cups plain (all-purpose) flour
- 225g/8oz/2 cups fine corn meal
- 50ml/10 tsp bicarbonate of soda (baking soda)
- 2.5ml/½ tsp salt
- 60ml/4 tbsp demerara (raw) sugar
- 450ml/¾ pint/scant 2 cups milk
- 2 eggs
- 50g/2oz/4 tbsp butter or margarine

COOK'S TIP
Because there is such a lot of bicarbonate of soda used in this recipe, the corn meal mixture begins to rise as soon as the liquid is added, so make sure you bake straight away.

1 Preheat the oven to 190°C/375°F/Gas 5 and grease either corn bread moulds, if you can find them, or a 900g/2lb loaf tin (pan).

2 Sift together the flour, corn meal, bicarbonate of soda, salt and sugar into a large bowl. In a separate bowl, whisk the milk and eggs, then stir into the flour mixture.

3 Melt the butter or margarine in a small pan and stir gradually into the corn meal mixture.

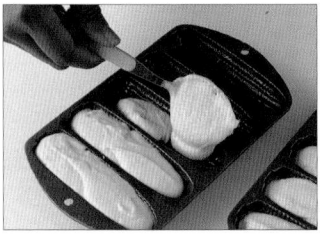

4 Carefully spoon the thick mixture into the moulds or tin. Bake the corn sticks for about 15 minutes. If using a loaf tin, you will need to bake for around 30–35 minutes, until the corn bread is golden and hollow sounding when tapped.

FRIED YELLOW PLANTAINS

WHEN PLANTAINS ARE YELLOW IT IS A SIGN THAT THEY ARE RIPE. THEY ARE OFTEN ADDED TO MEAT, FISH OR VEGETARIAN DISHES IN THE CARIBBEAN, OR SERVED AS A TASTY ACCOMPANIMENT.

SERVES FOUR

INGREDIENTS
- 2 yellow plantains
- oil, for shallow frying
- finely chopped chives, to garnish

1 Using a small sharp knife, trim the tops and tails of each plantain, then cut them in half.

2 Slit the skin along the natural ridges of each piece of plantain, and ease up using the tip of your thumb.

3 Peel away the entire plantain skin and discard. Thinly slice the plantains lengthways.

4 Heat a little oil in a frying pan and fry the plantain slices for 2–3 minutes on each side, until they are golden brown.

5 When the plantains are brown and crisp, drain on kitchen paper and serve sprinkled with chives.

COOK'S TIP

For the sweetest flavour, these gently fried plantain slices should be made using the ripest plantains available. The darker the skin, the riper the plantains are.

ARGENTINIAN BARBECUE SALSA

THIS COMBINATION OF FINELY CHOPPED VEGETABLES AND TART DRESSING IS THE PERFECT PARTNER FOR ALL TYPES OF GRILLED MEATS, SO IT IS NOT SURPRISING TO FIND BOWLS OF FRESH SALSA CREOLLA *ON THE TABLE WHENEVER A BARBECUE OR* ASADO *IS BEING PEPARED. SIMILAR BARBECUE SALSAS CAN ALSO BE FOUND IN BRAZIL, URUGUAY AND PARAGUAY.*

SERVES SIX

INGREDIENTS
- 2 fresh green chillies, seeded and very finely chopped
- 1 garlic clove, crushed
- 1 onion, very finely chopped
- 1 large tomato, peeled, seeded and very finely chopped
- 15ml/1 tbsp finely chopped fresh flat leaf parsley
- salt
- 105ml/7 tbsp olive oil
- 30ml/2 tbsp red wine vinegar

1 Combine the chopped chillies, crushed garlic, onion and tomato in a bowl. Stir in the chopped parsley and season to taste with salt.

2 Pour in the oil and vinegar and stir well. Allow the flavours to mingle for at least 1 hour before serving with grilled (broiled) or barbecued meats.

HOT CHILLI SALSA

CONTRARY TO POPULAR BELIEF, LATIN FOOD IS NOT INTRINSICALLY SPICY. IT IS THE HOT CHILLI OILS AND SALSAS, ADDED TO DISHES AT THE TABLE, THAT FAN THE FLAMES.

MAKES ONE SMALL JAR

INGREDIENTS
- 10 fresh red chillies, roughly chopped
- 1 large tomato, peeled and quartered
- 2 garlic cloves
- juice of 1 lime
- 60ml/4 tbsp olive oil
- salt

COOK'S TIP
Treat this salsa with extreme caution. Just the oil is enough to add serious heat to a dish, especially if the salsa has had a chance to age. A couple of drops of the oil are enough for most people!

1 Place the chillies, tomato and garlic in a food processor, then process the mixture until smooth.

2 Scrape the mixture into a small frying pan and place over a medium heat. Season with salt and cook, stirring, for 10 minutes, until the sauce is thick.

3 Remove from the heat and stir in the freshly squeezed lime juice. Transfer to a sterilized airtight jar and top with a thin film of olive oil before tightly screwing on the lid. As long as the sauce always has a film of oil on top, it will keep for ages at room temperature or in the refrigerator.

TAMARILLO SAUCE

THIS UNUSUAL PERUVIAN SAUCE MAKES A DELICIOUS DIP FOR SERVING WITH AREPAS *– THOSE IRRESISTIBLE CORN MEAL GRIDDLE CAKES THAT ARE FREQUENTLY FILLED WITH SOFT WHITE CHEESE. ALTERNATIVELY, ITS DELICIOUS, HOT AND SPICY FLAVOUR CONTRASTS BEAUTIFULLY WITH THE NATURAL SWEETNESS OF FRESH GRILLED SEAFOOD.*

SERVES FOUR

INGREDIENTS
- 450g/1lb fresh tamarillos
- 2.5ml/½ tsp ground ginger
- 1.5ml/¼ tsp ground cinnamon
- 1 fresh red chilli, seeded and chopped
- 1 small onion, finely chopped
- 5ml/1 tsp light brown sugar
- 105ml/7 tbsp water
- 30ml/2 tbsp olive oil
- salt

COOK'S TIP
If tamarillos are heavier than they look, they will be ripe and juicy.

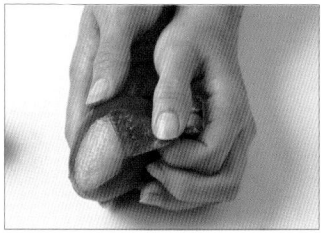

1 Place the whole fresh tamarillos in a large pan of boiling water for about 30 seconds. Drain, refresh in cold water, then carefully remove the peel with a sharp knife and discard it. Roughly chop the tamarillos.

2 Place the ginger and cinnamon in a small heavy pan over a low heat. Stir the mixture for 30 seconds, until the spices release their aroma. Add the chopped tamarillos, chilli, onion, sugar and water.

3 Bring to the boil, lower the heat, cover and simmer for 20 minutes. Remove the lid and continue cooking until the sauce thickens. Stir in the oil and season with salt. Serve with grilled (broiled) seafood.

AVOCADO SALSA

THERE ARE MANY VERSIONS OF AVOCADO SALSA, INCLUDING THE CLASSIC MEXICAN GUACAMOLE. *HERE THE INGREDIENTS ARE CHOPPED AND DICED, RATHER THAN MASHED, WHICH ADDS TEXTURE AND ALLOWS ALL THE DELICIOUS FLAVOURS TO REMAIN DISTINCT. PREPARE THIS SALSA AT THE LAST MINUTE TO AVOID THE AVOCADOS DISCOLOURING.*

SERVES FOUR

INGREDIENTS
- 1 large ripe avocado
- juice of 1 lime
- 15ml/1 tbsp red wine vinegar
- 1 tomato, peeled, seeded and chopped
- 1 green (bell) pepper, seeded and diced
- 1 red onion, finely chopped
- 1 fresh red chilli, seeded and finely chopped
- 45ml/3 tbsp olive oil
- salt

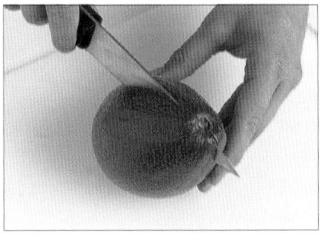

1 Prepare the avocado. Run a sharp knife around the whole length of the avocado, cutting right in until you touch the stone (pit). Twist the two sides of the split avocado in opposite directions to separate the two halves.

2 Use a large spoon to remove the large stone, then peel both halves of the avocado. Dice the flesh and put it in a bowl with the lime juice.

3 Stir the vinegar, tomato, pepper, onion and chilli into the avocado and lime juice mixture. Gradually add the olive oil, mixing well.

COOK'S TIP

If there is any delay before serving this salsa, add the avocado stone to the mixture. This will prevent any discoloration. Remember to remove the stone before serving though.

4 Season to taste with salt and serve with tortilla chips, or as an accompaniment to meat, fish or poultry.

Breads and Cakes

European-style breads and cakes are available in most parts of the Caribbean and Latin America, but the recipes have evolved to reflect regional traditions, with corn meal often being used instead of wheat flour. The breads make good accompaniments while the cakes are often eaten for breakfast or as snacks.

CORN TORTILLAS

TO MAKE THESE DELICIOUS MEXICAN SPECIALITIES, MAKE SURE YOU HAVE READY A TORTILLA PRESS AND A SMALL PLASTIC BAG, CUT OPEN AND HALVED CROSSWAYS.

MAKES ABOUT FOURTEEN

INGREDIENTS
- 275g/10oz/2½ cups *masa harina*
- 250–350ml/8–12fl oz/ 1–1½ cups water

COOK'S TIP
Tortillas are very easy to make but it is important to get the dough texture right. If it is too dry and crumbly, add a little water; if it is too wet, add more *masa harina*. If you misjudge the pressure needed for flattening the ball of dough to a neat circle on the tortilla press, just scrap it off, re-roll it and try again.

1 Put the *masa harina* into a bowl and stir in 250ml/8fl oz/1 cup of the water, mixing it to a soft dough that just holds together. If it is too dry, add a little more water. Cover the bowl with a cloth and set aside for 15 minutes.

2 Preheat the oven to 150°C/300°F/ Gas 2. Open the tortilla press and line both sides with the prepared plastic sheets. Preheat a griddle until hot.

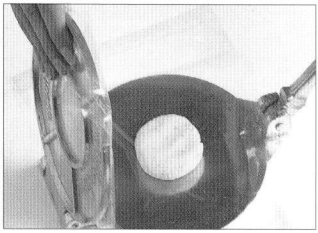

3 Knead the dough lightly and shape into 14 balls. Put a ball on the press and bring the top down firmly to flatten the dough out into a round.

4 Open the press. Peel off the top layer of plastic and, using the bottom layer, lift the tortilla out of the press. Peel off the bottom plastic and flip the tortilla on to the hot griddle.

5 Cook for 1 minute and turn over and cook for a minute more. Wrap in foil and keep warm. Repeat for the other tortillas.

FLOUR TORTILLAS

THESE ARE MORE COMMON THAN CORN TORTILLAS IN THE NORTH OF MEXICO, FROM SONORA TO CHIHUAHUA, WHERE WHEAT IS GROWN. FOR THE BEST RESULTS, USE A GOOD QUALITY PLAIN FLOUR.

MAKES ABOUT FOURTEEN

INGREDIENTS
- 225g/8oz/2 cups plain (all-purpose) flour
- 5ml/1 tsp salt
- 15ml/1 tbsp lard or vegetable fat
- 120ml/4fl oz/½ cup water

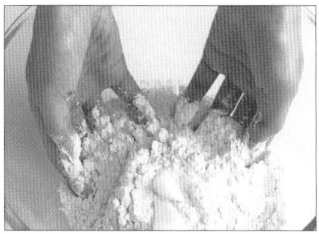

1 Sift the flour and salt into a large mixing bowl. Gradually rub in the lard or vegetable fat using your fingertips until the mixture resembles coarse breadcrumbs.

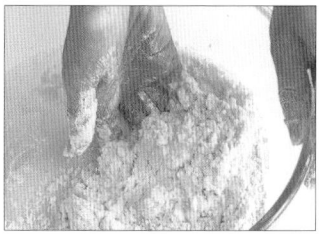

2 Gradually add the water and mix to a soft dough. Knead lightly, form into a ball, cover with a cloth and leave to rest for 15 minutes.

3 Carefully divide the dough into about 14 portions and form these portions into small balls. One by one, roll out each ball of dough on a lightly floured wooden board to a round measuring about 15cm/6in. Trim the rounds if necessary.

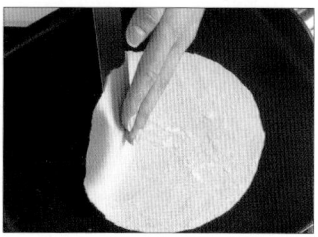

4 Heat an ungreased griddle or frying pan over a moderate heat. Cook the tortillas for about 1½–2 minutes on each side. Turn over with a palette knife or metal spatula when the bottom begins to brown. Wrap in foil and keep warm in the oven until ready to serve.

COOK'S TIP

Make flour tortillas whenever *masa harina* is difficult to find. To keep them soft and pliable, make sure they are kept warm until ready to serve, and eat as soon as possible.

DHAL PURI

KNOWN AS ROTI WHEN FILLED AND FOLDED, THESE TASTY FLAT BREADS CAN ALSO BE MADE WITH WHITE FLOUR. A TRADITIONAL CARIBBEAN FAVOURITE, DHAL PURI ARE DELICIOUS WITH MEAT, FISH OR VEGETABLE DISHES AND ARE IDEAL FOR MOPPING UP LEFTOVER SAUCES.

MAKES ABOUT FIFTEEN

INGREDIENTS
- 450g/1lb/4 cups self-raising (self-rising) flour
- 115g/4oz/1 cup wholemeal (whole-wheat) flour
- 350ml/12fl oz/1½ cups cold water
- 30ml/2 tbsp oil, plus extra for frying
- salt, to taste

For the filling
- 350g/12oz/1½ cups yellow split peas
- 15ml/1 tbsp ground cumin
- 2 garlic cloves, crushed

1 Sift the dry ingredients into a bowl, then tip in the grain remaining in the sieve. Add the water a little at a time, and knead gently until a soft dough forms. Continue kneading until supple, but do not over-work the dough.

2 Add the oil to the dough and continue to knead it until it is completely smooth. Put the dough in a polythene bag or wrap in clear film (plastic wrap). Place in a cool room or in the refrigerator and leave to rest for at least 30 minutes, or overnight if possible.

3 To make the filling, put the split peas in a large pan, pour over water to cover and cook for about 10–15 minutes, until half cooked – they should be tender on the outside, but still firm in the middle. Allow the water to evaporate during cooking, until the pan is almost dry, but add a little extra water to prevent burning, if necessary.

4 Spread out the peas on a tray. When cool, grind to a paste, using a mortar and pestle or food processor. Mix with the cumin and garlic.

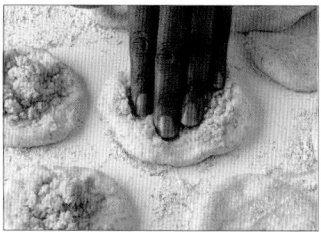

5 Divide the dough into about 15 balls, Slightly flatten each ball, put about 15ml/1 tbsp of the split pea mixture into the centre and fold over the edges.

6 Dust a rolling pin and a board with flour and roll out the dhal puri, taking care not to overstretch the dough, until they are about 18cm/7in in diameter.

7 Heat a little oil in a frying pan. Cook the dhal puris for about 3 minutes on each side until light brown. Serve as soon as the last one is cooked.

FRIED DUMPLINS

IN THE CARIBBEAN AND GUYANA THESE FRIED DUMPLINS ARE SIMPLY CALLED "BAKES". THEY ARE USUALLY SERVED WITH SALT FISH OR FRIED FISH, BUT CAN BE EATEN QUITE SIMPLY WITH BUTTER AND JAM OR CHEESE, WHICH CHILDREN ESPECIALLY LOVE.

MAKES ABOUT TEN

INGREDIENTS
- 450g/1lb/4 cups self-raising (self-rising) flour
- 10ml/2 tsp sugar
- 2.5ml/½ tsp salt
- 300ml/½ pint/1¼ cups milk
- oil, for frying

COOK'S TIP
Mix and knead the dough gently to avoid overworking it and making it tough. A quite light touch is all that is needed to make the dough smooth.

1 Sift the flour, sugar and salt into a large bowl, add the milk and mix and knead until a smooth dough forms.

2 Divide the dough into ten balls, kneading each ball with floured hands. Press the balls gently to flatten them into 7.5cm/3in rounds.

3 Heat a little oil in a non-stick frying pan over medium heat. Place half the dumplins in the pan, reduce the heat to low and fry for about 15 minutes, until they are golden brown, turning once.

4 Stand the dumplins on their sides for a few minutes to brown the edges, before removing them from the pan and draining thoroughly on kitchen paper. Serve immediately, while still warm.

CORN GRIDDLE CAKES

KNOWN AS AREPAS, *THESE ARE A STAPLE BREAD IN SEVERAL LATIN AMERICAN COUNTRIES, PARTICULARLY COLOMBIA AND VENEZUELA. EAT THEM FILLED WITH SOFT WHITE CHEESE, AS HERE, OR PLAIN AS AN ACCOMPANIMENT. WITH THEIR CRISP CRUST AND CHEWY INTERIOR,* AREPAS *CAN BECOME STALE VERY QUICKLY, SO ARE BEST EATEN PIPING HOT.*

MAKES FIFTEEN

INGREDIENTS

- 200g/7oz/1¾ cups *masarepa* (or *masa harina*)
- 2.5ml/½ tsp salt
- 300ml/½ pint/1¼ cups water
- 15ml/1 tbsp oil
- 200g/7oz fresh white cheese, such as queso fresco or mozzarella, roughly chopped

1 Combine the *masarepa* or *masa harina* and salt in a bowl. Gradually stir in the water to make a soft dough, then set aside for about 20 minutes.

2 Divide the dough into 15 equal-sized balls, then, using your fingers, flatten each ball into a circle, approximately 1cm/½in thick.

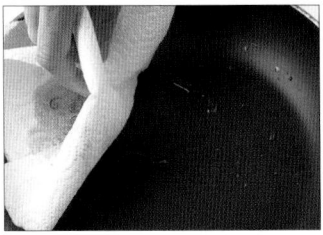

3 Heat 5ml/1 tsp of the oil in a large, heavy frying pan over a medium heat. Using a piece of kitchen paper, gently wipe the surface of the frying pan, leaving it just lightly greased.

4 Place five of the *arepas* in the frying pan. Cook for about 4 minutes, then flip over and cook for a further 4 minutes. The *arepas* should be lightly blistered on both sides.

5 Open the *arepas* and fill each with a few small pieces of fresh white cheese. Return to the pan to cook until the cheese begins to melt. Remove from the heat and keep warm.

6 Cook the remaining ten *arepas* in the same way, oiling the pan and wiping with kitchen paper in-between batches, to ensure it is always lightly greased. Serve the arepas while still warm so that the melted cheese is soft and runny.

COOK'S TIP

Masarepa is a flour made with the white corn grown in the Andes. Look for it in Latin American food stores. If not available, replace it with *masa harina*, the flour used to make tamales. The result will not be quite as delicate, but the *arepas* will be equally delicious.

VARIATION

Instead of cheese, try a delicious beef filling. Simply fry some minced (ground) beef in oil with ½ chopped onion, 1 small red chilli, finely chopped, 1 crushed garlic clove, ground black pepper and fresh thyme. When thoroughly cooked, stuff the mixture inside the *arepas*.

PARAGUAYAN CORN BREAD

THIS MOIST CORN MEAL BREAD IS SO RICH AND FLAVOURSOME THAT IT CAN EASILY BE EATEN ON ITS OWN. IT TASTES BEST WHEN EATEN WARM.

MAKES ONE LOAF

INGREDIENTS

- 75g/3oz/6 tbsp butter
- 1 large onion, finely chopped
- 400ml/14fl oz/1⅔ cups full-fat (whole) milk
- 225g/8oz/2 cups corn meal
- 175g/6oz mozzarella cheese, roughly grated
- 2 large eggs, separated
- salt and ground black pepper

1 Preheat the oven to 200°C/400°F/Gas 6. Using 15g/½oz/1 tbsp of the butter, grease a loaf tin (pan). Melt a further 25g/1oz/2 tbsp of the butter in a large pan over a low heat and fry the onions for 5 minutes until softened.

COOK'S TIP

If you can't get hold of corn meal, use instant polenta instead.

2 Pour in the milk and stir until heated, without allowing it to boil. Still stirring, add the corn meal in a steady stream. Continue to stir until the mixture is smooth.

3 Remove from the heat and stir in the cheese and remaining butter. When both have melted, season with salt and ground pepper.

4 Whisk the egg whites in a bowl until they hold their shape. Stir the egg yolks into the corn meal mixture, then gently fold in the egg whites.

5 Tip the mixture into the prepared loaf tin. Bake for 35–40 minutes, or until a skewer comes out clean when inserted in the bread. Turn out onto a wire rack to cool a little. Cut into slices and serve.

MEXICAN "BREAD OF THE DEAD"

A CELEBRATORY LOAF MADE FOR ALL SOULS' DAY, WHEN MEXICANS PAY THEIR RESPECTS TO THE SOULS OF THE DEAD, IT IS TRADITIONALLY DECORATED WITH A DOUGH SKULL, BONES AND TEARS.

MAKES ONE LARGE LOAF

INGREDIENTS
- 3 star anise
- 90ml/6 tbsp cold water
- 675g/1½lb/6 cups unbleached white bread flour, plus extra for sprinkling
- 5ml/1 tsp salt
- 115g/4oz/½ cup caster (superfine) sugar
- 25g/1oz fresh yeast
- 175ml/6fl oz/¾ cup lukewarm water
- 3 eggs
- 60ml/4 tbsp orange-flavoured liqueur
- 115g/4oz/½ cup butter, melted
- grated rind of 1 orange
- icing (confectioners') sugar, for dusting

1 Grease a 26cm/10½in fluted round cake tin (pan). Place the star anise in a small pan and add the cold water. Bring to the boil and boil for 3–4 minutes, or until the liquid has reduced to 45ml/3 tbsp. Discard the star anise and leave the liquid to cool.

2 Sift the flour and salt together into a large bowl. Stir in the sugar and make a well in the centre.

3 In a jug (pitcher), dissolve the yeast in the lukewarm water. Pour into the centre of the flour and mix in, using your fingers, until a smooth, thick batter forms. Sprinkle over a little more flour, cover with clear film (plastic wrap) and leave the batter in a warm place for 30 minutes, or until the mixture starts to bubble.

4 Beat the eggs, the reserved liquid flavoured with star anise, orange liqueur and melted butter together. Gradually incorporate into the flour mixture to form a smooth dough.

5 Turn out the dough on to a lightly floured surface and gently knead in the orange rind. Knead for 5–6 minutes until smooth and elastic.

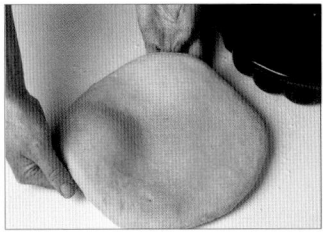

6 Shape the dough into a 26cm/10½in round and place in the prepared tin. Cover with lightly oiled clear film and leave to rise, in a warm place, for 2–3 hours, or until doubled in bulk.

7 Meanwhile, preheat the oven to 190°C/375°F/Gas 5. Bake the loaf for 45–50 minutes, or until golden. Turn out on to a wire rack to cool. Dust with icing sugar to serve.

VARIATION

Top the baked bread with orange-flavoured icing. Blend 60g/2oz/½ cup icing sugar and 15–30ml/1–2 tbsp orange liqueur. Pour the icing over the bread and let it dribble down the sides.

CARIBBEAN FRUIT AND RUM CAKE

THIS POPULAR CAKE IS EATEN AT CHRISTMAS, WEDDINGS AND OTHER SPECIAL OCCASIONS. IT IS KNOWN AS BLACK CAKE, BECAUSE THE TRADITIONAL RECIPE USES BURNT SUGAR.

MAKES ONE CAKE

INGREDIENTS

- 450g/1lb/2 cups currants
- 450g/1lb/3 cups raisins
- 225g/8oz/1 cup pitted prunes
- 115g/4oz/⅔ cup mixed (candied) peel
- 5ml/1 tsp ground mixed spice (pumpkin pie spice)
- 90ml/6 tbsp rum, plus more if needed
- 300ml/½ pint/1¼ cups sherry, plus more if needed
- 400g/14oz/1¾ cups soft dark brown sugar
- 450g/1lb/4 cups self-raising (self-rising) flour
- 450g/1lb/2 cups butter, softened
- 10 eggs, beaten
- 5ml/1 tsp natural vanilla essence (extract)

1 Wash the currants, raisins, prunes and mixed peel, then drain and pat dry. Place in a food processor and process until roughly chopped. Transfer to a large, bowl and add the the mixed spice, rum and sherry. Stir in 115g/4oz/½ cup of sugar. Mix well, then cover with a lid and set aside for anything from 2 weeks to 3 months – the longer it is left, the better the flavour will be.

2 Stir the fruit mixture occasionally, adding more alcohol, if you like, before replacing the cover.

3 Preheat the oven to 160°C/325°F/ Gas 3. Grease a 25cm/10in round cake tin (pan) and line with a double layer of greaseproof (waxed) paper or baking parchment.

4 Sift the flour into a bowl, and set it aside. In a large mixing bowl, cream the butter with the remaining sugar. Beat in the eggs until the mixture is smooth and creamy, adding a little of the flour if the mixture starts to curdle.

5 Add the fruit mixture, then gradually stir in the remaining flour and the vanilla essence. Mix well, adding 15–30ml/1–2 tbsp more sherry if the mixture is too stiff; it should just fall off the back of the spoon, but should not be too runny.

6 Spoon the mixture into the prepared pan, cover loosely with foil and bake for about 2½ hours, until the cake is firm and springy. Leave to cool in the pan overnight. Unless serving immediately, sprinkle the cake with more rum and wrap in greaseproof paper and foil to keep it moist.

COOK'S TIP

Although it is usual to roughly chop the dried fruits, they can be marinated whole if you prefer. If there is no time to marinate the fruit, simmer it gently in the alcohol mixture for about 30 minutes, and leave overnight.

APPLE AND CINNAMON CRUMBLE CAKE

THIS SCRUMPTIOUS CAKE, POPULAR IN THE CARIBBEAN, HAS LAYERS OF SPICY FRUIT AND CRUMBLE AND IS QUITE DELICIOUS WHEN SERVED WARM WITH FRESH CREAM.

MAKES ONE CAKE

INGREDIENTS

250g/9oz/1 cup plus 30ml/2 tbsp butter, softened
250g/9oz/1¼ cups caster (superfine) sugar
4 eggs
450g/1lb/4 cups self-raising (self-rising) flour
3 large cooking apples
2.5ml/½ tsp ground cinnamon

For the crumble topping

175g/6oz/¾ cup demerara (raw) sugar
125g/4¼oz/generous 1 cup plain (all-purpose) flour
5ml/1 tsp ground cinnamon
65g/2½oz/scant 1 cup desiccated (dry unsweetened shredded) coconut
115g/4oz/½ cup butter

1 Preheat the oven to 180°C/350°F/Gas 4. Grease and base-line a 25cm/10in round cake tin (pan). To make the crumble topping, mix the sugar, flour, cinnamon and coconut in a bowl, then rub in the butter with your fingertips until the mixture resembles breadcrumbs. Set aside.

2 Put the butter and sugar in a bowl and cream with an electric mixer until light and fluffy. Beat in the eggs, one at a time, beating well after each addition, and adding a little of the flour if the mixture starts to curdle.

3 Sift in half the remaining flour, mix well, then add the rest of the flour and stir until smooth.

4 Peel and core the apples, then grate them coarsely. Place the grated apples in a bowl and sprinkle with the cinnamon and set aside.

5 Spread half the cake mixture evenly over the base of the prepared tin. Spoon the apples on top and sprinkle over half the crumble topping.

6 Spread the remaining cake mixture over the crumble and finally top with the remaining crumble topping.

7 Bake for 1 hour 10 minutes–1 hour 20 minutes, covering the cake with foil if it browns too quickly. Leave in the pan for about 5 minutes before turning out on to a wire rack. Serve when cool.

BARBADIAN COCONUT SWEET BREAD

OFTEN MADE AT CHRISTMAS TIME IN BARBADOS, THIS DELICIOUS COCONUT BREAD IS MOST ENJOYABLE WITH A CUP OF HOT CHOCOLATE OR A GLASS OF FRUIT PUNCH.

MAKES TWO SMALL LOAVES

INGREDIENTS

- 175g/6oz/¾ cup butter or margarine
- 115g/4oz/½ cup demerara (raw) sugar
- 225g/8oz/2 cups self-raising (self-rising) flour
- 200g/7oz/scant 2 cups plain (all-purpose) flour
- 115g/4oz desiccated (dry unsweetened shredded) coconut
- 5ml/1 tsp mixed spice (pumpkin pie spice)
- 10ml/2 tsp vanilla essence (extract)
- 15ml/1 tbsp rum (optional)
- 2 eggs
- about 150ml/¼ pint/⅔ cup milk
- 15ml/1 tbsp caster (superfine) sugar, blended with 30ml/2 tbsp water, to glaze

1 Preheat the oven to 180°C/350°F/Gas 4. Grease two 450g/1lb loaf tins (pans) or one 900g/2lb tin.

2 Place the butter or margarine and sugar in a large mixing bowl and sift in all of the flour. Rub the ingredients together with your fingertips until the mixture begins to resemble fine breadcrumbs.

3 Add the coconut, mixed spice, vanilla essence, rum, if using, eggs and milk. Mix together well with your hands. If the mixture is too dry, add more milk. Knead on a floured board until firm and pliable.

4 Halve the mixture and place in the loaf tins. Glaze with sugared water and bake for about 1 hour, or until a skewer inserted into the loaf comes out clean.

DUCKANOO

THIS TASTY CARIBBEAN CAKE, WHICH HAS ITS ORIGINS IN WEST AFRICA, IS STEAMED IN FOIL PARCELS TO RETAIN MOISTURE. IT CONSISTS MAINLY OF CORN MEAL AND COCONUT AND IS DELICIOUS WITH FRESH CREAM.

MAKES SIX

INGREDIENTS

- 450g/1lb/3 cups fine corn meal
- 350g/12oz fresh coconut, chopped
- 600ml/1 pint/2½ cups fresh milk
- 115g/4oz currants or raisins
- 50g/2oz/¼ cup butter or margarine, melted
- 115g/4oz/½ cup demerara (raw) sugar
- 60ml/4 tbsp water
- 1.5ml/¼ tsp freshly grated nutmeg
- 2.5ml/½ tsp ground cinnamon
- 5ml/1 tsp vanilla essence (extract)

1 Place the corn meal in a large bowl. Blend the coconut and the milk in a blender or food processor until smooth. Stir the coconut mixture into the corn meal, then add all of the remaining ingredients and stir well.

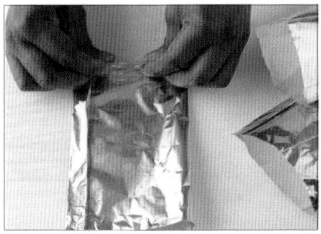

2 Take 6 pieces of foil and fold into 13 x 15cm/5 x 6in pockets leaving an opening on one short side. Fold over the edges of the remaining sides tightly to ensure that they are well sealed. This will prevent liquid seeping in.

3 Put one or two spoonfuls of the corn meal mixture into each foil pocket and fold over the final edge of foil to seal tightly.

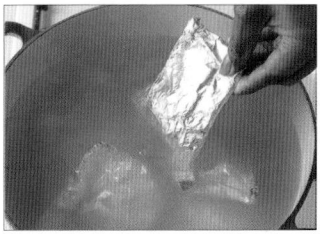

4 Place the foil pockets in a large pan of boiling water. Cover and simmer for about 45–60 minutes. Lift the pockets out of the water and carefully remove the foil. Serve the duckanoo alone or with fresh cream.

CORN MEAL AND FENNEL SEED CAKE

BEING A STAPLE FOOD, CORN MEAL IS OFTEN USED IN BAKING. HERE IT MAKES A DELICIOUS TEA CAKE OR AFTER-SCHOOL SNACK FOR THE CHILDREN.

MAKES ONE LOAF

INGREDIENTS
- 40g/1½oz/3 tbsp unsalted (sweet) butter, softened
- 200g/7oz/1 cup caster (superfine) sugar
- 200g/7oz/1⅓ cups coarse corn meal
- 200g/7oz/1¾ cups plain (all-purpose) flour
- 350ml/12fl oz/1½ cups full-fat (whole) milk
- 10ml/2 tsp baking powder
- 5ml/1 tsp salt
- 4 eggs
- 5ml/1 tsp fennel seeds

COOK'S TIP
The cake batter will seem very runny before baking. Don't let this worry you; the result will be a well-risen, moist cake.

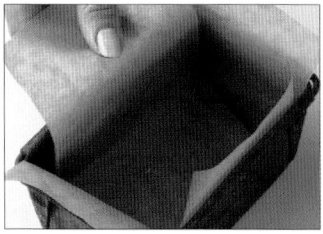

1 Preheat the oven to 180°C/350°F/Gas 4. Grease a 23 x 13cm/9 x 5in loaf tin (pan) and line with baking parchment.

VARIATION
A popular version of this cake is made with the addition of grated fresh white cheese. Stir 150g/5oz into the cake batter before baking. The result will be much creamier and even more moist.

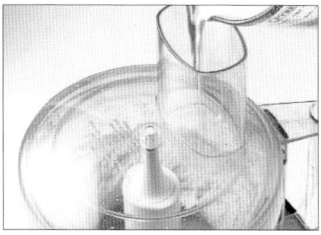

2 Cream the butter and sugar in a food processor until thoroughly combined. Add the remaining ingredients to the food processor and blend again to make a thin cake batter.

3 Pour the batter into the prepared loaf tin and bake for 40–45 minutes, or until a skewer inserted in the centre of the cake comes out clean. Allow to cool slightly, then transfer to a wire rack. Serve at room temperature.

BANANA BREAD

THIS IS MORE OF A CAKE THAN A BREAD, AND IS DELICIOUS EATEN ON ITS OWN FOR BREAKFAST OR AS AN AFTERNOON SNACK. IT ALSO MAKES AN IMPRESSIVE INFORMAL DESSERT WHEN TOASTED, BUTTERED AND SERVED WITH LASHINGS OF BRANDY CREAM.

MAKES ONE LOAF

INGREDIENTS
- 2 ripe bananas
- 115g/4oz/½ cup butter, softened, plus extra for greasing
- 75g/3oz/6 tbsp light brown sugar
- 2.5ml/½ tsp ground cinnamon
- 2.5ml/½ tsp ground ginger
- large pinch of ground cloves
- 2 eggs, lightly beaten
- 175g/6oz/1½ cups self-raising (self-rising) flour
- 15ml/1 tbsp milk (optional)
- 50g/2oz/½ cup walnut pieces

1 Preheat the oven to 180°C/350°F/Gas 4. Grease a 23 x 13cm/9 x 5in loaf tin (pan) and line with baking parchment. Mash the bananas with a fork and set them aside.

2 Cream the butter with the sugar by hand or in a food processor until light and creamy. Add the spices, eggs and flour and blend again until thoroughly combined. The mixture should be thin enough to fall reluctantly off a spoon. If it is too thick, stir in the milk.

COOK'S TIP
Do not blend the banana in a food processor – it will become too runny.

3 Fold the mashed bananas and walnut pieces into the mixture, then tip it into the prepared loaf tin. Bake the banana bread for about 1 hour, or until a skewer inserted in the centre comes out clean. Transfer to a wire rack to cool.

DESSERTS

The abundant supply of sweet and juicy tropical fruit available in Latin America and the Caribbean means that dessert usually consists of fresh fruit. Otherwise, desserts tend to be rice dishes based on eggs and sugar and are usually of Spanish and Portuguese origin, where rich custard tarts and crème caramels have always been popular.

FRUITS OF THE TROPICS SALAD

CANNED GUAVAS DO NOT HAVE QUITE THE SAME FLAVOUR AS FRESH ONES, BUT ARE AN EXCELLENT INGREDIENT IN THEIR OWN RIGHT – DELICIOUS IN THIS CARIBBEAN FRUIT SALAD.

2 Chop the stem ginger and add it to the pineapple mixture.

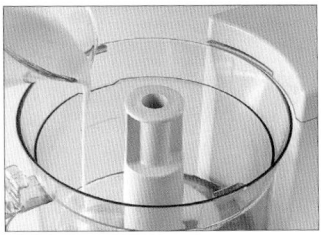

3 Pour the ginger syrup into a blender or food processor. Add the remaining banana, the coconut milk and the sugar. Pour in the reserved guava syrup and blend to a smooth creamy purée.

SERVES SIX

INGREDIENTS

- 1 medium pineapple
- 400g/14oz can guava halves in syrup
- 2 bananas, sliced
- 1 large mango, peeled, stoned (pitted) and diced
- 115g/4oz preserved stem ginger plus 30ml/2 tbsp of the syrup from the jar
- 60ml/4 tbsp thick coconut milk
- 10ml/2 tsp sugar
- 2.5ml/½ tsp freshly grated nutmeg
- 2.5ml/½ tsp ground cinnamon
- strips of coconut, to decorate

1 Remove the leafy top of the pineapple, saving it to decorate the serving platter if you like. Cut the pineapple lengthways into quarters, then remove the peel and core from each piece. Cube the pineapple, and place in a serving bowl. Drain the guavas, reserving the syrup, and chop. Add the guavas to the bowl with half the bananas and all the mango.

4 Pour the banana and coconut dressing over the fruit, add a little grated nutmeg and a sprinkling of cinnamon. Cover and chill.

5 Serve the salad chilled, decorated with fresh strips of coconut. If you are serving the mixture on a large platter, the pineapple top can be placed in the centre as a decoration.

Coconut Ice Cream

This heavenly ice cream, popular throughout the Caribbean, is easy to make and uses storecupboard ingredients, so is perfect for easy entertaining.

SERVES EIGHT

INGREDIENTS
- 400g/14oz can evaporated (unsweetened condensed) milk
- 400g/14oz can condensed milk
- 400g/14oz can coconut milk
- freshly grated nutmeg
- 5ml/1 tsp almond essence (extract)
- fresh lemon balm sprigs, lime slices and shredded coconut, to decorate

COOK'S TIP
If using an ice-cream maker, mix the ingredients in a jug (pitcher), chill in the freezer for 30 minutes. Pour into the ice-cream maker and churn as directed.

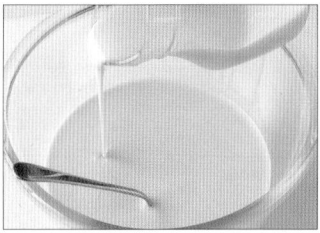

1 Mix the evaporated, condensed and coconut milk in a large freezerproof bowl until thoroughly combined.

2 Stir in the grated nutmeg and almond essence. Place the bowl in the freezer and chill the mixture for about 1–2 hours or until semi-frozen.

3 Remove the bowl from the freezer and whisk the mixture vigorously until it is light and fluffy and has almost doubled in volume.

4 Pour into a freezer container, then cover and freeze. Soften slightly before serving, decorated with lemon balm, lime slices and shredded coconut.

MANGO SORBET

THIS FOOLPROOF RECIPE IS INCREDIBLY EASY TO MAKE WITHOUT AN ICE-CREAM MAKER. A SMOOTH TEXTURE AND FRUITY, CONCENTRATED FLAVOUR IS GUARANTEED.

SERVES SIX

INGREDIENTS

- 200g/7oz/1 cup caster (superfine) sugar
- 150ml/¼ pint/⅔ cup water
- 3 large ripe mangoes
- juice of 1 lime
- 1 egg white

COOK'S TIP

Home-made sorbets (sherbets) tend to set more solidly than bought versions, so always transfer them to the refrigerator to thaw slightly before serving.

VARIATION

The sorbet can be made with ripe papayas instead of mangoes. Add the grated rind of the lime as well as the juice.

1 Dissolve the sugar in the water in a small pan over a low heat. Allow to cool.

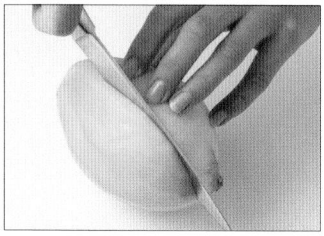

2 Cut off a thick lengthways slice from either side of each mango. Cut off any flesh, peel and chop it roughly. Put the mango flesh in a food processor or blender and process until smooth.

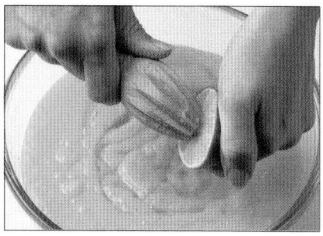

3 Scrape into a freezerproof bowl and stir in the syrup and lime juice. Freeze for 2–4 hours until almost solid.

4 Scoop into a food processor and blend until soft. Pour in the egg white and blend until combined. Return to the bowl, cover and freeze until firm.

COLOMBIAN PINEAPPLE CUSTARD

THESE PINEAPPLE CRÈME CARAMELS ARE THE PERFECT DINNER PARTY DESSERT. THEY ARE VERY EASY TO MAKE, ESPECIALLY IF YOU BUY PREPARED FRESH PINEAPPLE FROM THE SUPERMARKET.

MAKES SIX

INGREDIENTS
- 350g/12oz peeled fresh pineapple, chopped
- 150g/5oz/⅔ cup caster (superfine) sugar
- 4 eggs, lightly beaten

For the caramel
- 60ml/4 tbsp granulated sugar
- juice of 1 lime

1 Put the pineapple in a blender or food processor and process until smooth. Scrape the purée into a pan and add the sugar. Cook for 5 minutes or until reduced by one-third. The mixture should be thick but not jam-like, so add a little water if it is too thick. Transfer to a bowl and leave to cool.

COOK'S TIP
Avoid over-whisking the eggs. Gently stir them into the pineapple mixture without incorporating air.

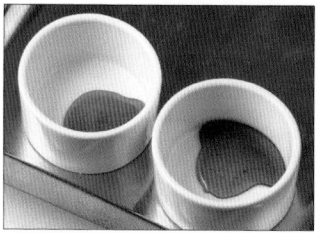

2 Meanwhile make the caramel. Place the granulated sugar in a heavy pan over a medium heat. As the sugar starts to caramelize around the edges, shake the pan to mix the sugar, but do not stir. Remove the pan from the heat as soon as all the sugar has dissolved and the caramel has become golden brown. Immediately stir in the lime juice taking care not to burn yourself. The hot caramel will spit when the lime juice is added, but this will stop. Divide the caramel among six ramekins and turn them so that they are coated evenly.

3 Preheat the oven to 180°C/350°F/Gas 4. Stir the eggs into the cool pineapple mixture. Divide the mixture equally among the ramekins. Place the moulds in a roasting pan and pour in warm water to come halfway up their sides. Cover with foil and bake for 45 minutes, until set. Allow to cool.

4 Just before serving, unmould the custards directly on to dessert plates. Loosen the edges with a knife, invert a dessert plate on top of each mould and turn both over.

TAPIOCA PUDDING

THIS IS ONE OF THOSE DESSERTS THAT PROVOKES STRONG REACTIONS. MOST PEOPLE EITHER LOVE IT OR LOATHE IT, BUT IT IS VERY POPULAR THROUGHOUT LATIN AMERICA. FOR ITS MANY FANS, THERE IS NOTHING NICER THAN THIS CREAMY DESSERT STREWN WITH CRUNCHY CASHEWS.

SERVES SIX

INGREDIENTS
- 90g/3½oz/generous ½ cup tapioca
- 750ml/1¼ pints/3 cups full-fat (whole) milk
- 1 cinnamon stick, bruised
- 45ml/3 tbsp caster (superfine) sugar
- 30ml/2 tbsp chopped cashew nuts

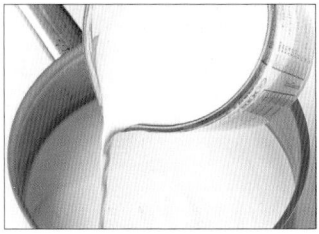

1 Put the tapioca in a strainer and rinse under cold running water. Drain and tip into a heavy pan.

VARIATION

For coconut-flavoured tapioca pudding, simply replace the milk with the same quantity of coconut milk.

2 Pour in the milk and soak for 30 minutes. Place the pan over a medium heat and bring to the boil. Add the bruised cinnamon stick, then lower the heat and simmer gently for 30 minutes, or until most of the milk has been absorbed. Stir occasionally to prevent the tapioca from sticking.

3 Stir in the sugar and gently simmer for a further 10 minutes. Carefully remove the cinnamon stick and spoon the pudding into individual dessert bowls. Lightly toast the cashew nuts in a dry frying pan, taking care not to burn them, and scatter over the puddings. Serve warm rather than hot or cold.

FRIED BANANAS WITH SUGAR AND RUM

CHILDREN LOVE FRIED BANANAS, BUT THIS CARIBBEAN VERSION WITH RUM DELIVERS AN EXTRA KICK AND IS STRICTLY FOR GROWN-UPS. FRIED BANANAS CAN BE INCREDIBLY SWEET, BUT THE LIME JUICE CUTS THROUGH THE SWEETNESS WITH DELICIOUS RESULTS.

SERVES FOUR

INGREDIENTS

- 50g/2oz/¼ cup caster (superfine) sugar
- 45ml/3 tbsp rum
- 65g/2½oz/5 tbsp unsalted (sweet) butter
- grated rind and juice of 1 lime
- 4 bananas, peeled
- vanilla ice cream, to serve

1 Place the sugar, rum, butter, grated lime rind and lime juice in a large heavy frying pan over a low heat. Cook for a few minutes, stirring occasionally, until the sugar has completely dissolved.

COOK'S TIP

Avoid using bananas that are too ripe, otherwise they may break apart in the pan before they get a chance to colour.

2 Add the bananas to the pan, turning to coat them in the sauce. Cook over a medium heat for 5 minutes on each side, or until the bananas are golden.

3 Remove from the heat and cut the bananas in half. Serve two pieces of banana per person with a scoop of vanilla ice cream and a generous drizzle of the hot sauce.

COCONUT AND PUMPKIN COMPOTE

LATIN AMERICANS LOVE WHOLE PRESERVED FRUITS IN SYRUP. ALSO POPULAR ARE COMPOTES LIKE THIS ONE, TRADITIONALLY SERVED WITH FRESH CHEESE.

SERVES SIX

INGREDIENTS
- 800g/1¾lb pumpkin, peeled and seeded
- 450g/1lb/2¼ cups caster (superfine) sugar
- 4 cloves
- 350ml/12fl oz/1½ cups water
- 115g/4oz/1⅓ cups desiccated (dry unsweetened shredded) coconut
- ricotta cheese, to serve

VARIATION
This preserve is more traditionally made without coconut. For pure pumpkin compote, leave out the coconut and double the quantity of pumpkin.

1 Cut the pumpkin into even-size pieces and place in a heavy pan. Add the sugar, cloves and water. Heat gently, without bringing to the boil, until the sugar has dissolved.

2 Increase the heat to medium. Simmer the mixture for 30–35 minutes, until the pumpkin is soft. Using a fork mash the cooked pumpkin until it is reduced to a rough purée.

3 Stir in the coconut and simmer for a further 15 minutes. The mixture should be thick but still liquid, so add more water if necessary. Leave to cool, then transfer to an airtight container and store in the refrigerator for up to 2 weeks.

4 Spoon the compote into a serving bowl and allow it to come to room temperature before serving with a fresh white cheese, such as ricotta.

DULCE DE LECHE

SPANISH IN ORIGIN, THIS TOFFEE-LIKE DESSERT IS A CHILDREN'S FAVOURITE THROUGHOUT LATIN AMERICA. LITERALLY TRANSLATED AS "CARAMELIZED MILK", IT IS TRADITIONALLY MADE WITH MILK AND SUGAR, BUT THIS VERSION IS MUCH QUICKER AND JUST AS DELICIOUS.

SERVES SIX

INGREDIENTS
- 400g/14oz can condensed milk
- 400g/14oz can evaporated (unsweetened condensed) milk

VARIATION
A classic trick to making low-maintenance *dulce de leche* is to cook a whole, closed can of condensed milk in a pan of boiling water for 30 minutes, but this must be done with care as the can could explode if not continuously immersed in water. South American cooks often add a can of condensed milk to the pan when cooking beans, so side dish and dessert cook together.

1 Combine the condensed and evaporated milk in a heavy pan. Place over a medium heat and bring to the boil. Reduce the heat slightly and cook, stirring constantly, for 30–35 minutes until thickened and toffee coloured. Use a relatively large pan, as the milk has a tendency to boil over.

2 Pour into a sterilized jar and seal. *Dulce de leche* will keep for months, but with time, the texture will alter and won't be as smooth.

3 Serve with ice cream, as a filling for pancakes or cakes, or even with a white cheese, such as ricotta.

CARIBBEAN SPICED RICE PUDDING

SOME RECIPES FROM THE CARIBBEAN CAN BE EXTREMELY SWEET, PARTICULARLY DESSERTS. IF THIS RICE PUDDING IS A LITTLE TOO SWEET FOR YOUR TASTE, SIMPLY REDUCE THE SUGAR QUANTITY AND RELY UPON THE NATURAL SWEETNESS OF THE FRUIT.

SERVES SIX

INGREDIENTS
- 25g/1oz/2 tbsp butter
- 1 cinnamon stick
- 115g/4oz/½ cup soft brown sugar
- 115g/4oz/⅔ cup ground rice
- 1.2 litres/2 pints/5 cups milk
- 2.5ml/½ tsp allspice
- 50g/2oz/⅓ cup sultanas (golden raisins)
- 75g/3oz mandarin oranges, chopped
- 75g/3oz pineapple, chopped

1 Melt the butter in a non-stick pan. Add the cinnamon stick and sugar. Heat over a medium heat until the sugar just begins to caramelize. Remove from the heat.

2 Carefully stir in the rice and three-quarters of the milk. Slowly bring to the boil, stirring all the time, being careful not to let the milk burn. Reduce the heat and simmer gently for about 10 minutes, or until the rice is cooked, stirring constantly.

3 Add the remaining milk, the allspice and the sultanas. Leave to simmer for 5 minutes, stirring occasionally.

4 When the rice is thick and creamy, allow to cool slightly, then stir in the mandarin and pineapple pieces.

JAMAICAN FRUIT TRIFLE

THIS TRIFLE IS ACTUALLY BASED ON A CARIBBEAN FOOL THAT CONSISTS OF FRUIT STIRRED INTO THICK VANILLA-FLAVOURED CREAM. THIS VERSION IS MUCH LESS RICH, REDRESSING THE BALANCE WITH PLENTY OF FRUIT, AND WITH CRÈME FRAÎCHE REPLACING SOME OF THE CREAM.

SERVES EIGHT

INGREDIENTS

- 1 large pineapple, peeled and cored
- 300ml/½ pint/1¼ cups double (heavy) cream
- 200ml/7fl oz/scant 1 cup crème fraîche
- 60ml/4 tbsp icing (confectioners') sugar, sifted
- 10ml/2 tsp pure vanilla essence (extract)
- 30ml/2 tbsp white or coconut rum
- 3 papayas, peeled, seeded and chopped
- 3 mangoes, peeled, stoned (pitted) and chopped
- thinly pared rind and juice of 1 lime
- 25g/1oz/⅓ cup coarsely shredded or flaked coconut, toasted

1 Cut the pineapple into large chunks, place in a food processor or blender and process briefly until chopped. Tip into a sieve placed over a bowl and leave for 5 minutes so that most of the juice drains from the fruit.

2 Whip the double cream to soft peaks, then fold in the crème fraîche, sifted icing sugar, vanilla extract and rum.

3 Fold the drained chopped pineapple into the cream mixture. Place the chopped papayas and mangoes in a large bowl and pour over the lime juice. Gently stir the fruit mixture to combine. Shred the pared lime rind.

4 Divide the fruit mixture and the pineapple cream among eight dessert plates. Decorate with the lime shreds, toasted coconut and a few small pineapple leaves, if you like, and serve at once.

COOK'S TIP

It is important to let the pineapple purée drain thoroughly, otherwise, the pineapple cream will be watery. Don't throw away the drained pineapple juice – mix it with fizzy mineral water for a refreshing drink.

BRAZILIAN COCONUT FLAN

THIS IS A SOMEWHAT UNCONVENTIONAL BUT VERY SUCCESSFUL RECIPE FOR QUINDAO, *A CLASSIC BRAZILIAN DESSERT MADE WITH NO FEWER THAN 18 EGG YOLKS. IT IS AVAILABLE AS A PACKET MIX THROUGHOUT LATIN AMERICA, BUT IT IS MUCH MORE DELICIOUS IF YOU MAKE YOUR OWN.*

SERVES TWELVE

INGREDIENTS

- 150g/5oz/1⅔ cups desiccated (dry unsweetened shredded) coconut
- 200ml/7fl oz/scant 1 cup full-fat (whole) milk
- 40g/1½oz/3 tbsp unsalted (sweet) butter, softened
- 400g/14oz/2 cups caster (superfine) sugar, plus extra for dusting
- 18 egg yolks

1 Put the desiccated coconut in a bowl. Pour over the milk and leave to stand for about 15 minutes, or until all the milk has been absorbed.

2 Meanwhile, grease a 23cm/9in ring mould with some of the butter and then lightly dust with a sprinkling of caster sugar.

3 Put the remaining butter in a large bowl. Add the sugar and soaked coconut, and mix vigorously until thoroughly combined.

4 Using a wooden spoon, gently stir in the egg yolks, one at a time. When the ingredients are thoroughly combined, cover the bowl with a clean dishtowel and leave the mixture to stand in a cool place for about 1 hour.

5 Tip the coconut mixture into the prepared ring mould and place this in the centre of a large, deep roasting pan. Pour in enough warm water to come halfway up the outside of the mould. Place this bain marie and its pudding in a cold oven.

6 Heat the oven to 220°C/425°F/Gas 7 and bake the flan for about 1 hour, or until the surface is a dark golden, caramelized brown. Remove from the oven and leave to cool in the water in the roasting pan.

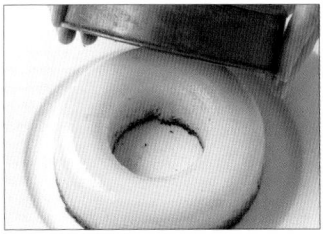

7 When the flan is cold, loosen the edges carefully with a palette knife. Cover with an upturned serving platter and turn the ring mould gently upside down. Gently lift off the ring mould, being careful not to let it touch the top of the flan. Serve cut in thick slices.

VARIATIONS

When available, use finely grated fresh coconut instead of desiccated. There is no need to soak the fresh coconut in the milk; just add both ingredients to the butter and sugar. For a more fragrant, even sweeter flan, try adding a whole vanilla pod to the egg and coconut mixture before it is left to stand. Make sure you remove it before cooking.

DRINKS

Nothing is more refreshing or nutritious than freshly squeezed fruit juice or coconut juice straight from the shell. Fruit bars serving these juices are found throughout the Caribbean and Latin America. The region is also famous for its cocktails, and every country has its favourite spirit – there's Brazilian cachaça, Peruvian pisco, Caribbean rum and Mexican tequila.

MANGO SHAKE

CHILDREN LOVE FRESH FRUIT SHAKES, AND WITH THE VARIETY OF TROPICAL FRUIT AVAILABLE THROUGHOUT THE REGION, THEY ARE SPOILT FOR CHOICE.

MAKES 1 LITRE/1¾ PINTS/4 CUPS

INGREDIENTS
- 2 large ripe mangoes
- 750ml/1¼ pints/3 cups full-fat (whole) milk
- juice of ½ lime
- caster (superfine) sugar, to taste

VARIATION
In Brazil, a similar drink is made with avocados. Simply use 2 ripe avocados in place of the mangoes. Until recently, Brazilians viewed avocados as fruit and would not have dreamed of eating them in savoury dishes. Once you have tasted this unusual, delicious variation, you will understand why.

1 Place each mango in turn on a board with the narrow side down. Cut off a thick lengthways slice, keeping as close to the stone (pit) as possible. Turn the mango around and repeat on the other side. Cut off the flesh that is still attached to the stone. Remove the peel and chop the flesh roughly.

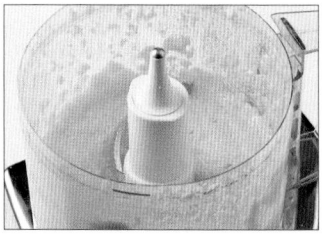

2 Put the chopped mango in a blender or food processor and add the milk and lime juice. Process until smooth.

3 Pour the mango shake into a jug (pitcher), stir in sugar to taste and chill in the refrigerator. Serve in tall glasses with ice cubes.

PINEAPPLE AND MINT JUICE

THIS DRINK IS PERFECTLY REFRESHING ON A SUNNY DAY – THE MINT REALLY BRINGS OUT THE SWEETNESS OF THE FRUIT, AND ADDED SUGAR IS RARELY REQUIRED.

MAKES 1 LITRE/1¾ PINTS/4 CUPS

INGREDIENTS
- 1kg/2¼lb pineapples
- 10 fresh mint leaves
- crushed ice
- caster (superfine) sugar, to taste

VARIATION
To make a pineapple and mint granita, pour the juice into a shallow metal container and place in the freezer until almost firm. Break up the mixture using a fork and return it to the freezer. Repeat this procedure two or three times, until the mixture is semi-frozen, then serve.

1 Cut the top and base off each pineapple, then cut off the skin, being careful to remove all the "eyes". Discard the skin and cut the pineapple, including the core, into large chunks.

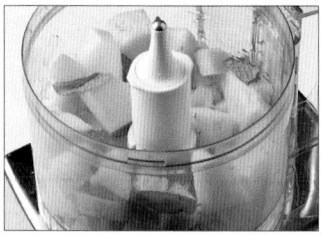

2 Blend the pineapple chunks with the mint leaves in a blender or food processor until smooth. Pour into a jug (pitcher) and stir in the crushed ice. Stir until the ice has dissolved slightly.

CASHEW NUT MILK

IN MAINLAND SPAIN AND MEXICO A SIMILAR DRINK – HORCHATA – IS MADE WITH ALMONDS, BUT THIS CUBAN VARIATION WITH CASHEWS IS EVEN MORE DELICIOUS. THE RESULT IS RICH AND CREAMY. IT IS GREAT FOR KIDS AND EVEN BETTER FOR ADULTS WHO NEED A HANGOVER CURE.

1 Finely grind the cashews in a food processor. Add the sugar and cinnamon and grind the mixture again to make a smooth paste.

2 With the motor still running, gradually pour in 900ml/1½ pints/3¾ cups of boiling water, until the drink becomes smooth and frothy. Scrape down the mixture occasionally, if necessary.

3 Pour the cashew nut milk into a jug (pitcher). Cover and chill in the refrigerator. Stir well before serving in tall glasses. Float ice cubes in each glass. As the ice melts, it will dilute the drink, giving it a lighter texture.

MAKES 1.2 LITRES/2 PINTS/5 CUPS

INGREDIENTS
- 400g/14oz/3½ cups blanched cashews
- 225g/8oz/generous 1 cup caster (superfine) sugar
- 1.5ml/¼ tsp ground cinnamon

COOK'S TIP
For a smooth drink, make this the night before, allow it to stand in the refrigerator overnight, and strain before serving.

PASSION FRUIT BATIDA

BRAZILIAN BATIDAS *CAN BE MADE WITH A VARIETY OF JUICES, SUCH AS LIME OR COCONUT MILK. DO NOT BE FOOLED BY THE FRUITY SWEETNESS: A SMALL GLASS OF* BATIDA, *SIPPED SLOWLY, IS MORE THAN ENOUGH TO GET THE PARTY STARTED.*

MAKES TWO

INGREDIENTS
- 8 passion fruit
- 200ml/7fl oz/scant 1 cup *cachaça*
- 30ml/2 tbsp caster (superfine) sugar
- 3 ice cubes

1 Cut the passion fruit in half and scoop the flesh and seeds into a cocktail shaker or mixing jug (pitcher).

2 Add the remaining ingredients, including the ice cubes, and shake vigorously or stir thoroughly.

3 Strain into two cocktail glasses and serve the *batida* immediately.

VARIATIONS

- Two other flavours of *batida* that are also very popular are lime and coconut. Simply replace the passion fruit with 60ml/4 tbsp lime juice or coconut milk.
- If you are unable to find *cachaça*, replace with equal quantities of vodka.

PISCO SOUR

THIS COCKTAIL, ENJOYED IN PERU, BOLIVIA, ECUADOR AND CHILE, GETS ITS NAME FROM THE PERUVIAN BRANDY WITH WHICH IT IS MADE. GIVE THE COCKTAIL A GOOD SHAKE TO ENCOURAGE THE EGG WHITES TO FOAM UP, AND FINISH WITH THE BITTER, SPICY TASTE OF ANGOSTURA.

MAKES TWO

INGREDIENTS
- 105ml/7 tbsp pisco
- 10ml/2 tsp egg white
- 30ml/2 tbsp caster (superfine) sugar
- juice of 1 lime
- 6 ice cubes
- Angostura bitters

COOK'S TIPS
- Don't stir the cocktail after adding the Angostura bitters, so each sip tastes slightly different.
- If you prefer not to eat raw egg white, the drink can be made without it.

1 Chill two tumblers in the freezer for 10 minutes.

2 Combine all the ingredients, except for the Angostura bitters, in a cocktail shaker and shake vigorously for about 30 seconds.

3 Strain into the chilled glasses and shake 2–3 drops of the bitters on top. Serve immediately.

CAIPIRINHA

THIS BRAZILIAN DRINK CAN BE ENJOYED AT ANY TIME OF DAY – ON THE BEACH WHILE SNACKING ON SEAFOOD, AS AN APERITIF BEFORE A MEAL AND EVEN WITH STEAK AT A BARBECUE. AS ANY TOURIST TO BRAZIL WILL KNOW, ONCE YOU HAVE TASTED IT, YOU ARE HOOKED FOR LIFE!

MAKES TWO

INGREDIENTS
- 2 limes
- 30ml/2 tbsp caster (superfine) sugar
- 105ml/7 tbsp *cachaça*
- crushed ice

VARIATION
Use the same recipe to make *caipiroska*, with vodka replacing the cachaça, or *caipirissima*, using white rum.

1 Wash the limes thoroughly, scrubbing the rind to remove any artificial wax coating that might have been applied, then cut into large chunks.

2 Place the lime chunks in two cocktail tumblers and divide the sugar equally between them. Pound the sugar and lime together with a pestle. The skill lies in being vigorous enough to extract the juice and oil from the rind, yet delicate enough not to break the glass.

3 Top with the crushed ice and divide the cachaça equally between the glasses. Stir vigorously and serve.

MOJITO

A REFRESHING CUBAN COCKTAIL, THIS INCORPORATES RUM, MINT AND LIME. TAKE YOUR TIME DRINKING IT AND THE FLAVOUR OF THE MINT WILL GRADUALLY INTENSIFY.

MAKES ONE

INGREDIENTS
- juice of 1 lime
- 15ml/1 tbsp caster (superfine) sugar
- 4 fresh mint sprigs
- 75ml/5 tbsp white rum
- crushed ice
- 90ml/6 tbsp soda water (club soda)

COOK'S TIPS

- If you don't have a refrigerator that delivers crushed ice or a blender with sufficiently tough blades, put the ice in a freezer bag, wrap it in a dishtowel and beat it against the kitchen work surface – it's noisy, but it works.
- Shaking the cocktail bruises the mint leaves, releasing their flavour. If you do not have a cocktail shaker, bruise the mint leaves by hand before adding them.

1 Mix the lime juice and sugar in a cocktail shaker and shake until the sugar has dissolved.

2 Add three of the mint sprigs, the rum and some crushed ice and shake vigorously. Pour into a tall glass, top with the soda water and decorate with the remaining mint.

CUBA LIBRE

THIS SIMPLE COCKTAIL HAS ALWAYS BEEN VERY POPULAR, BUT SINCE CASTRO TOOK POWER IN 1959 ITS NAME IS SEEN AS POLITICALLY INCORRECT. CUBAN EXILES HAVE SARCASTICALLY RENAMED IT MENTIRITA, *MEANING "LITTLE LIE".*

MAKES ONE

INGREDIENTS
- crushed ice
- 45ml/3 tbsp white rum
- 75ml/5 tbsp cola
- 1 lime wedge, optional

COOK'S TIPS

Rum is made by fermenting and distilling the thick brown liquid (molasses) that is left behind after extracting sugar from sugar cane.

1 Spoon the crushed ice into a tall glass and top with the white rum.

2 Pour in the cola and decorate with a wedge of lime. Serve immediately.

DEMERARA RUM PUNCH

THE INSPIRATION FOR THIS PUNCH CAME FROM THE RUM DISTILLERY AT PLANTATION DIAMOND ESTATE IN GUYANA, WHERE SOME OF THE FINEST RUM IN THE WORLD IS MADE, AND THE TANTALIZING AROMAS OF SUGAR CANE AND RUM PERVADE THE AIR.

SERVES FOUR

INGREDIENTS
- 150ml/¼ pint/⅔ cup orange juice
- 150ml/¼ pint/⅔ cup pineapple juice
- 150ml/¼ pint/⅔ cup mango juice
- 120ml/4fl oz/½ cup water
- 250ml/8fl oz/1 cup dark rum
- a shake of angostura bitters
- freshly grated nutmeg
- 25g/1oz/2 tbsp demerara (raw) sugar
- 1 small banana
- 1 large orange

1 Pour the orange, pineapple and mango juices into a large punch bowl. Stir in the water.

2 Add the rum, angostura bitters, nutmeg and sugar. Stir gently for a few minutes until the sugar has dissolved.

3 Slice the banana thinly and stir the slices gently into the punch.

4 Slice the orange and add to the punch. Chill and serve in tumblers with ice.

VARIATIONS

You can use white rum instead of dark, if you prefer. To make a stronger punch, simply add more rum.

CARIBBEAN CREAM STOUT PUNCH

THIS FAIRLY UNUSUAL PUNCH, MADE USING STOUT, CONDENSED MILK AND SHERRY, IS A WELL-KNOWN "PICK-ME-UP" THAT IS POPULAR ALL OVER THE CARIBBEAN. WITH A SWEET, HEADY AROMA OF VANILLA, IT SOOTHES AND REVIVES TIRED MINDS AND BODIES.

SERVES TWO

INGREDIENTS
- 475ml/16fl oz/2 cups stout
- 300ml/½ pint/1¼ cups evaporated (unsweetened condensed) milk
- 75ml/5 tbsp condensed milk
- 75ml/5 tbsp sherry
- 2 or 3 drops vanilla essence (extract)
- freshly grated nutmeg

1 Mix together the stout, evaporated and condensed milks, sherry and vanilla essence in a blender or food processor, or whisk together in a large mixing bowl, until creamy.

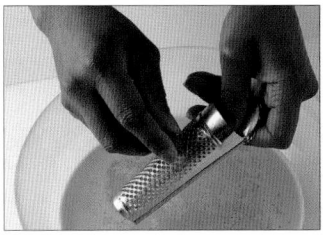

2 Add a little grated nutmeg to the stout mixture and blend or whisk thoroughly again for a few minutes.

3 Chill for at least 45 minutes, or until really cold, before ladling into small glasses to serve.

NUTRITIONAL INFORMATION

The nutritional analysis below is per portion, unless otherwise stated.

p68 Cassava Chips Energy 453Kcal/1900kJ; Protein 3g; Carbohydrate 56.4g, of which sugars 1.4g; Fat 25.6g, of which saturates 3.8g; Cholesterol 0mg; Calcium 30mg; Fibre 2.6g; Sodium 4mg

p69 Cheese Tamales Energy 197Kcal/825kJ; Protein 3.3g; Carbohydrate 21.2g, of which sugars 0.3g; Fat 11.6g, of which saturates 5.8g; Cholesterol 21mg; Calcium 80mg; Fibre 0.0g; Sodium 560mg

p70 Plantain and Sweet Potato Chips Energy 396Kcal/1658kJ; Protein 1.7g; Carbohydrate 51.5g, of which sugars 12.6g; Fat 21.7g, of which saturates 2.5g; Cholesterol 0mg; Calcium 11mg; Fibre 2.8g; Sodium 11mg

p70 Coconut King Prawns Energy 186Kcal/774kJ; Protein 11.2g; Carbohydrate 3.1g, of which sugars 2.6g; Fat 14.5g, of which saturates 8.4g; Cholesterol 182mg; Calcium 111mg; Fibre 1.7g; Sodium 443mg

p72 Tamales de Picadillo Energy 188Kcal/785kJ; Protein 7.8g; Carbohydrate 14.7g, of which sugars 3.0g; Fat 11.3g, of which saturates 4.4g; Cholesterol 26mg; Calcium 13mg; Fibre 0.4g; Sodium 175mg

p73 Mixed Tostadas Energy 253Kcal/1068kJ; Protein 14.7g; Carbohydrate 32.8g, of which sugars 3.4g; Fat 7.9g, of which saturates 2.8g; Cholesterol 25mg; Calcium 192mg; Fibre 3.0g; Sodium 424mg

p74 Cheesy Eggs Energy 167Kcal/693kJ; Protein 9.9g; Carbohydrate 0.1g, of which sugars 0.1g; Fat 14.2g, of which saturates 4.7g; Cholesterol 240mg; Calcium 108mg; Fibre 0g; Sodium 179mg

p75 Crab Cakes Energy 240Kcal/997kJ; Protein 5.9g; Carbohydrate 13.3g, of which sugars 8.9g; Fat 18.6g, of which saturates 8.7g; Cholesterol 58mg; Calcium 58mg; Fibre 2.8g; Sodium 197mg

p76 Pan-fried Squid Energy 250Kcal/1043kJ; Protein 32.8g; Carbohydrate 2.6g, of which sugars 0.1g; Fat 9.2g, of which saturates 1.5g; Cholesterol 500mg; Calcium 33mg; Fibre 0g; Sodium 475mg

p76 Fried Whitebait with Cayenne Pepper Energy 328Kcal/1359kJ; Protein 12.2g; Carbohydrate 3.3g, of which sugars 0.1g; Fat 29.7g, of which saturates 5.9g; Cholesterol 0mg; Calcium 538mg; Fibre 0.1g; Sodium 144mg

p78 Black Eyed Bean and Shrimp Fritters Energy 136Kcal/570kJ; Protein 7.7g; Carbohydrate 14.7g, of which sugars 1.6g; Fat 5.5g, of which saturates 0.7g; Cholesterol 10mg; Calcium 33mg; Fibre 2.3g; Sodium 83mg

p79 Beef Empanadas Energy 138Kcal/579kJ; Protein 6.6g; Carbohydrate 12.7g, of which sugars 0.8g; Fat 7.1g, of which saturates 3.1g; Cholesterol 23mg; Calcium 20mg; Fibre 0.7g; Sodium 102mg

p80 Nut Brittle Energy 239Kcal/1005kJ; Protein 6.5g; Carbohydrate 29.3g, of which sugars 27.2g; Fat 11.5g, of which saturates 2.2g; Cholesterol 00mg; Calcium 22mg; Fibre 1.5g; Sodium 2mg

p80 Coconut Sweets Energy 40Kcal/168kJ; Protein 0.1g; Carbohydrate 7.4g, of which sugars 7.4g; Fat 1.2g, of which saturates 1.1g; Cholesterol 0mg; Calcium 3mg; Fibre 0.3g; Sodium 1mg

p84 Vermicelli Soup Energy 128Kcal/537kJ; Protein 4.4g; Carbohydrate 10.5g, of which sugars 5.7g; Fat 8.0g, of which saturates 2.1g; Cholesterol 6mg; Calcium 86mg; Fibre 1.9g; Sodium 101mg

p84 Tomato Soup Energy 78Kcal/327kJ; Protein 2.1g; Carbohydrate 10.0g, of which sugars 9.0g; Fat 3.6g, of which saturates 0.6g; Cholesterol 0mg; Calcium 26mg; Fibre 2.8g; Sodium 103mg

p86 Creamy Heart of Palm Soup Energy 441Kcal/1824kJ; Protein 4.9g; Carbohydrate 13.1g, of which sugars 7.1g; Fat 41.4g, of which saturates 24.5g; Cholesterol 99mg; Calcium 91mg; Fibre 4.5g; Sodium 219mg

p87 Peanut and Potato Soup with Coriander Energy 259Kcal/1076kJ; Protein 8.1g; Carbohydrate 14.5g, of which sugars 6.1g; Fat 19.2g, of which saturates 3.7g; Cholesterol 0mg; Calcium 30mg; Fibre 3.0g; Sodium 141mg

p88 Fish and Sweet Potato Soup Energy 125Kcal/528kJ; Protein 11.6g; Carbohydrate 16.7g, of which sugars 5.0g; Fat 1.7g, of which saturates 0.3g; Cholesterol 20mg; Calcium 44mg; Fibre 8.4g; Sodium 223mg

p88 Caribbean Vegetable Soup Energy 195Kcal/820kJ; Protein 3.8g; Carbohydrate 33.7g, of which sugars 16.0g; Fat 5.9g, of which saturates 3.4g; Cholesterol 13mg; Calcium 52mg; Fibre 3.4g; Sodium 62mg

p90 Crab, Coconut and Coriander Soup Energy 232Kcal/972kJ; Protein 23.8g; Carbohydrate 7.4g, of which sugars 6.5g; Fat 12.2g, of which saturates 3.7g; Cholesterol 90mg; Calcium 188mg; Fibre 1.0g; Sodium 937mg

p91 Chilli Clam Broth Energy 141Kcal/595kJ; Protein 8.8g; Carbohydrate 11.0g, of which sugars 4.1g; Fat 4.3g, of which saturates 0.7g; Cholesterol 31mg; Calcium 74mg; Fibre 1.2g; Sodium 403mg

p92 Chunky Prawn Chupe Energy 259Kcal/1089kJ; Protein 23.2g; Carbohydrate 26.8g, of which sugars 7.3g; Fat 7.3g, of which saturates 1.1g; Cholesterol 233mg; Calcium 125mg; Fibre 3.7g; Sodium 1.4g

p92 Corn Soup Energy 561Kcal/2330kJ; Protein 5.6g; Carbohydrate 39.2g, of which sugars 16.3g; Fat 43.6g, of which saturates 26.3g; Cholesterol 107mg; Calcium 54mg; Fibre 2.6g; Sodium 577mg

p94 Beef and Cassava Soup Energy 332Kcal/1400kJ; Protein 27.3g; Carbohydrate 28.6g, of which sugars 8.7g; Fat 7.8g, of which saturates 3.1g; Cholesterol 78mg; Calcium 62mg; Fibre 2.4g; Sodium 295mg

p95 Lamb and Lentil Soup Energy 530Kcal/2225kJ; Protein 57.0g; Carbohydrate 35.2g, of which sugars 2.8g; Fat 18.8g, of which saturates 8.0g; Cholesterol 167mg; Calcium 57mg; Fibre 3.0g; Sodium 180mg

p98 Baked Sea Bass with Coconut Energy 227Kcal/961kJ; Protein 38.2g; Carbohydrate 5.4g, of which sugars 4.6g; Fat 6.1g, of which saturates 0.9g; Cholesterol 95mg; Calcium 125mg; Fibre 0.5g; Sodium 326mg

p98 Pan-Fried Sea Bream with Lime and Tomato Salsa Energy 208Kcal/870kJ; Protein 28.1g; Carbohydrate 2.5g, of which sugars 2.5g; Fat 9.5g, of which saturates 1.4g; Cholesterol 69mg; Calcium 21mg; Fibre 0.8g; Sodium 97mg

p100 Halibut with Peppers and Coconut Milk Energy 279Kcal/1175kJ; Protein 23.8g; Carbohydrate 19.9g, of which sugars 7.5g; Fat 12.3g, of which saturates 5.6g; Cholesterol 41mg; Calcium 48mg; Fibre 2.3g; Sodium 122mg

p101 Prawn and Potato Omelette Energy 195Kcal/814kJ; Protein 16.0g; Carbohydrate 9.0g, of which sugars 3.4g; Fat 10.8g, of which saturates 2.5g; Cholesterol 320mg; Calcium 85mg; Fibre 1.2g; Sodium 659mg

p102 Salmon in Mango and Ginger Sauce Energy 718Kcal/2999kJ; Protein 56.8g; Carbohydrate 32.6g, of which sugars 32.3g; Fat 40.9g, of which saturates 11.9g; Cholesterol 164mg; Calcium 79mg; Fibre 2.5g; Sodium 359mg

p102 Fried Snapper with Avocado Energy 294Kcal/1223kJ; Protein 27.0g; Carbohydrate 0.9g, of which sugars 0.3g; Fat 20.2g, of which saturates 3.5g; Cholesterol 90mg; Calcium 31mg; Fibre 1.7g; Sodium 146mg

p104 Trout in Wine Sauce with Plantain Energy 324Kcal/1353kJ; Protein 22.0g; Carbohydrate 17.6g, of which sugars 6.1g; Fat 16.2g, of which saturates 5.2g; Cholesterol 83g; Calcium 28mg; Fibre 0.6g; Sodium 139g

p105 Eschovished Fish Energy 210Kcal/879kJ; Protein 28.0g; Carbohydrate 5.4g, of which sugars 4.7g; Fat 8.5g, of which saturates 1.1g; Cholesterol 69mg; Calcium 28mg; Fibre 0.8g; Sodium 91mg

p106 Sea Bass Ceviche Energy 183Kcal/776kJ; Protein 30.6g; Carbohydrate 9.7g, of which sugars 8.9g; Fat 2.8g, of which saturates 0.4g; Cholesterol 101mg; Calcium 51mg; Fibre 1.0g; Sodium 171mg

p107 Mackerel Escabeche Energy 576Kcal/2393kJ; Protein 38.5g; Carbohydrate 8.4g, of which sugars 1.5g; Fat 43.3g, of which saturates 8.2g; Cholesterol 108mg; Calcium 40mg; Fibre 0.6g; Sodium 127mg

p108 Marinated Red Mullet Energy 338Kcal/1408kJ; Protein 29.9g; Carbohydrate 12.3g, of which sugars 7.2g; Fat 19.1g, of which saturates 2.8g; Cholesterol 69mg; Calcium 60mg; Fibre 3.9g; Sodium 636mg

p109 Cod Caramba Energy 307Kcal/1286kJ; Protein 20.6g; Carbohydrate 18.5g, of which sugars 7.1g; Fat 14.1g, of which saturates 6.9g; Cholesterol 78mg; Calcium 119mg; Fibre 2.7g; Sodium 720mg

p110 Pumpkin and Prawns with Dried Shrimp Energy 210Kcal/877kJ; Protein 17.5g; Carbohydrate 8.7g, of which sugars 6.9g; Fat 11.9g, of which saturates 4.3g; Cholesterol 187mg; Calcium 147mg; Fibre 3.0g; Sodium 1g

p111 Salt Fish and Ackee Energy 292Kcal/1225kJ; Protein 38.4g; Carbohydrate 7.7g, of which sugars 6.2g; Fat 12.2g, of which saturates 4.3g; Cholesterol 80mg; Calcium 78mg; Fibre 2.4g; Sodium 494mg

p112 Jamaican Fish Curry Energy 695Kcal/2921kJ; Protein 39.5g; Carbohydrate 69.7g, of which sugars 11.2g; Fat 30.7g, of which saturates 19.3g; Cholesterol 51mg; Calcium 112mg; Fibre 3.3g; Sodium 216mg

p114 King Prawns in a Coconut and Nut Cream Energy 496Kcal/2072kJ; Protein 46.5g; Carbohydrate 18.1g, of which sugars 6.4g; Fat 26.8g, of which saturates 12.5g; Cholesterol 448mg; Calcium 254mg; Fibre 2.3g; Sodium 2.8g

p115 Stuffed Crab Energy 162Kcal/680kJ; Protein 15.9g; Carbohydrate 8.7g, of which sugars 3.5g; Fat 7.3g, of which saturates 3.7g; Cholesterol 129mg; Calcium 162mg; Fibre 0.9g; Sodium 475mg

p116 Crab and Corn Gumbo Energy 274Kcal/1144kJ; Protein 9.8g; Carbohydrate 24.2g, of which sugars 6.8g; Fat 11.4g, of which saturates 4.1g; Cholesterol 31mg; Calcium 77mg; Fibre 3.4g; Sodium 349mg

p117 Creole Fish Stew Energy 172Kcal/724kJ; Protein 17.8g; Carbohydrate 5.8g, of which sugars 5.1g; Fat 8.7g, of which saturates 1.9g; Cholesterol 45.8mg; Calcium 59mg; Fibre 1.8g; Sodium 222mg

p118 Cuban Seafood Rice Energy 326Kcal/1379kJ; Protein 28.4g; Carbohydrate 40.9g, of which sugars 1.1g; Fat 6.6g, of which saturates 1.2g; Cholesterol 286mg; Calcium 112mg; Fibre 0.5g; Sodium 1.2g

p120 Chilean Squid Casserole Energy 260Kcal/1089kJ; Protein 19.9g; Carbohydrate 17.2g, of which sugars 3.5g; Fat 8.1g, of which saturates 1.3g; Cholesterol 267mg; Calcium 42mg; Fibre 1.5g; Sodium 333mg

p121 Chilean Seafood Platter Energy 205Kcal/863kJ; Protein 32.7g; Carbohydrate 3.5g, of which sugars 0.5g; Fat 6.8g, of which saturates 1.1g; Cholesterol 267mg; Calcium 146mg; Fibre 0.4g; Sodium 1.6g

p124 The Gaucho Barbecue Energy 839Kcal/3501kJ; Protein 88.1g; Carbohydrate 3.8g, of which sugars 1.1g; Fat 52.5g, of which saturates 22.5g; Cholesterol 249mg; Calcium 63mg; Fibre 0.4g; Sodium 1.2g

p125 Beef Stuffed with Eggs and Spinach Energy 318Kcal/1328kJ; Protein 39.0g; Carbohydrate 3.4g, of which sugars 2.8g; Fat 16.7g, of which saturates 4.6g; Cholesterol 161mg; Calcium 103mg; Fibre 1.6g; Sodium 299mg

p126 Carbonada Criolla Energy 505Kcal/2124kJ; Protein 46.1g; Carbohydrate 33.6g, of which sugars 11.4g; Fat 18.3g, of which saturates 6.1g; Cholesterol 125mg; Calcium 44mg; Fibre 3.6g; Sodium 175mg

p128 Peppered Steak in Sherry Cream Sauce Energy 427Kcal/1780kJ; Protein 38.1g; Carbohydrate 8.4g, of which sugars 3.3g; Fat 23.3g, of which saturates 10.7g; Cholesterol 115mg; Calcium 40mg; Fibre 7.4g; Sodium 142mg

p129 Oxtail and Butter Beans Energy 773Kcal/3240kJ; Protein 88.0g; Carbohydrate 29.6g, of which sugars 6.2g; Fat 34.4g, of which saturates 0.2g; Cholesterol 275mg; Calcium 92mg; Fibre 4.8g; Sodium 522mg

p130 Black Bean Chilli con Carne Energy 374Kcal/1575kJ; Protein 39.0g; Carbohydrate 27.9g, of which sugars 7.4g; Fat 12.6g, of which saturates 4.1g; Cholesterol 83mg; Calcium 60mg; Fibre 4.7g; Sodium 111mg

p131 Mexican Spicy Beef Tortilla Energy 595Kcal/2516kJ; Protein 30.3g; Carbohydrate 91.2g, of which sugars 11.5g; Fat 14.7g, of which saturates 4.7g; Cholesterol 53mg; Calcium 153mg; Fibre 4.0g; Sodium 379mg

p132 Feijoada Energy 779Kcal/3262kJ; Protein 58.0g; Carbohydrate 49.9g, of which sugars 3.8g; Fat 39.9g, of which saturates 13.5g; Cholesterol 142mg; Calcium 135mg; Fibre 7.3g; Sodium 1.5g

p134 Spicy Meatballs with Tomato Sauce Energy 552Kcal/2296kJ; Protein 29.9g; Carbohydrate 21.8g, of which sugars 6.0g; Fat 39.0g, of which saturates 11.6g; Cholesterol 132mg; Calcium 75mg; Fibre 2.0g; Sodium 268mg

p135 Scrambled Eggs with Chorizo Energy 322Kcal/1335kJ; Protein 20.3g; Carbohydrate 5.7g, of which sugars 0.6g; Fat 24.3g, of which saturates 7.6g; Cholesterol 472mg; Calcium 101mg; Fibre 0.3g; Sodium 687mg

p136 Hearty Beef Stew Energy 515Kcal/2158kJ; Protein 62.6g; Carbohydrate 13.0g, of which sugars 6.7g; Fat 22.9g, of which saturates 10.9g; Cholesterol 186mg; Calcium 70mg; Fibre 1.5g; Sodium 245mg

p137 Caribbean Lamb Curry Energy 338Kcal/1409kJ; Protein 30.8g; Carbohydrate 3.2g, of which sugars 2.3g; Fat 22.6g, of which saturates 10.1g; Cholesterol 128mg; Calcium 29mg; Fibre 0.5g; Sodium 229mg

p138 "Seasoned-up" Lamb in Spinach Sauce Energy 331Kcal/1380kJ; Protein 35.6g; Carbohydrate 4.0g, of which sugars 3.1g; Fat 19.4g, of which saturates 6.7g; Cholesterol 125mg; Calcium 80mg; Fibre 1.2g; Sodium 241mg

p138 Lamb Pelau Energy 652Kcal/2726kJ; Protein 32.1g; Carbohydrate 96.3g, of which sugars 5.7g; Fat 15.0g, of which saturates 7.3g; Cholesterol 97mg; Calcium 51mg; Fibre 1.0g; Sodium 231mg

p140 Spiced Roast Leg of Lamb Energy 470Kcal/1962kJ; Protein 37.2g; Carbohydrate 22.6g, of which sugars 6.5g; Fat 24.9g, of which saturates 9.1g; Cholesterol 117mg; Calcium 38mg; Fibre 7.4g; Sodium 651mg

p141 Rabbit in Coconut Milk Energy 301Kcal/1260kJ; Protein 29.9g; Carbohydrate 10.8g, of which sugars 9.2g; Fat 15.7g, of which saturates 4.0g; Cholesterol 68mg; Calcium 73mg; Fibre 1.5g; Sodium 236mg

p142 Pork Roasted wtih Herbs, Spices and Rum Energy 410Kcal/1712kJ; Protein 42.4g; Carbohydrate 3.9g, of which sugars 3.8g; Fat 21.4g, of which saturates 8.2g; Cholesterol 132mg; Calcium 16mg; Fibre 0.1g; Sodium 577mg

p143 Pork with Pineapple Energy 492Kcal/2041kJ; Protein 28.7g; Carbohydrate 12.9g, of which sugars 12.2g; Fat 36.4g, of which saturates 12.6g; Cholesterol 92g; Calcium 30mg; Fibre 1.2g; Sodium 136g

p144 Pork in Milk Energy 472Kcal/1957kJ; Protein 27.2g; Carbohydrate 7.5g, of which sugars 7.5g; Fat 37.1g, of which saturates 15.9g; Cholesterol 103g; Calcium 209mg; Fibre 0g; Sodium 159g

p144 Baked Ham with Orange and Lime Energy 348Kcal/1448kJ; Protein 43.8g; Carbohydrate 0.6g, of which sugars 0.6g; Fat 18.8g, of which saturates 6.3g; Cholesterol 58g; Calcium 18mg; Fibre 0g; Sodium 2201g

p148 Cuban Chicken Pie Energy 521Kcal/2814kJ; Protein 39.8g; Carbohydrate 35.2g, of which sugars 20.1g; Fat 25.6g, of which saturates 10.8g; Cholesterol 324g; Calcium 62mg; Fibre 2.5g; Sodium 0.19g

p149 Chicken with Okra Energy 122Kcal/511kJ; Protein 10.8g; Carbohydrate 9.7g, of which sugars 7.9g; Fat 4.8g, of which saturates 1.0g; Cholesterol 32g; Calcium 162mg; Fibre 5.1g; Sodium 0.04g

p150 Colombian Chicken Hot-pot Energy 368Kcal/1559kJ; Protein 29.2g; Carbohydrate 49.6g, of which sugars 6.5g; Fat 7.2g, of which saturates 1.8g; Cholesterol 107; Calcium 29mg; Fibre 3.7g; Sodium 0.19g

p152 Barbecued Jerk Chicken Energy 460Kcal/1924kJ; Protein 59.7g; Carbohydrate 2.2g, of which sugars 2.2g; Fat 23.6g, of which saturates 6.4g; Cholesterol 254g; Calcium 26mg; Fibre 0.0g; Sodium 0.21g

p153 Thyme and Lime Chicken Energy 495Kcal/2053kJ; Protein 31.6g; Carbohydrate 0.4g, of which sugars 0.4g; Fat 40.8g, of which saturates 16.7g; Cholesterol 212g; Calcium 24mg; Fibre 0.1g; Sodium 0.25g

p154 Chicken, Pork and Potatoes in Peanut Sauce Energy 405Kcal/1697kJ; Protein 41.1g; Carbohydrate 18.2g, of which sugars 4.1g; Fat 19.0g, of which saturates 3.8g; Cholesterol 105g; Calcium 40mg; Fibre 2.5g; Sodium 0.44g

p156 Spicy Fried Chicken Energy 345Kcal/1442kJ; Protein 35.5g; Carbohydrate 6.7g, of which sugars 1.0g; Fat 19.8g, of which saturates 4.5g; Cholesterol 177g; Calcium 54mg; Fibre 0.2g; Sodium 0.17g

p157 Sunday Roast Chicken Energy 348Kcal/1455kJ; Protein 37.5g; Carbohydrate 7.8g, of which sugars 7.8g; Fat 18.8g, of which saturates 8.8g; Cholesterol 155mg; Calcium 18mg; Fibre 0.0g; Sodium 200mg

p158 Peanut Chicken Energy 326Kcal/1374kJ; Protein 55.5g; Carbohydrate 4.2g, of which sugars 3.1g; Fat 9.8g, of which saturates 4.5g; Cholesterol 171mg; Calcium 25mg; Fibre 0.9g; Sodium 190mg

p158 Breasts of Turkey with Mango and Wine Energy 351Kcal/1476kJ; Protein 49.9g; Carbohydrate 9.0g, of which sugars 6.4g; Fat 10.4g, of which saturates 6.0g; Cholesterol 135mg; Calcium 29mg; Fibre 1.5g; Sodium 190mg

p160 Peruvian Duck with Rice Energy 527Kcal/2207kJ; Protein 17.6g; Carbohydrate 55.2g, of which sugars 2.8g; Fat 24.6g, of which saturates 7.2g; Cholesterol 58mg; Calcium 62mg; Fibre 1.8g; Sodium 100mg

p160 Drunken Duck Energy 693Kcal/2895kJ; Protein 24.7g; Carbohydrate 45.5g, of which sugars 14.9g; Fat 41.7g, of which saturates 12.5g; Cholesterol 106mg; Calcium 91mg; Fibre 5.6g; Sodium 220mg

p164 Corn Soufflé Energy 385Kcal/1605kJ; Protein 15.2g; Carbohydrate 25.3g, of which sugars 8.7g; Fat 25.5g, of which saturates 13.7g; Cholesterol 246mg; Calcium 246mg; Fibre 2.5g; Sodium 480mg

p165 Layered Potato Bake with Cheese Energy 442Kcal/1831kJ; Protein 12.2g; Carbohydrate 16.3g, of which sugars 4.1g; Fat 36.9g, of which saturates 7.2g; Cholesterol 132mg; Calcium 137mg; Fibre 2.4g; Sodium 610mg

p166 Heart of Palm Pie Energy 566Kcal/2361kJ; Protein 10.8g; Carbohydrate 57.1g, of which sugars 6.3g; Fat 34.2g, of which saturates 18.2g; Cholesterol 139mg; Calcium 164mg; Fibre 4.4g; Sodium 430,g

p168 Macaroni Cheese Pie Energy 609Kcal/2553kJ; Protein 25.1g; Carbohydrate 60.0g, of which sugars 9.9g; Fat 31.6g, of which saturates 18.6g; Cholesterol 135mg; Calcium 494mg; Fibre 2.4g; Sodium 560mg

p169 Red Bean Chilli Energy 291Kcal/1224kJ; Protein 12.7g; Carbohydrate 35.7g, of which sugars 11.0g; Fat 6.5g, of which saturates 0.8g; Cholesterol 0mg; Calcium 86mg; Fibre 6.1g; Sodium 1.2g

p170 Peppers Stuffed with Beans Energy 528Kcal/2201kJ; Protein 26.1g; Carbohydrate 32.3g, of which sugars 6.8g; Fat 33.6g, of which saturates 12.1g; Cholesterol 118mg; Calcium 286mg; Fibre 10.1g; Sodium 360mg

p171 Green Bean and Sweet Red Pepper Salad Energy 283Kcal/1168kJ; Protein 3.0g; Carbohydrate 11.0g, of which sugars 8.5g; Fat 25.4g, of which saturates 3.6g; Cholesterol 0mg; Calcium 74mg; Fibre 5.5g; Sodium 120mg

p172 Spicy Vegetable Chow Mein Energy 414Kcal/1740kJ; Protein 12.4g; Carbohydrate 62.5g, of which sugars 8.5g; Fat 14.4g, of which saturates 2.7g; Cholesterol 23mg; Calcium 74mg; Fibre 4.7g; Sodium 266mg

p172 Aubergines Stuffed with Sweet Potato Energy 249Kcal/1013kJ; Protein 8.1g; Carbohydrate 24.6g, of which sugars 7.9g; Fat 13.1g, of which saturates 5.1g; Cholesterol 15mg; Calcium 186mg; Fibre 5.0g; Sodium 170mg

p174 Spinach Plantain Rounds Energy 266Kcal/1113kJ; Protein 5.9g; Carbohydrate 30.8g, of which sugars 7.6g; Fat 14.1g, of which saturates 3.6g; Cholesterol 65mg; Calcium 207mg; Fibre 3.6g; Sodium 205mg

p175 Peppery Bean Salad Energy 248Kcal/1046kJ; Protein 14.0g; Carbohydrate 35.4g, of which sugars 6.5g; Fat 6.5g, of which saturates 0.9g; Cholesterol 0mg; Calcium 122mg; Fibre 11.0g; Sodium 660mg

p176 Avocado and Grapefruit Salad Energy 351Kcal/1448kJ; Protein 2.5g; Carbohydrate 5.4g, of which sugars 4.0g; Fat 35.7g, of which saturates 6.4g; Cholesterol 0mg; Calcium 28mg; Fibre 4.1g; Sodium 80mg

p177 Quinoa Salad with Citrus Dressing Energy 225Kcal/938kJ; Protein 4.1g; Carbohydrate 22.1g, of which sugars 3.1g; Fat 13.9g, of which saturates 2.1g; Cholesterol 0mg; Calcium 40mg; Fibre 3.0g; Sodium 10mg

p178 Okra and Tomato Salad Energy 154Kcal/639kJ; Protein 3.7g; Carbohydrate 7.9g, of which sugars 6.6g; Fat 12.3g, of which saturates 1.9g; Cholesterol 0mg; Calcium 174mg; Fibre 5.2g; Sodium 15mg

p178 Tomato, Heart of Palm and Onion Salad Energy 152Kcal/632kJ; Protein 2.8g; Carbohydrate 8.7g, of which sugars 7.7g; Fat 12.0g, of which saturates 1.8g; Cholesterol 0mg; Calcium 38mg; Fibre 3.9g; Sodium 16mg

p180 Spicy Potato Salad Energy 184Kcal/776kJ; Protein 3.9g; Carbohydrate 30.0g, of which sugars 7.0g; Fat 6.2g, of which saturates 1.0g; Cholesterol 6mg; Calcium 32mg; Fibre 3.7g; Sodium 100mg

p181 Mango, Tomato and Red Onion Salad Energy 93Kcal/390kJ; Protein 1.0g; Carbohydrate 10.1g, of which sugars 9.5g; Fat 5.8g, of which saturates 0.7g; Cholesterol 0mg; Calcium 17mg; Fibre 2.1g; Sodium 6mg

p182 Peruvian Salad Energy 226Kcal/945kJ; Protein 6.2g; Carbohydrate 23.1g, of which sugars 4.6g; Fat 12.7g, of which saturates 2.6g; Cholesterol 78mg; Calcium 59mg; Fibre 3.3g; Sodium 570mg

p183 Pumpkin Salad Energy 384Kcal/1583kJ; Protein 2.2g; Carbohydrate 8.7g, of which sugars 6.5g; Fat 38.1g, of which saturates 5.5g; Cholesterol 0mg; Calcium 84mg; Fibre 3.0g; Sodium 10mg

186 Plain Rice Energy 241Kcal/1018kJ; Protein 3.7g; Carbohydrate 42.9g, of which sugars 0g; Fat 7.3g, of which saturates 1.1g; Cholesterol 0mg; Calcium 26mg; Fibre 0.2g; Sodium 0mg

p186 Black Beans Energy 319Kcal/1347kJ; Protein 20.7g; Carbohydrate 40.6g, of which sugars 2.2g; Fat 9.4g, of which saturates 2.4g; Cholesterol 12mg; Calcium 62mg; Fibre 6.2g; Sodium 250mg

p188 Coconut Rice Energy 337Kcal/1435kJ; Protein 5.5g; Carbohydrate 69.4g, of which sugars 15.8g; Fat 6.2g, of which saturates 3.1g; Cholesterol 8mg; Calcium 120mg; Fibre 0.3g; Sodium 400mg

p189 Toasted Cassava Flour with Egg and Bacon Energy 218Kcal/918kJ; Protein 8.4g; Carbohydrate 29.2g, of which sugars 0.6g; Fat 8.3g, of which saturates 3.2g; Cholesterol 93mg; Calcium 67mg; Fibre 1.2g; Sodium 230mg

p190 Rice and Peas Energy 449Kcal/1903kJ; Protein 13.9g; Carbohydrate 83.3g, of which sugars 4.4g; Fat 9.1g, of which saturates 5.7g; Cholesterol 0mg; Calcium 82mg; Fibre 6.3g; Sodium 10mg

p191 Cou-Cou Energy 264Kcal/1115kJ; Protein 1.2g; Carbohydrate 52.7g, of which sugars 0.8g; Fat 6.8g, of which saturates 4.1g; Cholesterol 16mg; Calcium 56mg; Fibre 1.2g; Sodium 80mg

p192 Buttered Spinach and Rice Energy 520Kcal/2169kJ; Protein 11.5g; Carbohydrate 95.4g, of which sugars 4.6g; Fat 9.7g, of which saturates 5.3g; Cholesterol 21mg; Calcium 184mg; Fibre 2.7g; Sodium 190mg

p192 Creamed Sweet Potatoes Energy 313Kcal/1321kJ; Protein 4.4g; Carbohydrate 51.1g, of which sugars 13.4g; Fat 11.6g, of which saturates 6.8g; Cholesterol 27mg; Calcium 74mg; Fibre 9.6g; Sodium 170mg

p194 Colombian Cheesy Potatoes Energy 448Kcal/1882kJ; Protein 11.5g; Carbohydrate 55.8g, of which sugars 6.5g; Fat 21.4g, of which saturates 13g; Cholesterol 52mg; Calcium 166mg; Fibre 3.8g; Sodium 150mg

p195 Caribbean Potato Salad Energy 167Kcal/705kJ; Protein 3.7g; Carbohydrate 30.2g, of which sugars 7.1g; Fat 4.3g, of which saturates 0.7g; Cholesterol 4mg; Calcium 24mg; Fibre 3.5g; Sodium 90mg

p196 Okra Fried Rice Energy 305Kcal/1286kJ; Protein 4.7g; Carbohydrate 50.6g, of which sugars 1.9g; Fat 10.7g, of which saturates 3.1g; Cholesterol 8mg; Calcium 35mg; Fibre 0.5g; Sodium 65mg

p196 Aubergines with Garlic and Spring Onions Energy 132Kcal/551kJ; Protein 3.2g; Carbohydrate 9.3g, of which sugars 8.7g; Fat 9.5g, of which saturates 1.3g; Cholesterol 0mg; Calcium 36mg; Fibre 5.7g; Sodium 550mg

p198 Cassava with a Citrus Salsa Energy 305Kcal/1294kJ; Protein 3g; Carbohydrate 57.2g, of which sugars 2.2g; Fat 8.9g, of which saturates 1.4g; Cholesterol 0mg; Calcium 31mg; Fibre 2.6g; Sodium 0mg

p199 Stir-Fried Spring Greens Energy 111Kcal/459kJ; Protein 6.3g; Carbohydrate 2.5g, of which sugars 2g; Fat 8.5g, of which saturates 2.3g; Cholesterol 16mg; Calcium 159mg; Fibre 2.6g; Sodium330mg

p200 Corn Sticks Energy 64Kcal/272kJ; Protein 1.4g; Carbohydrate 11.7g, of which sugars 1.9g; Fat 1.7g, of which saturates 0.9g; Cholesterol 15mg; Calcium 36mg; Fibre 0.2g; Sodium 160mg

p201 Fried Yellow Plantains Energy 267Kcal/1126kJ; Protein 1.5g; Carbohydrate 47.5g, of which sugars 11.5g; Fat 9.2g, of which saturates 1g; Cholesterol 0mg; Calcium 6mg; Fibre 2.3g; Sodium 0mg

p202 Argentinian Barbecue Salsa Energy 132Kcal/543kJ; Protein 0.7g; Carbohydrate 3.2g, of which sugars 2.6g; Fat 13g, of which saturates 1.9g; Cholesterol 0mg; Calcium 10mg; Fibre 0.8g; Sodium 0mg

p202 Hot Chilli Salsa Energy 441Kcal/1820kJ; Protein 3.8g; Carbohydrate 5.8g, of which sugars 5.8g; Fat 45g, of which saturates 6.4g; Cholesterol 0mg; Calcium 40mg; Fibre 1.5g; Sodium 20mg

p204 Tamarillo Sauce Energy 112Kcal/468kJ; Protein 0.7g; Carbohydrate 15.5g, of which sugars 15.2g; Fat 5.7g, of which saturates 0.8g; Cholesterol 0mg; Calcium 9mg; Fibre 2.2g; Sodium 0mg

p205 Avocado Salsa Energy 190Kcal/786kJ; Protein 1.9g; Carbohydrate 5.6g, of which sugars 4g; Fat 18g, of which saturates 3.2g; Cholesterol 0mg; Calcium 20mg; Fibre 3g; Sodium 10mg

p208 Corn Tortillas Energy 70Kcal/296kJ; Protein 0.1g; Carbohydrate 18.1g, of which sugars 0g; Fat 0.1g, of which saturates 0g; Cholesterol 0mg; Calcium 3mg; Fibre 0g; Sodium 10mg

p209 Flour Tortillas Energy 64Kcal/272kJ; Protein 1.5g; Carbohydrate 12.5g, of which sugars 0.2g; Fat 1.3g, of which saturates 0.5g; Cholesterol 1mg; Calcium 23mg; Fibre 0.5g; Sodium 140mg

p210 Dhal Puri Energy 237Kcal/1004kJ; Protein 9.2g; Carbohydrate 40.8g, of which sugars 1.1g; Fat 5.2g, of which saturates 0.6g; Cholesterol 0mg; Calcium 120mg; Fibre 2.8g; Sodium 120mg

p211 Fried Dumplins Energy 205Kcal/868kJ; Protein 5g; Carbohydrate 36.3g, of which sugars 2.8g; Fat 5.4g, of which saturates 0.9g; Cholesterol 2mg; Calcium 194mg; Fibre 1.4g; Sodium 270mg

p212 Corn Griddle Cakes Energy 87Kcal/366kJ; Protein 2.2g; Carbohydrate 12.5g, of which sugars 0.2g; Fat 3.5g, of which saturates 1.9g; Cholesterol 9mg; Calcium 50mg; Fibre 0g; Sodium 260mg

p214 Paraguayan Corn Bread Energy 232Kcal/971kJ; Protein 6.0g; Carbohydrate 24.7g, of which sugars 3.4g; Fat 12.8g, of which saturates 7.6g; Cholesterol 80mg; Calcium 128mg; Fibre 0.3g; Sodium 340mg

p215 Mexican "Bread of the Dead" (per loaf) Energy 4071Kcal/17154kJ; Protein 86.6g; Carbohydrate 660.6g, of which sugars 146.2g; Fat 123.5g, of which saturates 67g; Cholesterol 949mg; Calcium 1080mg; Fibre 20.9g; Sodium 2.9g

p216 Caribbean Fruit and Rum Cake (per cake) Energy 10871Kcal/45678kJ; Protein 146.1g; Carbohydrate 1526.5g, of which sugars 1192.2g; Fat 448g, of which saturates 254.6g; Cholesterol 3.3g; Calcium 2987mg; Fibre 49.8g; Sodium 5.92g

p217 Apple and Cinnamon Crumble Cake (per cake) Energy 7217Kcal/30269kJ; Protein 89.9g; Carbohydrate 929.9g, of which sugars 500.3g; Fat 374.7g, of which saturates 233.7g; Cholesterol 1.7g; Calcium 2062mg; Fibre 34.1g; Sodium 4.22g

p218 Barbadian Coconut Sweet Bread (per cake) Energy 4078Kcal/17076kJ; Protein 59.2g; Carbohydrate 473.7g, of which sugars 154.2g; Fat 229.5g, of which saturates 156.9g; Cholesterol 609mg; Calcium 1373mg; Fibre 28.9g; Sodium 2.06g

p219 Duckanoo Energy 827Kcal/3499kJ; Protein 7.3g; Carbohydrate 161.4g, of which sugars 57.9g; Fat 21.5g, of which saturates 15g; Cholesterol 36mg; Calcium 224mg; Fibre 2.4g; Sodium 220mg

p220 Corn meal and Fennel Seed Cake Energy 514Kcal/2170kJ; Protein 10.4g; Carbohydrate 94.7g, of which sugars 38.2g; Fat 12.9g, of which saturates 6.3g; Cholesterol 179mg; Calcium 163mg; Fibre 1.1g; Sodium 630mg

p220 Banana Bread (per loaf) Energy 2444Kcal/10218kJ; Protein 41.4g; Carbohydrate 259.4g, of which sugars 124.4g; Fat 144.9g, of which saturates 67.1g; Cholesterol 714mg; Calcium 782mg; Fibre 9.4g; Sodium 1.5g

p224 Fruits of the Tropics Salad Energy 154Kcal/658kJ; Protein 1.3g; Carbohydrate 39.0g, of which sugars 38.1g; Fat 0.4g, of which saturates 0.1g; Cholesterol 0mg; Calcium 31mg; Fibre 4.1g; Sodium 40mg

p225 Coconut Ice Cream Energy 253Kcal/1065kJ; Protein 8.6g; Carbohydrate 34.5g, of which sugars 34.5g; Fat 9.9g, of which saturates 6.2g; Cholesterol 35mg; Calcium 305mg; Fibre 0g; Sodium 220mg

p226 Mango Sorbet Energy 176Kcal/753kJ; Protein 1g; Carbohydrate 45.6g, of which sugars 45.4g; Fat 0.2g, of which saturates 0.1g; Cholesterol 0mg; Calcium 13mg; Fibre 2g; Sodium 10mg

p227 Colombian Pineapple Custard Energy 214Kcal/908kJ; Protein 5.3g; Carbohydrate 40.5g, of which sugars 40.5g; Fat 4.6g, of which saturates 1.3g; Cholesterol 156mg; Calcium 38mg; Fibre 0.7g; Sodium 60mg

p228 Tapioca Pudding Energy 190Kcal/799kJ; Protein 6.1g; Carbohydrate 25.2g, of which sugars 13.8g; Fat 7.9g, of which saturates 3.7g; Cholesterol 18mg; Calcium 156mg; Fibre 0.2g; Sodium 70mg

p229 Fried Bananas with Sugar and Rum Energy 290Kcal/1213kJ; Protein 1.3g; Carbohydrate 36.4g, of which sugars 34.1g; Fat 13.7g, of which saturates 8.6g; Cholesterol 35mg; Calcium 10mg; Fibre 1.1g; Sodium 100mg

p230 Coconut and Pumpkin Compote Energy 429Kcal/1811kJ; Protein 2g; Carbohydrate 82.9g, of which sugars 82.2g; Fat 12.2g, of which saturates 10.4g; Cholesterol 0mg; Calcium 51mg; Fibre 4g; Sodium 100mg

p230 Dulce de Leche Energy 323Kcal/1357kJ; Protein 11.3g; Carbohydrate 42.7g, of which sugars 42.7g; Fat 13g, of which saturates 8.1g; Cholesterol 47mg; Calcium 387mg; Fibre 0g; Sodium 210mg

p232 Caribbean Spiced Rice Pudding Energy 304Kcal/1288kJ; Protein 8.6g; Carbohydrate 53.9g, of which sugars 37.4g; Fat 7.6g, of which saturates 4.5g; Cholesterol 20mg; Calcium 266mg; Fibre 0.4g; Sodium 110mg

p233 Jamaican Fruit Trifle Energy 400Kcal/1664kJ; Protein 2.2g; Carbohydrate 29.1g, of which sugars 28.9g; Fat 30.4g, of which saturates 19.4g; Cholesterol 80mg; Calcium 70mg; Fibre 3.9g; Sodium 20mg

p234 Brazilian Coconut Flan Energy 334Kcal/1398kJ; Protein 5.6g; Carbohydrate 36.6g, of which sugars 36.6g; Fat 19.4g, of which saturates 11.2g; Cholesterol 312mg; Calcium 62mg; Fibre 1.7g; Sodium 50mg

p238 Mango Shake Energy 667Kcal/2793kJ; Protein 26.9g; Carbohydrate 76.2g, of which sugars 75.3g; Fat 29.9g, of which saturates 19.1g; Cholesterol 105mg; Calcium 922mg; Fibre 7.8g; Sodium330mg

p238 Pineapple and Mint Juice Energy 113Kcal/485kJ; Protein 2g; Carbohydrate 26.6g, of which sugars 25.3g; Fat 0.7g, of which saturates 0g; Cholesterol 0mg; Calcium 98mg; Fibre 3g; Sodium 10mg

p240 Cashew Nut Milk Energy 805Kcal/3397kJ; Protein 29.4g; Carbohydrate 136.6g, of which sugars 133g; Fat 19.2g, of which saturates 2.4g; Cholesterol 0mg; Calcium 192mg; Fibre 2.4g; Sodium 390mg

p241 Passion Fruit Batida Energy 151Kcal/631kJ; Protein 0.8g; Carbohydrate 9.6g, of which sugars 9.6g; Fat 0.1g, of which saturates 0g; Cholesterol 0mg; Calcium 4mg; Fibre 1g; Sodium 10mg

p242 Pisco Sour Energy 187Kcal/783kJ; Protein 2.9g; Carbohydrate 15.8g, of which sugars 15.8g; Fat 0g, of which saturates 0g; Cholesterol 0mg; Calcium 3mg; Fibre 0g; Sodium 60mg

p242 Caipirinha Energy 176Kcal/736kJ; Protein 0g; Carbohydrate 15.8g, of which sugars 15.8g; Fat 0g, of which saturates 0g; Cholesterol 0mg; Calcium 2mg; Fibre 0g; Sodium 0mg

p244 Mojito Energy 226Kcal/941kJ; Protein 0g; Carbohydrate 15.8g, of which sugars 15.8g; Fat 0g, of which saturates 0g; Cholesterol 0mg; Calcium 2mg; Fibre 0g; Sodium 0mg

p244 Cubre Libre Energy 130Kcal/542kJ; Protein 0g; Carbohydrate 8.1g, of which sugars 8.1g; Fat 0g, of which saturates 0g; Cholesterol 0mg; Calcium 4mg; Fibre 0g; Sodium 0mg

p246 Demarara Rum Punch Energy 237Kcal/993kJ; Protein 1.4g; Carbohydrate 24.1g, of which sugars 24.1g; Fat 0.3g, of which saturates 0g; Cholesterol 0g; Calcium 20mg; Fibre 0mg; Sodium 10mg

p247 Caribbean Cream Stout Punch Energy 466Kcal/1950kJ; Protein 16.8g; Carbohydrate 37.7g, of which sugars 37.7g; Fat 17.9g, of which saturates 11.2g; Cholesterol 65mg; Calcium 556mg; Fibre 0g; Sodium 340mg

INDEX

A
abalone 57
ackees 48
  salt fish and ackee 111
African influence 7, 22, 196
almonds 49
annatto (achiote) 24, 50, 140
añu 42
apple and cinnamon crumble cake 217
Argentina 16–17, 64
  Argentinian barbecue salsa 202–3
  beef stuffed with eggs and spinach 125
  carbonada criolla 126–7
  wine 64
asadero 52
aubergines stuffed with sweet potato 172–3
aubergines with garlic and spring onions 196–7
avocadoes 24, 43
  avocado and grapefruit salad 176
  avocado salsa 205
  fried snapper with avocado 102–3
Aztecs 6, 18

B
Bacardi, Facundo 11
Bajan bread and butter custard 53
baked ham with orange and lime 144–5
baked sea bass with coconut 98–9
bananas 10, 47
  banana bread 220–1
  fried bananas with sugar and rum 229
Barbadian coconut sweet bread 218
barbecued jerk chicken 152
beans 6, 8, 24, 34–5
  black bean chilli con carne 130
  black beans 186–7
  black-eyed bean and shrimp fritters 78
  green bean and sweet red pepper salad 171
  oxtail and butter beans 129
  peppers stuffed with beans 170

  peppery bean salad 175
  Peruvian salad 182
  red bean chilli 169
beef 16, 58
  beef and cassava soup 94
  beef empanadas 79
  beef stuffed with eggs and spinach 125
  black bean chilli con carne 130
  carbonada criolla 126–7
  feijoada 132–3
  Gaucho barbecue 124
  hearty beef stew 136
  Mexican spicy beef tortilla 131
  oxtail and butter beans 129
  peppered steak in sherry cream sauce 128
  spicy meatballs with tomato sauce 134
beer 65
black bean chilli con carne 130
black beans 186–7
black-eyed bean and shrimp fritters 78
Bolivia 18–19
  peanut and potato soup with coriander 87
  pisco sour 242–3
Brazil 12–15, 202
  black-eyed bean and shrimp fritters 78
  Brazil nuts 49
  Brazilian coconut flan 234–5
  caipirinha 242–3
  chicken with okra 149
  crab, coconut and coriander soup 90
  feijoada 132–3
  halibut with peppers and coconut milk 100
  king prawns in a coconut and nut cream 114
  nut brittle 80–1
  passion fruit *batida* 241
  stir-fried spring greens 199
  toasted cassava flour with egg and bacon 189
bread 206–21
  Bajan bread and butter custard 53
  banana bread 220–1
  Barbadian coconut sweet bread 218
  dhal puri 210
  fried dumplins 211
  Mexican bread of the dead 215
  Paraguayan corn bread 214
breadfruit 48
breast of turkey with mango and wine 158–9
buttered spinach and rice 192–3

C
Cabral, Pedro 6, 12
caipirinha 242–3
cake 206–21
  apple and cinnamon crumble cake 217
  Caribbean fruit and rum cake 216
  corn griddle cakes 212–13
  corn meal and fennel seed cake 220–1
carbonada criolla 126–7
Caribbean 6, 8–11
  apple and cinnamon crumble cake 217
  aubergines stuffed with sweet potato 172–3
  Barbadian coconut sweet bread 218
  barbecued jerk chicken 152

  breast of turkey with mango and wine 158–9
  buttered spinach and rice 192–3
  Caribbean cream stout punch 247
  Caribbean fruit and rum cake 216
  Caribbean lamb curry 137
  Caribbean potato salad 195
  Caribbean spiced rice pudding 232
  Caribbean vegetable soup 88–9
  cheesy eggs 74
  coconut ice cream 225
  coconut king prawns 70–1
  corn sticks 200
  cou-cou 191
  crab and corn gumbo 116
  crab cakes 75
  creamed sweet potatoes 192–3
  dhal puri 210
  duckanoo 219
  eschovished fish 105
  fish and sweet potato soup 88–9
  fried bananas with sugar and rum 229
  fried dumplins 211
  fried snapper with avocado 102–3
  fried yellow plantains 201
  fruits of the tropics salad 224
  hearty beef stew 136
  hot sauces 39
  Jamaican fish curry 112–13
  Jamaican fruit trifle 233
  lamb and lentil soup 95
  lamb pelau 138–9
  macaroni cheese pie 168
  mango, tomato and red onion salad 181
  oxtail and butter beans 129
  peanut chicken 158-9
  peppery bean salad 175
  plantain and sweet potato chips 70–1
  pork roasted with herbs, spices and rum 142
  pumpkin and prawns with dried shrimps 110
  red bean chilli 169
  rice and peas 190
  salt fish and ackee 111

"seasoned-up" lamb in spinach sauce 138–9
spice mixes 51
spicy fried chicken 156
spicy potato salad 180
spinach plantain rounds 174
thyme and lime chicken 153
trout in wine sauce with plantain 104
carnitas 59
cashew nuts 49
cashew nut milk 240
cassava 8, 16, 41, 132
beef and cassava soup 94
cassava chips 68
cassava with citrus salsa 198
toasted cassava flour with egg and bacon 189
Central America 23
ceviche 7, 19
sea bass ceviche 106
chayotes 40
cheese 52
cheese tamales 69
cheesy eggs 74
Colombian cheesy potatoes 194
layered potato bake with cheese 165
macaroni cheese pie 168
cherimoyas 48
chicken 60
barbecued jerk chicken 152
chicken with okra 149
chicken, pork and potatoes in peanut sauce 154–5
Colombian chicken hot-pot 150–1
Cuban chicken pie 148
peanut chicken 158-9
spicy fried chicken 156
Sunday roast chicken 157
thyme and lime chicken 153
Chile 20–1, 64
Chilean seafood platter 121
Chilean squid casserole 120
pisco sour 242-3
wine 64
chillies 6, 7, 14, 24, 36–9, 117
Argentinian barbecue salsa 202–3
black bean chilli con carne 130
chilli clam broth 91
hot chilli salsa 202–3
pebre 50
red bean chilli 169
Chinese influence 22
chocolate 24, 63
chorizo 59
scrambled eggs with chorizo 135
chunky prawn chupe 92–3
cilantro *see* coriander
cinnamon and apple crumble cake 217
citrus fruits 46–7
cassava with citrus salsa 198
quinoa salad with citrus dressing 177
clams 56
chilli clam broth 91
cocoa 7, 24
coconuts 10, 49
baked sea bass with coconut 98–9
Barbadian coconut sweet bread 218
Brazilian coconut flan 234–5
coconut and pumpkin compote 230–1
coconut ice cream 225
coconut king prawns 70–1
coconut rice 188
coconut sweets 80–1
crab, coconut and coriander soup 90
duckanoo 219
halibut with peppers and coconut milk 100
king prawns in a coconut and nut cream 114
rabbit in coconut milk 141
cod caramba 109
coffee 10, 12, 14, 62–3
Colombia 22
baked sea bass with coconut 98–9

beef empanadas 79
chilli clam broth 91
coconut rice 188
Colombian cheesy potatoes 194
Colombian chicken hot-pot 150–1
Colombian pineapple custard 227
corn griddle cakes 212–13
rabbit in coconut milk 141
Columbus, Christopher 6, 8, 10, 22, 23
comal 29
conch 57
congrio 55
coriander 51
crab, coconut and coriander soup 90
peanut and potato soup with coriander 87
pebre 50
corn 6, 8, 12, 16, 18, 24, 30–1
corn griddle cakes 212–13
corn meal and fennel seed cake 220–1
corn soufflé 164
corn soup 92-3
corn sticks 200
corn tortillas 208
cou-cou 191
crab and corn gumbo 116
duckanoo 219
Paraguayan corn bread 214
tamales de picadillo 72
Cortés, Hernán 6, 24
cou-cou 191
courgettes (zucchini) 40
crab 56
crab and corn gumbo 116
crab cakes 75
crab, coconut and coriander soup 90
stuffed crab 115
creamed sweet potatoes 192–3
creamy heart of palm soup 86
Creole cooking 9, 116
Creole fish stew 117
Cuba
cashew nut milk 240
cassava with citrus salsa 198
Cuba libre 244–5
Cuban chicken pie 148
Cuban seafood rice 118–19
mojito 244–5
curanto 21, 56, 57
cuscuzeiro 29

D

dairy products 52–3
demarara rum punch 246
dendê oil 13
desserts 222–35
dhal puri 210
diamonds 13
dried meat 58
drinks 62–5, 236–47
caipirinha 242–3
Caribbean cream stout punch 247
cashew nut milk 240
Cuba libre 244–5
demerara rum punch 246
mango shake 238–9
mojito 244–5
passion fruit *batida* 241
pineapple and mint juice 238–9
pisco sour 242–3
duck 60
drunken duck 160–1
Peruvian duck with rice 160–1
dulce de guayaba 46
dulce de leche 21, 53, 230–1

E

earthenware dishes 29
Ecuador 18–19
peanut and potato soup with coriander 87
pisco sour 242–3
eggs 53, 172
beef stuffed with eggs and spinach 125
Brazilian coconut flan 234–5
cheesy eggs 74

Colombian pineapple custard 227
prawn and potato omelette 101
scrambled eggs with chorizo 135
toasted cassava flour with egg and bacon 189
El Dorado 22
epazote 50
equipment 28–9
eschovished fish 105

F

farinherra 29
feasts and festivals
Argentina 17
Bolivia 19
Brazil 15
Caribbean 11
Chile 21
Ecuador 19
Mexico 25
Paraguay 17
Peru 19
Uruguay 17
feijoada 132–3
fennel seed and corn meal cake 220–1
fish 19, 54–5, 96–121
baked sea bass with coconut 98–9
cod caramba 109
Creole fish stew 117
eschovished fish 105
fish and sweet potato soup 88–9
fried snapper with avocado 102–3
fried whitebait with cayenne pepper 76–7
halibut with peppers and coconut milk 100
Jamaican fish curry 112–13
marinated red mullet 108
pan-fried sea bream with lime and tomato salsa 98–9
salmon in mango and ginger sauce 102–3
salt fish and ackee 111
sea bass ceviche 106
trout in wine sauce with plantain 104
flour tortillas 209
flying fish 55
food and drink
Argentina 17
Bolivia 18–19
Brazil 14–15
Caribbean 9–10
Central America 22
Chile 21
Colombia 22
Ecuador 18–19
Mexico 24–5
Paraguay 17
Peru 18–19
Uruguay 17
Venezuela 22
fried bananas with sugar and rum 229
fried dumplins 211
fried snapper with avocado 102–3
fried whitebait with cayenne pepper 76–7
fried yellow plantains 201
fruit 23, 43, 44–8
Caribbean fruit and rum cake 216
fruit drinks 62
fruits of the tropics salad 224
Jamaican fruit trifle 233

G

game birds 61
garlic 7
aubergines with garlic and spring onions 196–7
Gaucho barbecue 124
German influence 14
ginger and mango sauce with salmon 102–3
gold 13, 16, 22
grapefruit 46, 47
avocado and grapefruit salad 176
green bean and sweet red pepper salad 171
grouper 54
guascas 51
guavas 46
dulce de guayaba 46
guinea pigs 19, 61
Guyana
demerara rum punch 246
fried dumplins 211
spicy vegetable chow mein 172–3

H

halibut with peppers and coconut milk 100
heart of palm pie 166–7
hearty beef stew 136
herbs 50–1
pork roasted with herbs, spices and rum 142
hot chilli salsa 202–3
huacatay 51
huitlacoche (corn truffles) 7, 31

I

ice cream, coconut 225
Incas 6, 18
Indian (Asian) influence 22, 138, 210
Italian influence 52, 144

J

Jamaican fish curry 112–13
Jamaican fruit trifle 233
jicama 42

K

kid 59
king prawns in a coconut and nut cream 114

L

lamb 59
Caribbean lamb curry 137
lamb and lentil soup 95
lamb pelau 138–9
"seasoned-up" lamb in spinach sauce 138–9
Latin America 6–7
layered potato bake with cheese 165
lemons 46–7
lentil and lamb soup 95
limes 46–7
baked ham with orange and lime 144–5
pan-fried sea bream with lime and tomato salsa 98–9
thyme and lime chicken 153
liqueurs 65

M

macaroni cheese pie 168
mackerel escabeche 107
mahi mahi (dolphin fish) 54
mangoes 45
breast of turkey with mango and wine 158–9
mango shake 238–9
mango sorbet 226
mango, tomato and red onion salad 181
salmon in mango and ginger sauce 102–3
marinated red mullet 108
masa harina 69
Mayas 6, 24
meat 58–9, 122–45
mescal 65
metate 28
Mexico 6, 24–5
black bean chilli con carne 130
cod caramba 109
corn tortillas 208
flour tortillas 209
green bean and sweet red pepper salad 171
Mexican "bread of the dead" 215
Mexican spicy beef tortilla 131
mixed tostadas 73
peppers stuffed with beans 170
pork with pineapple 143
scrambled eggs with chorizo 135

tamales de picadillo 72
tomato soup 84–5
vermicelli soup 84–5
milk 53
Bajan bread and butter custard 53
dulce de leche 21, 53, 230–1
pork in milk 144–5
mint 51
pineapple and mint juice 238–9
mixed tostadas 73
mojito 244–5
molcajete 28
mullet, marinated red 108
mussels 56

N

nutritional information 252–5
nuts 49
king prawns in a coconut and nut cream 114
nut brittle 80–1

O

oca 42
offal 59
Ojeda, Alonso de 8
okra 10, 13, 42
chicken with okra 149
cou-cou 191
okra and tomato salad 178–9
okra fried rice 196–7
onions 7
aubergines with garlic and spring onions 196–7
mango, tomato and red onion salad 181
tomato, heart of palm and onion salad 178–9
oranges 10, 46, 47
baked ham with orange and lime 144–5
oxtail and butter beans 129

P

palillo 51
palm hearts 42
creamy heart of palm soup 86
heart of palm pie 166–7
tomato, heart of palm and onion salad 178–9
pampas 16–17

pan-fried sea bream with lime and tomato salsa 98–9
pan-fried squid 76–7
papayas 44–5
Paraguay 16–17, 202
Paraguayan corn bread 214
passion fruit *batida* 241
Patagonian toothfish 54
peanuts 49
chicken, pork and potatoes in peanut sauce 154–5
peanut and potato soup with coriander 87
peanut chicken 158–9
peas 13, 35
rice and peas 190
pebre 50
pecan nuts 49
peppered steak in sherry cream sauce 128
peppers 8, 36–9
green bean and sweet red pepper salad 171
halibut with peppers and coconut milk 100
peppers stuffed with beans 170
peppery bean salad 175
Peruvian salad 182
Peru 6, 18–19
chicken, pork and potatoes in peanut sauce 154–5
layered potato bake with cheese 165
Peruvian duck with rice 160–1
Peruvian salad 182
pisco sour 242–3
pork in milk 144–5
sea bass ceviche 106
tamarillo sauce 204
pheasant in green pipian sauce 61
pine nuts 49
pineapples 44, 233
Colombian pineapple custard 227
pineapple and mint juice 238–9
pork with pineapple 143
pisco 65
pisco sour 242–3
Pizarro, Francisco 6, 16, 18
plain rice 186–7
plantains 10, 48
fried yellow plantains 201
plantain and sweet potato chips 70–1
spinach plantain rounds 174
trout in wine sauce with plantain 104
pompano 55
pork 59
baked ham with orange and lime 144–5
feijoda 132–3
Gaucho barbecue 124
pork in milk 144–5
pork roasted with herbs, spices and rum 142
pork with pineapple 143
toasted cassava flour with egg and bacon 189
Portugal 6–7, 12–13
potatoes 18, 19, 33
chicken, pork and potatoes in peanut sauce 154–5
Colombian cheesy potatoes 194
layered potato bake with cheese 165
peanut and potato soup with coriander 87
prawn and potato omelette 101
spicy potato salad 180

poultry 60–1, 146–61
prawns 56
chunky prawn chupe 92–3
coconut king prawns 70–1
king prawns in a coconut and nut cream 114
prawn and potato omelette 101
pumpkin and prawns with dried shrimps 110
prickly pears 48
pumpkins 40
carbonada criolla 126–7
coconut and pumpkin compote 230–1
pumpkin and prawns with dried shrimps 110
pumpkin salad 183

Q

queso anejo 52
queso blanco 52
queso chihuaha 52
queso fresco 52
quinoa salad with citrus dressing 177

R

rabbit in coconut milk 141
red bean chilli 169
rice 7, 32
buttered spinach and rice 192–3
Caribbean spiced rice pudding 232
coconut rice 188
Cuban seafood rice 118–19
lamb pelau 138–9
okra fried rice 196–7
Peruvian duck with rice 160–1
Peruvian salad 182
plain rice 186–7
rice and peas 190
rum 9, 11, 65
Caribbean fruit and rum cake 216
demerara rum punch 246
fried bananas with sugar and rum 229
pork roasted with herbs, spices and rum 142

S
salmon in mango and ginger sauce 102–3
salsas 184–205
salt cod 55
salt fish and ackee 111
sausages 59
scallops 57
scrambled eggs with chorizo 135
sea bass 54
baked sea bass with coconut 98–9
sea bass ceviche 106
sea bream with lime and tomato salsa 98–9
sea urchins 57
seafood *see* shellfish and fish
seasoned-up lamb in spinach sauce 138–9
shellfish 10, 21, 56–7, 96–121
black-eyed bean and shrimp fritters 78
Chilean seafood platter 121
Chilean squid casserole 120
chilli clam broth 91
chunky prawn chupe 92–3
coconut king prawns 70–1
crab and corn gumbo 116
crab cakes 75
crab, coconut and coriander soup 90
Cuban seafood rice 118–19
king prawns in a coconut and nut cream 114
pan-fried squid 76–7
prawn and potato omelette 101
pumpkin and prawns with dried shrimp 110
stuffed crab 115
shrimp 56
black-eyed bean and shrimp fritters 78
pumpkin and prawns with dried shrimps 110
side dishes 184–205
silver 16
slavery 7, 10, 13
snacks 66–81
Argentina 17
Bolivia 19
Brazil 15
Caribbean 10
Chile 21
Ecuador 19
Mexico 25
Paraguay 17
Peru 19
Uruguay 17
snapper 54
fried snapper with avocado 102–3
sorbet, mango 226
soups 82–95
Spain 6–7, 9, 16, 18, 20, 24–5, 52
spices 51
Caribbean spiced rice pudding 232
Mexican spicy beef tortilla 131
pork roasted with herbs, spices and rum 142
spiced roast leg of lamb 140
spicy fried chicken 156
spicy meatballs with tomato sauce 134
spicy potato salad 180
spicy vegetable chow mein 172–3
spinach
beef stuffed with eggs and spinach 125
buttered spinach and rice 192–3
"seasoned-up" lamb in spinach sauce 138–9
spinach plantain rounds 174
spirits 65
spring greens, stir-fried 199
squash 6, 8, 12, 24, 40
squid 57
Chilean squid casserole 120
pan-fried squid 76–7
stir-fried spring greens 199
street food 66–81
Argentina 17
Bolivia 19
Brazil 15
Caribbean 10
Chile 21
Ecuador 19
Mexico 25
Paraguay 17
Peru 19
Uruguay 17
stuffed crab 115
sugar cane 6, 10, 13, 51
Sunday roast chicken 157
sweet potatoes 8, 12, 16, 41, 112
aubergines stuffed with sweet potato 172–3
creamed sweet potatoes 192–3
fish and sweet potato soup 88–9
plantain and sweet potato chips 70–1
swordfish 55

T
tamales de picadillo 72
tamarillos 48
tamarillo sauce 204
tapioca pudding 228
tejolote 28
tequila 65
Tex-Mex cooking 24, 130
thyme 51
thyme and lime chicken 153
toasted cassava flour with egg and bacon 189
tomatoes 6, 7, 43
mango, tomato and red onion salad 181
okra and tomato salad 178–9
pan-fried sea bream with lime and tomato salsa 98–9
spicy meatballs with tomato sauce 134
tomato soup 84–5
tomato, heart of palm and onion salad 178–9
tortillas
corn tortillas 208
flour tortillas 209
Mexican spicy beef tortilla 131
mixed tostadas 73
tortilla press 28, 29
trout 55
trout in wine sauce with plantain 104
turkey 60-1
breast of turkey with mango and wine 158–9

U
Uruguay 16–17, 202

V
vegetables 40–2, 43, 162–83
Caribbean vegetable soup 88–9
spicy vegetable chow mein 172–3
Venezuela 22
corn griddle cakes 212–13
vermicelli soup 84–5

W
walnuts 49
wine 6, 64
breast of turkey with mango and wine 158–9
peppered steak in sherry cream sauce 128
trout in wine sauce with plantain 104

Y
yacón 42
yams 8, 10, 13, 41
yerba maté 17, 63

Notes

Notes

Notes

Notes

Notes

Notes

Notes

Notes